2540q215

BT
93
F37
-1992

NARRATIVE
THEOLOGY
AFTER
AUSCHWITZ

FROM ALIENATION
TO ETHICS

DISCARDED

DARRELL J.
FASCHING

FORTRESS PRESS

AUG 0 1 2002

NORMANDALE COMMUNITY COLLEGE
MINNEAPOLIS
9700 FRANCE AVENUE SOUTH
BLOOMINGTON, MN 55431-4399

D0814262

NARRATIVE THEOLOGY AFTER AUSCHWITZ
From Alienation to Ethics

Copyright © 1992 Augsburg Fortress. All rights reserved. Except for brief quotations in critical articles or reviews, no part of this book may be reproduced in any manner without prior written permission from the publisher. Write to: Permissions, Augsburg Fortress, 426 S. Fifth St., Box 1209, Minneapolis, MN 55440.

Scripture quotations are from the New Revised Standard Version of the Bible, copyright © 1989 by the Division of Christian Education of the National Council of the Churches of Christ in the United States of America. Used with permission.

Excerpts from *Job*, The Anchor Bible, copyright © 1965, are reprinted by permission of Doubleday, a division of Bantam, Dell Publishing Group, Inc.

Excerpts from "The Relationship of Judaism: Toward a New Organic Model" by Irving Greenberg in *Quarterly Review* 4, no. 4 (Winter 1984), are reprinted by permission of *Quarterly Review*.

Excerpts from "*Hutzpa K'lapei Shamaya*: A Christian Response to the Jewish Tradition of Arguing with God" by Belden Lane in *Journal of Ecumenical Studies* 4 (Fall 1986), copyright © 1986 *Journal of Ecumenical Studies*, are reprinted by permission of the copyright holder.

Cover design: Terry Bentley

Library of Congress Cataloging-in-Publication Data

Fasching, Darrell J., 1944–
    Narrative theology after Auschwitz : from alienation to ethics /
Darrell J. Fasching.
        p.   cm.
    Includes bibliographical references and index.
    ISBN 0-8006-2531-7
    1. Holocaust (Christian theology)   2. Holocaust, Jewish
(1939–1945)—Moral and ethical aspects.   3. Christianity and other
religions—Judaism.   4. Judaism—Relations—Christianity.
I. Title.
BT93.F37   1992
231.7'6—dc20   92-6689
                                                                                    CIP

The paper used in this publication meets the minimum requirements of American National Standard for Information Sciences—Permanence of Paper for Printed Library Materials, ANSI Z329.48-1984.   ∞™

Manufactured in the U.S.A.   AF 1-2531
96   95   94   93   92   1   2   3   4   5   6   7   8   9   10

For
Laura Lyn Gushin
and
Irving Greenberg

To the Waconia Public
Library with gratitude
for fostering my love of
books.

7-24-2001

CONTENTS

Preface   vii

Prologue: Wrestling with the Stranger   1

1. Theology after Auschwitz:
   Re-forming the Christian Story   17
   The Narrative Tradition of Supersession
   The Holocaust as Hermeneutical Rupture
   On Paul, Job, and the Burning Children
   Beyond the Sacred and the Secular

2. Ethics after Auschwitz: Christians and the
   Jewish Narrative Tradition of Chutzpah   49
   Unquestioning Obedience and Iconoclastic Audacity
   Wrestling with God
   The Ethical Failure of Christianity
   A Narrative Ethic of Audacity

3. The Challenge of Auschwitz: Rethinking Christian
   Narrative Ethics   89
   Narrative as a Mode of Ethical Reflection
   Albert Speer's Self-Deception
   The Shoah, the Gospel Story, and Self-Deception

Augustine's Confessions *as a Model for Narrative Truth*
Doubt: The Eschatological Norm of Narrative Truth

4. Demythologizing the Demonic   129
    The Myth of Demonic Invincibility
    Demonic Doubling among the Nazi Doctors
    Demonic Doubling and Luther's Two-Kingdom Ethic
    Demythologizing the Demonic
    Conversion—Reclaiming the Double

5. Reconstructing Christian Narrative Ethics   153
    Ethical Paradox after Auschwitz
    From Alienation to Ethical Audacity
    Ethics and the Social Ecology of Conscience
    Personal and Professional Responsibility after Auschwitz

Epilogue: On Wrestling and Reconciliation   187

Indexes   195

PREFACE

This book is dedicated to my wife, Laura, who entered my life in 1974 and changed it forever. As a Christian I had never given serious thought to the history of Jewish-Christian relations until I married her. Love has the power to open not only the heart but the mind. Suddenly I found myself tied to the history of the Jews in a very personal way by my love for my wife. That was for me the beginning of a long and painful journey of discovery—uncovering the history of Christian anti-Judaism—a journey that made me an alien and a stranger to my own tradition. I can never thank her enough for the gift of that experience.

This book is also dedicated to my rabbi, Irving Greenberg. No, I have not become a Jew. My destiny lies in the reform of my own tradition not in its abandonment. But if a rabbi is a "teacher," then surely Irving Greenberg is my rabbi. In 1974 I went to a conference where I happened to hear Greenberg speak. His words were devastating, penetrating, illuminating. If I was now a stranger to my own tradition, with his help I was able to see both my tradition and his with new eyes. His influence on this book and on my future work is pervasive and obvious. His friendship and encouragement means a great deal to me. Intermarriage between Christians and Jews is a delicate issue. Maintaining Jewish identity in our world is urgent. I realize that Rabbi Greenberg spends a great deal of his life trying to strengthen Jewish identity. I do not want to compromise in any way the integrity of his views and the continuing distinctiveness of his faith. I report these facts of my biography (which, I confess, I have not previously admitted to him), because they explain how this book came about.

There are others to whom I am deeply indebted: Harold and Lillian Gushin, who welcomed me into the House of Israel even though I was a stranger; Gabriel Vahanian, under whom I studied at Syracuse University and whose influence pervades the way I wrestle with theological and ethical issues; Jim Williams, who also was my mentor at Syracuse University and who first introduced me to the profundity of the book of Job; and Jonathan Paradise and A. Thomas Kraabel, who laid the foundations when I was an undergraduate at the University of Minnesota.

At the University of South Florida, where I now teach, I owe a special debt to Bill Shea (who has since moved on to St. Louis University), whose encouragement caused me to think I might have something to say about theology and ethics after the Holocaust, and to Bill Tremmel, for his constant support and encouragement. Others elsewhere gave me such encouragement as well, especially Franklin Littell and Alice and Roy Eckardt. Their support and inspiration have meant more than I can say. Franklin Littell's work first drew my attention to the lessons that Christians need to learn from the tradition of wrestling with God. Roy and Alice Eckardt pioneered the theological rethinking of the meaning of the tragic, historical wrestling match between the elder and younger brothers.

I owe special thanks as well to a former student, Jim David, who was instrumental in making it possible for me to attend the international conference on the Holocaust, "Remembering for the Future," at Oxford University in the summer of 1988. The paper I prepared for that conference and the conversations I had there, especially with Alice Eckardt, Richard Rubenstein, and Marc Ellis, led me to conceive this book. Indeed, I drafted the first outline of this book while at that conference. I wish also to thank J. Patout Burns at Washington University, Michael Fishbane at the University of Chicago, and Stanley Hauerwas at Duke University for reading portions of this manuscript and offering both encouragement and constructive criticism.

I owe a debt of gratitude as well to another former student, Janet Bank, for her careful reading of the manuscript and her helpful suggestions. Also, my thanks to those graduate students at the University of South Florida who worked through an earlier draft of this manuscript with me in one of my seminars: Tracy Stewart, Robin Tuthill, Janet Nelson, and Alice Hutton. I must also thank Michael West, Academic Editor at Fortress Press, who encouraged me to pursue the writing of this book when it was no more than a sketchy proposal. His encouragement then and throughout the project has meant a great deal to me. I wish, finally, to express my appreciation to my friend M. Richard (Rick) Malivuk, pastor of All Saints Lutheran Church, who listened patiently to the ideas put forward here over countless Saturday morning breakfasts, offering good-humored encouragement and criticism.

I also wish to thank *Horizons* for permission to use material from "Can Christian Faith Survive Auschwitz" in chapter 1 and Pergamon Press, who published the proceedings of the Oxford conference "Remembering for the Future," for permission to use material from "Faith and Ethics after Auschwitz—What Christians Can Learn from Jews" in chapter 2, and also the *Journal of Ecumenical Studies,* which reprinted a version of this essay in vol. 27, no. 3, Summer 1990. Material in chapter 5 on the work of Jacques Ellul first appeared in volumes 10 and 11 of *Research in Philosophy and Technology* (JAI Press). I also wish to acknowledge permission from the *Journal of the American Association of Rabbis,* for the use of material from "Ethics after Auschwitz and Hiroshima: The Challenge of the 'Other' for Jews, Christians, Buddhists, and Other Strangers in a Technological Civilization." Finally, I wish to express my appreciation for the assistance provided me by the University of South Florida, for this book was made possible in part by two University grants—a research grant for the summer of 1989 and a sabbatical grant for the fall of 1989.

PROLOGUE

WRESTLING WITH THE STRANGER

That same night [Jacob] got up and took his two wives, his two maids, and his eleven children, and crossed the ford of the Jab'bok. He took them and sent them across the stream, and likewise everything that he had. Jacob was left alone; and a man wrestled with him until daybreak. When the man saw that he did not prevail against Jacob, he struck him on the hip socket; and Jacob's hip was put out of joint as he wrestled with him. Then he [the stranger] said, "Let me go, for the day is breaking." But Jacob said, "I will not let you go, unless you bless me." So he [the stranger] said to him, "What is your name?" And he said, "Jacob." Then the man said, "You shall no longer be called Jacob, but Israel, for you have striven with God and with humans, and have prevailed." Then Jacob asked him, "Please tell me your name." But he [the stranger] said, "Why is it that you ask my name?" And there he blessed him. So Jacob called the place Peni'el, saying, "For I have seen God face to face, and yet my life is preserved."

(Gen. 32:22-30)

Theology, as I understand it, belongs not only to the church or synagogue but also to the university—to the humanities. For it is the task of the humanities to wrestle with the ever-elusive question of human identity. Echoing the theology of Augustine, Calvin in his introduction to the *Institutes* states that knowledge of God and knowledge of ourselves are so closely intertwined that it is difficult to discern which one precedes and brings forth the other.[1] But the Augustinian formulation does not articulate

1. See John Calvin, *The Institutes of Christian Religion*, ed. John McNeill, trans. Ford Lewis Battles (Philadelphia: Westminster Press, 1960), 35.

1

the complexity of that truth as well as the story of Jacob wrestling with the stranger does. For what the Genesis story makes clear is that self-knowledge is never just a private affair between God and the individual. On the contrary, it is only when we wrestle with the stranger, whether it be our neighbor or our enemy, that we can begin to grasp both who we are and who God is. It is this complexity that also makes theology an inherently ethical discipline. The ethical measure of a theology is, as I shall argue, whether it welcomes the stranger and audaciously protects the dignity and well-being of the stranger.

When we wrestle with the stranger, the biblical story implies, we wrestle with the infinite unfathomability of both the divine and the human. We wrestle with the God who can neither be named nor imaged but, para-doxically, in whose image we are created. The moment that realization dawns upon us we understand that the stranger is not just "the other," for in that moment we realize that we are strangers even to ourselves. Neither God nor our selves can be named and imaged. Our human dignity lies in mirroring an infinite that, although expressed through the finite, can never be reduced and confined to the finite. When we wrestle with God we become strangers to ourselves and thus are able to identify with the ex-perience of the stranger and welcome the stranger into our lives as the one whose very strangeness or otherness mediates the presence of the Wholly Other. Through the story of Jacob's encounter with the stranger we come to learn that wrestling with the one who is alien or different does not have to lead to the victory of one over the other. It can lead instead to mutual respect. Not all wrestling matches are zero-sum games in which there can be only one winner. Jacob wins; he prevails, but the stranger is not defeated and blesses him before departing. There is a lesson for doing theology and ethics in this story. Theology is not so much a matter of metaphysics as it is a task of reflecting on our encounter with the "other" as the occasion for understanding our relationship to the Wholly Other—and of coming to understand ourselves and what is required of us through this double en-counter. Theology is rooted in our experience of alienation, for it is our experience of being a stranger (even to ourselves) that opens us up to the possibility of welcoming the stranger as the "holy other."

This book is an experiment in decentered or alienated theology. Alienated theology is the opposite of apologetic theology. Apologetic theology seeks to defend the "truth" and "superiority" of one's own tradition against the "false," "inferior," and "alien" views of other traditions. By contrast, alienated theology is theology done as if one were a stranger to one's own tradition; one sees and critiques one's own tradition from the vantage point of the other's tradition. It is my conviction that alienated theology is the appropriate mode for theology in an emerging world civilization—a civilization tottering in the balance between apocalyptic self-annihilation and utopian renewal. There are two ways to enter world history, according to the contemporary author John Dunne: You can be dragged in by way of world war or you can walk in by way of mutual understanding. By the first path global civilization emerges as a totalitarian project of dominance that risks a total nuclear apocalypse. By the second path we prevent the first and create global civilization through an expansion of our understanding of what it means to be human. This understanding occurs when we pass over to another's religion and culture and come back with new insight into our own.

Gandhi is an example of one who passed over to the Sermon on the Mount and came back to the Hindu *Gita* to gain new insight into it as a scripture of nonviolence. Gandhi never considered becoming a Christian, but his Hinduism was radically altered by his encounter with Christianity. One could say the same (reversing the directions) for Martin Luther King, Jr., who was deeply influenced by Gandhi's understanding of nonviolent resistance in the *Gita*. When we pass over (whether through travel, friendship, or disciplined study and imagination) we become "strangers in a strange land" as well as strangers to ourselves, seeing ourselves through the eyes of another. Assuming the perspective of a stranger is an occasion for insight and the sharing of insight. Such cross-cultural interactions build bridges of understanding and action between persons and cultures that make cooperation possible and conquest unnecessary. Passing over short-circuits apocalyptic confrontation and inaugurates utopian new beginnings—new beginnings for the postmodern world of the coming third millennium. Gandhi and King are symbols of a possible style for a postmodern alienated theology.

To be an alien is to be a stranger. To be alienated is to be a stranger to oneself. We live in a world of ideological conflict in which far too many individuals (whether theists or atheists) practice a centered theology in which they are too sure of who they are and what they must do. Such a world has far too many answers and not nearly enough questions and self-questioning. A world divided by its answers is headed for an inevitable apocalyptic destiny. When we are willing to become strangers to ourselves (or when we unwillingly become so), however, new possibilities open up where before everything was closed and hopeless.

Centered theologies, whether sacred or secular, theist or atheist, are ethnocentric theologies that can tolerate the alien or other, if at all, only as a potential candidate for conversion to sameness. Centered theologies are exercises in narcissism that inevitably lead down apocalyptic paths like those that led to Auschwitz and Hiroshima. Why? Because such theologies, whether sacred or secular, cannot permit there to be others in the world whose way of being might, by sheer contrast, cause self-doubt and self-questioning.

When as a student I read Paul Tillich, I found it hard to believe him when he said that the questions were more important than the answers. I was so taken with his answers that I was sure he was just trying to be modest. Since then, I have realized that answers always seem more important and more certain to those who have come by them without wrestling with the questions. I know now that Tillich was quite serious and quite right—the questions are indeed more important. I have found a fullness in the doubts and questions of my life that I once thought could only be found in the answers. After Auschwitz I distrust all final answers—all final solutions. Mercifully, doubts and questions have come to be so fulfilling that I find myself suspicious of answers, not because they are necessarily false or irrelevant, but because even when relevant and true they are, and can only be, partial. It is doubt and questioning that always lure me on to broader horizons and deeper insights through an openness to the infinite that leaves me contentedly discontent.

Alienated theology understands doubt and the questions that arise from it as our most fundamental experience of the infinite. For, like the infinite, our questions are unending, always inviting us to transcend our present horizon of understanding. Likewise, the presence of the stranger calls us into question and invites us to transcend the present horizon of the egocentric and ethnocentric answers that structure our identities. An alienated theology understands that only a faith that requires one to welcome the alien or stranger is truly a utopian faith capable of transforming us into "new beings" who can create a new world of pluralistic human interdependence. According to the Genesis story of the Tower of Babel (Gen. 11:1-9), human beings sought to grasp transcendence through a single language and the common technological project of building a tower to heaven. God, however, upset their efforts by confusing their tongues, so that they could not understand each other. They became strangers to one another and so could not complete their task. The popular interpretation of this story is that the confusion of tongues was a curse and a punishment for the human sin of pride. But I am convinced that this is a serious misunderstanding of its meaning. I would suggest, rather, that human beings misunderstood where transcendence lay and God simply redirected them to the true experience of transcendence, which can occur only when there are strangers to be welcomed into our lives.

To put it in terms closest to home for myself: as a Christian who seeks to come to grips with Auschwitz in the light of the history of Christian anti-Judaism, I cannot be a Christian unless I am prepared to welcome Jews into my life. The very attempt to convert them would destroy the authenticity of my own faith by robbing me of the chance to welcome the stranger (the one who is different from me and a permanent witness of the Wholly Other in my life), who is given to me as an invitation to self-transcendence. For the literal meaning of "transcendence" is "to go beyond"—to go beyond ourselves (individually and communally) as we are to become something more and something new. To be human is to have a utopian capacity to create new worlds. When we deny ourselves that possibility, we plant the seeds of our apocalyptic self-destruction. The tragedy of human existence revealed by Auschwitz and again by Hiroshima is that we continue to misread our situation. Given the opportunity for self-transcendence, the opportunity to be carried beyond ourselves into a new, global, human community, we have too often insisted on a technological solution, a MAD (Mutual Assured Destruction) solution. This, at best, leads to a global stalemate between cultures and at worst to an attempt at global conquest. In either case we place ourselves under the dark and threatening cloud of a nuclear apocalypse, which such a path may well bring.

Alienated theology is an attempt to critique one's own tradition by imaginatively experiencing it through the eyes of the other who stands outside one's tradition, as if one were the other who has been, or will be, affected by it. This book is a project in, and an invitation to, decentered or alienated theology. The task is not so much one of correctly understanding what alien communities have thought about each other as it is one of creating new insights and new meanings through a process of shared insights. The task is not primarily the historical one of recalling the past (although that must be done), but the ethical task of constructing the future. We are engaged less in the description of being than in the making of being. We are not so much interested in what Judaism, Christianity, and Buddhism (and other a-theisms) have been as what they will become as a result of engaging in the process of alienated theology.

To speak personally, I write as an alienated Christian living in what has often been called an age of alienation. I used to think that the experience of alienation was a problem in need of resolution. I have come to see it, however, as a promising opportunity, for when we become strangers to ourselves we experience a new vulnerability and a new openness to the other—other persons, other ideas, other cultures, and other ways of life. To the degree that secularization alienates us from our sacred traditions, it presents us with utopian possibilities. It also presents us with apocalyptic dangers. The greatest danger created by alienation seems to be that we shall become lost in a sea of relativism, of assuming that one way is as good as another. This relativism is just as destructive as those centered theologies that assume there is only one way. It is my conviction, however, that there is a path between these extremes of relativism and absolutism: the way of doubt and self-questioning that accompanies passing over and coming back. As a permanent way I believe it prevents one from settling into either a self-complacent absolutism or a self-complacent relativism; it replaces both with the experience of self-transcendence as a surrender to doubt and its social correlate, openness to the stranger.

This book is part of a project on theological ethics after Auschwitz and Hiroshima, intended to be an experiment in theology of culture as an approach to comparative religious ethics. From the perspective of a narrative-ethics approach, I attempt to restructure the Christian narrative tradition, in the light of Auschwitz, through a dialogue with the strand of post-Holocaust Jewish theology and ethics that draws upon the Jewish narrative tradition of *chutzpah*. This volume culminates in an ethic of personal and professional responsibility proposed as a strategy for restraining the human capacity for the demonic.

In the next volume, *The Ethical Challenge of Auschwitz and Hiroshima—Apocalypse or Utopia?* (SUNY Press, 1993), I continue the narrative-ethics approach but extend the ethical focus of the discussion to encompass religion, technology, and public policy in a cross-cultural perspective. There I argue that the dominant myth or narrative of our modern global technological civilization is the Janus-faced myth of "Apocalypse or Utopia." This mythic narrative tends to render us ethically impotent, for, mesmerized by the power of technology, we become trapped in the manic-depressive rhythms of a sacral awe—of fascination and dread. When we are caught up in the utopian euphoria created by the marvelous promises of technology, we do not wish to change anything. When, in our darker moments, we fear that this same technology is out of control and leading us to our own apocalyptic self-destruction, we feel overwhelmed and unable to do anything. The paradox is that the very strength of our literal utopian euphoria sends us careening toward some literal apocalyptic final solution. I also suggest that the narrative theme of the demonic that dominated Auschwitz—killing in order to heal—has become globalized and incorporated into the Janus-faced technological mythos that emerged out of Hiroshima. This mythic narrative underlies and structures much of public policy in our nuclear age. Finally, I extend the Jewish-Christian dialogue of this volume to include Buddhism, in order to suggest a cross-cultural coalition for an ethic of human dignity, human rights, and human liberation in response to this technological globalization of the demonic. At the heart of my position is the conviction that the *kairos* of our time calls forth the badly neglected ethic of welcoming the stranger, which underlies the biblical tradition, and analogously welcoming the outcast, which underlies the Buddhist tradition. This care for the stranger and the outcast provides the critical norm for an ethic of human dignity, human rights, and human liberation.

I want to construct a theory of theology of culture as comparative religious ethics. However, the theory I am developing and the conclusions I reach concerning a cross-cultural pluralistic ethic of human rights in response to Auschwitz and Hiroshima would be impossible unless I first come to grips with Auschwitz as a singular event for Western religion, culture, and ethics. My immediate goal in this volume is to span the abyss between Jews and Christians in a suggested coalition against the unprecedented power of the demonic that has erupted in this century. My ultimate goal, in the next volume, is to expand this coalition so as to bridge not only the abyss between religions, East and West, but also between religious and secular ethics.

The total project, then, is about religion, ethics, and public policy after Auschwitz and Hiroshima. It is about: (a) rethinking the meaning of civilization and public order in an emerging pluralistic world civilization as we approach the end of a millennium; (b) the need of a cross-cultural ethic in a world racked by ethical relativism and ideological conflict; and (c) the mythologies of the sacred and the secular in a technological civilization and the appropriate role for religion in the shaping of public values in a "secular" world.

I write from the perspective of theology. However, it is not "Christian" theology, although it is assuredly theology written by a Christian. It is not "confessional theology" but theology understood as an academic discipline within the humanities whose purpose is the illumination of the human experience (individual and communal) of transcendence as self-transcendence. Obviously, the same subject matter would be treated differently had this project been written by a Buddhist or some other more "secular" a-theist, or by a Hindu, Jew, or Muslim rather than a Christian. Yet I intend it to be a theology that has something to say not only to Christians but also to Jews and Buddhists without being either a Jewish or Buddhist theology. And I mean it to be a theology relevant to secular or humanistic atheists as well.

What I am engaged in is "theology of culture," a discipline first introduced by Paul Tillich in his 1920 essay, "On the Idea of a Theology of Culture," with which he inaugurated his career.[2] Theology of culture is the appropriate discipline for both the secular university and an emerging world civilization. For, as Tillich insists, the theologian of culture is no "confessional theologian" but rather a "free agent" who takes as his or her task the identification and elucidation of the relationship between religion and culture in all its diversity. Theology of culture could equally be called "philosophy of religion," provided that discipline were able to break free of its nearly exclusive bias as a tradition of commentary on the logic of Western theism rather than on religion as a transcultural human phenomenon. Theology of culture, as I understand it, exists at the intersection of philosophy and the history of religions, as a form of comparative religious ethics. It separates itself from some forms of comparative religious ethics

2. Paul Tillich, "On the Idea of a Theology of Culture," in *What Is Religion?* (New York: Harper Torchbooks, 1969), 155–81.

in that it goes beyond description to prescription. Its task is nothing less than a total critique of culture.

Doing ethics requires not just philosophical reflection but also historical, sociological, and psychological reflection. Paul Tillich's proposal for a theology of culture draws these diverse elements into a unified whole that replaces traditional ethics with the new and uniquely modern task of the critique of culture. In premodern cultures, society was viewed as an extension of the sacred, normative, and unchangeable order of nature. Only in the modern period did human beings become self-conscious of society and culture as realms separate from the order of nature, that is, as the product of human decisions and commitments. Only in the light of such self-consciousness is a social ethic even conceivable as the project of critiquing the institutional order and cultural values that define the horizons of human action. The critique of culture "as a whole" presents a unique problem. For if we live, move, and have our being within culture, how is it possible to transcend it so as to critique it? From what vantage point can we "stand outside it"? Such a critique presupposes the identification of values that, in some sense, transcend the cultures in which they are embedded. I believe such values can be identified. However, they do not exist in a vacuum. They are embodied in particular types of narrative carried by specific types of communal traditions that, in some sense, stand apart from the cultures in which they find themselves. The ultimate goal of theology of culture is to identify those religious experiences, forms of religious community, and narrative traditions that have transcended the historical epoch and cultural milieu of their origin in order to influence other times and places. For these traditions will have proven themselves both religiously and culturally transcendent and therefore may offer possible norms for the critique of both religions and cultures.

The frame of reference for the formation of this thesis is shaped in important ways by Eric Voegelin, who makes a fundamental distinction between two types of social/ethical order—cosmological and anthropological. Voegelin takes the Socratic experience as a model for these distinctions. For the polytheistic civilization in which Socrates grew up society was viewed as "the cosmos writ small," and humanity's task was to conform to the divinely sanctioned sacred order of nature. Into this order Socrates introduced a new, *anthropological ethic*, a humanistic ethic in which society is understood as "man [or, the human] writ large." In this view, society is to be more than simply the cosmos in miniature (i.e., a sacred cosmic order). It should, rather, make "the human" the measure of every just social order so long as (unlike the Sophists) the measure of the human is the *unseen* measure of the Good. This Good transcends the cosmos (and human imagination) and yet reveals itself experientially within the self or soul as the "sensorium of transcendence."[3] An anthropological ethic is an ethic of human dignity grounded in an inner experience of openness to the infinite—that which is Wholly Other than this cosmos.

More radical but parallel forms of this ethical experience emerged in Judaism and Buddhism through the formation of holy communities where this type of ethical consciousness was sustained by stronger traditions of myth and ritual than those offered by the philosophical schools of the Greeks. Whereas cosmological societies are monistic (i.e., the whole of society forms one continuous sacred order of gods and humans in unity with the cosmos), anthropological communities promote a dualism of "this world" and the "other world" (or "this world" and the eschatological "world to come" or the "wheel of Samsara" and the "wheel of Dharma"). This dualism in each instance is mirrored in the structure of society in which the iconoclastic and utopian values of the "other world" are embodied in the holy (i.e., separated) community, which functions as a desacralizing (or secularizing) presence within the sacred social order of "this world." Whereas the false utopianism of a sacred society makes the finite absolute by identifying "the way things are" as the way they ought to be (i.e., Is = Ought), the authentic utopianism of a holy community represents an opening up of the human to an infinite that cannot be contained in any finite order and therefore opposes an "otherworldly ought" to the way things are (Ought vs. Is) and creates a fermenting presence for social transformation. Such anthropological communities, set apart from society, are the social carriers of culturally transcendent values. Shaped by an openness to the infinite, they are capable of influencing diverse cultures and historical epochs. The sociological intersection of these two ethical realms (i.e., the sacred and the holy) and the working out of a "two-kingdom" ethic is not a problem unique to Christianity. It is inherent in

---

3. Eric Voegelin, *The New Science of Politics* (Chicago: Univ. of Chicago Press, 1952), 75. See his discussion on discovery of the soul, 67–75. Voegelin's most important work is his five-volume *Order and History* (Baton Rouge: Louisiana State Univ. Press, 1956–1987).

the very nature of anthropological ethics in all its forms, even in its philosophical forms (as when Plato sought to work out the relation between philosophers and kings). In every case, the counterpositioning of the holy community (e.g., synagogue, church, *sangha*, philosophical schools) in relation to a sacred society produces the need to work out an ethic of two realms or two kingdoms.

The ethical importance of such mythological or metaphysical dualisms, so long as they remain dialectical and not dualistic, is that they introduce an element of negation and doubt that can desacralize the status quo and prepare a society for utopian transformation. For instance, when Socrates separated the Is from the Ought, he brought an "otherworldly Ought" to bear in judgment of the existing social order and thereby made "the human good" rather than "sacred order" the measure of a just society. Perceived as a dangerous secularizing influence on society, Socrates was executed for impiety toward the gods (and hence toward the sacred order of society) and corrupting the youth (i.e., seducing them into asking the critical question: Is what society defines as the good really the good?).

According to Voegelin, the ethical challenge of the two realms is to keep the two orders in dialectical balance. Every society must be both the cosmos writ small and the human writ large. Ethical wisdom requires that we embrace both truths in a paradoxical dialectic. Individual and social self-transcendence can occur only if there is a mutually limiting dialectical tension between these the two orders. Authentic social self-transcendence combines respect for reality with the iconoclastic utopian impulse constantly to question and test the limits of reality so as to open up new possibilities for transformation. This dialectic respects the unfinished or utopian dimension of the human reality in its openness to the infinite. It respects the finitude of the body (individually and communally) while keeping both self and society open to the infinite possibilities of the human for transformation and renewal.

Although this project in comparative religious ethics attempts to identify the positive and negative value of several types of religious experience, I do not pretend to write from some neutral, Archimedean vantage point. As Tillich insisted, no theologian of culture can escape his or her own religious and cultural history. Indeed, every scholar in the social sciences and humanities is a participant observer in the human condition being studied. There is no neutral vantage point from which to begin. One must acknowledge one's starting position and work outward from there. This is as true for the psychologist or anthropologist as it is for the political scientist, philosopher, and theologian. My own starting point is that of an alienated Christian, alienated by my encounter with the Holocaust and the history of anti-Judaism that paved the way to it. Confessionally, my stand in Christianity, like Tillich's, is Lutheran. But like Tillich I seek to be an objective scholar, making philosophically fair statements and evaluations about a wide diversity of religious and cultural phenomena in order to construct a social ethic that can sustain a total critique of modern culture.

In this volume, I make the case for alienated theology as a way of doing comparative religious ethics by passing over into the narrative traditions of post-Holocaust Judaism and coming back to post-Holocaust Christianity in order to construct an ethic of personal and professional responsibility after Auschwitz. In the process of doing this I found myself forced to expand my vision of the project beyond Auschwitz and Western culture. As I studied the post-Holocaust Jewish theologians who are responding to the Shoah, in the same breath with "Auschwitz" the name "Hiroshima" kept coming up. The link between Auschwitz and Hiroshima turns out to be an inner link demanded by the analysis of those who were, directly or indirectly, the victims of the Holocaust. It is as if those who know something of the desolation of Auschwitz recognize that in some sense they have a kinship with those who know the desolation of Hiroshima. Also, more than once I have encountered an awareness of a logical as well as a psychological link between the two. This link is the progressive unfolding of a desacralized and desacralizing technological civilization that no longer holds anything sacred, not even human life—nothing, that is, except what Jacques Ellul calls "the technical imperative": If it can be done, it must be done.[4] The death camps were technically feasible and they came to pass. The atom bomb was technically feasible and it came to pass. A final apocalyptic nuclear annihilation of the earth is technically feasible. . . .

At Auschwitz technical power was still limited in scope and capable of being demonically directed at targeted populations such as Gypsies and Jews. With the coming of the bomb, however, technical power has become autonomous. It has outstripped human intentionality. If there is a next time after Hiroshima and Nagasaki, it will not matter who the good guys and

---

4. Jacques Ellul, *The Technological System* (New York: Continuum, 1980), 334.

who the bad guys are. The threat of apocalypse that erupted at Auschwitz is no longer limited to the West. Hiroshima symbolizes the globalization of the demonic in its technological form, a globalization that forces a meeting of East and West.

The movement from Auschwitz to Hiroshima is psychological, logical, and finally mythological. For Auschwitz and Hiroshima have assumed the mythological status of sacred events that orient human consciousness. They have become transhistorical and transcultural events that are shaping a public consciousness of our common humanity. The horrifying irony is that they are not manifestations of the divine but of the demonic, and the common awareness they are creating is structured by dread. As Arthur Cohen suggests, the task of theology in our time is to excavate the abyss of the demonic and build a bridge of transcendence over it.[5] We need a common hope to unite us as a global human community, one that can carry us beyond our common dread. Perhaps excavating the abyss will motivate us to build a bridge—a bridge built by passing over the abyss and into other religions and cultures in order to come back with new insight into ourselves and our own culture.

Auschwitz and Hiroshima warn of the danger of dividing the world into sacred and profane populations, as the Nazis did with the categories of the "pure Aryan race" and the "subhuman races." For such divisions can lead to a "killing in order to heal" or the extermination of all who "are not worthy of life," as the Nazis put it. In such a context the dialogue between Christians and Jews in response to Auschwitz, with which this book begins, leads to the inclusion of Buddhists as inevitably as Auschwitz leads to Hiroshima. Despite their dramatic differences, these three traditions have an inner affinity with each other as holy communities, separated from society by their experiences of transcendence but united with each other in their complementary ethical traditions of welcoming the stranger and the outcast. The movement from Auschwitz to Hiroshima provides a prophetic warning of what the future holds if we fail to create a cross-cultural public order that can find unity in diversity. The apocalyptic threat of our time is that we shall be swallowed up in the abyss of the demonic. Our utopian hope lies in passing over and coming back. Our hope lies in creating

5. Arthur Cohen, *The Tremendum* (New York: Crossroad, 1981). See esp. chap. 4, "The Bridge over the Abyss."

a new world where strangers are welcome, a world where bonds of cross-cultural understanding could alter our relation to the technical order and at the same time make total destruction of the other unthinkable. I believe such a world is possible, based on a new social-ethical coalition of Jews, Christians, Buddhists, and other (secular) a-theists—one that can transform the rest of the world. I propose not so much a set of answers to the problems of the modern world as a process to engage in, through which, at the intersection of religions and cultures, we might find our way into the future together. It is not my intent to provide "final solutions" to the world's problems. "Final solutions" and "having a future," I fear, are incompatible goals. For my part, I prefer living in an unfinished world—one open to the utopian possibilities of the human. My goal is simply to identify and to promote a process of transcendence, and a transcendence in process, which I believe is already at work in world history as we approach the coming of the third millennium.

The argument that I make in *The Ethical Challenge of Auschwitz and Hiroshima—Apocalypse or Utopia?* suggests that all public order is structured by the experience of the sacred, which legitimates a given social order. As a consequence, the notion that we live in a purely secular civilization needs to be qualified. The particular form of sacred order that dominates modern civilization assumes a secular guise. It is a demonic form rooted in the normlessness of modern cultural relativism and expressed in the paradoxical formula "nothing is any longer sacred, not even human life." Since culture, like nature, abhors a vacuum, such relativism inevitably defaults in some arbitrary form of absolutism that refuses to tolerate the pluralism to which it is a reaction. When all values are viewed as equally arbitrary, no good reasons can be offered for one option over another, and the will to power takes over. In a technological civilization, the autonomous secular rationality of technique, symbolized by Auschwitz and Hiroshima, expresses this arbitrary will to power.

Before we can productively confront the global threat of technical rationality and nuclear annihilation presented to us by Hiroshima (i.e., the escalation of genocide into the threat of omnicide), we need to confront its incubation in Western religion and culture, a process that gave birth to Auschwitz and all the death camps of Europe. In order to make my case, I apply the model of alienated theology to Christian theology and ethics in the light of Auschwitz. Chapter 1 reviews the role that the Christian narrative traditions of supersession played in creating the path that led to Auschwitz and the moral unacceptability of that narrative tradition after Auschwitz. It goes on to suggest a new hermeneutic or interpretive criterion for Christian theology after Auschwitz. Drawn from the work of Irving Greenberg, this criterion is: "No statement, theological or otherwise, should be made that would not be credible in the presence of the burning children."[6] In the light of this criterion, I suggest a new canon within the canon of Christian Scriptures, one with two foci: the book of Job read as a post-Holocaust parable and an exegesis of Paul's Letter to the Romans derived primarily from the recent work of Krister Stendahl, E. P. Sanders, and Lloyd Gaston. The purpose of this canon within the canon is to suggest a normative form for the Christian story after Auschwitz. Chapter 2 then contrasts the ethical consequences of different narrative interpretations of faith. I critique the role of Luther's two-kingdom ethic, with its emphasis on unquestioning obedience, in promoting Christian complicity with the Nazi genocidal program. In response I suggest a new norm for Christian ethics based on the post-Shoah Jewish theology and ethics of such figures as Emil Fackenheim, Elie Wiesel, and especially Irving Greenberg. This norm, rooted in the Jewish narrative tradition of chutzpah[7] (i.e., the audacity to question all authority—sacred or secular, divine or human—in defense of the dignity of the stranger), is also succinctly stated by Greenberg, who suggests that "nothing dare evoke our absolute, unquestioning loyalty, not even our God, for this leads to possibilities of SS loyalties."[8]

The remaining chapters seek to reconstruct Christian faith and ethics under the guidance of these suggested hermeneutical and ethical norms. Chapters 3 and 4 engage in the revision of Christian ethics through a critique and reconstruction of the Christian narrative tradition of Augustine and Luther. Stanley Hauerwas's narrative approach to Christian ethics is used to help formulate this reconstruction. In the process I engage in a critique and reconstruction of Hauerwas's theory of narrative ethics as well. The result sets the stage for the development of a model of social ethics

6. Irving Greenberg, "Cloud of Smoke, Pillar of Fire: Judaism, Christianity, and Modernity after the Holocaust," in *Auschwitz: Beginning of a New Era?* ed. Eva Fleischner (New York: KTAV, 1977), 23.

7. "Chutzpah," for those unfamiliar with the term, should not be pronounced the way it looks. The "ch" should be pronounced as an aspirated "h" and the first syllable (chutz), should rhyme with "foots," not "huts."

8. Ibid., 38.

that responds directly to the demonic dimension of technobureaucratic institutions revealed at Auschwitz. Here Hauerwas's study of Albert Speer (in chap. 3) and Robert Jay Lifton's study of the Nazi doctors (in chap. 4) provide the data for my analysis of the human capacity for the demonic in relation to the narrative theme—killing in order to heal.

In chapter 5, then, I reconstruct Luther's two-kingdom ethic in relation to the Jewish ethical tradition of audacity (chutzpah) on behalf of the stranger as a counterstrategy to this capacity for the demonic. This reconstruction allows me to suggest an ethical model for personal and professional responsibility after Auschwitz structured in terms of a socioecology of conscience. Finally, in the epilogue I tie the theological and ethical dimensions of my argument together by placing the story of Jacob wrestling with the stranger back within its larger context—the story of the rivalry of Jacob and Esau and their reconciliation. I do this in order to demonstrate that this story of Jacob's attempt to usurp the identity and inheritance of his older brother and his ultimate repentance and their reconciliation actually governs the theological construction of Paul's Letter to the Romans. The result, I hope, suggests the possibility of a common coalition between Jews and Christians against any future eruptions of the demonic. In *The Ethical Challenge of Auschwitz and Hiroshima*, I will attempt to extend this coalition and suggest a cross-cultural ethic of human dignity, human rights, and human liberation through the synergy of the diverse narrative traditions (East and West, religious and secular) of hospitality, whose common theme is welcoming the stranger. Contrary to the usual critique of human rights (launched by narrative ethicists) as an attempt to impose a single, universal, storyless ethic on the whole human race, I argue that an ethic of human dignity and human rights requires just the opposite, namely, a pluralistic coalition of the narrative traditions of holy communities that need to share only one thing in common—hospitality to the stranger.

CHAPTER ONE

THEOLOGY AFTER AUSCHWITZ

RE-FORMING THE CHRISTIAN STORY

THE NARRATIVE TRADITION OF SUPERSESSION

According to Adolf Hitler, two Catholic bishops once came to see him to protest his treatment of the Jews. His response, he boasted, was that he did not understand their protest since he was just finishing what the church had started.[1] While it would be a mistake to suggest that one could completely explain the Holocaust in terms of the history of Christian anti-Judaism, it cannot be explained without it. The history of Christian anti-Judaism set precedents for the Holocaust. It created an aura of acceptability for anti-Jewish ideas, which Hitler was able to use and manipulate to catapult himself into power. Christian anti-Judaism was a necessary but not sufficient condition for the time of desolation. The genocidal attack on the Jews could not have happened without that history, even though other historical factors (political, social, economic) had also to occur. That the Holocaust could occur is a judgment on all the institutions and resources of Western civilization, but it is an especially devastating judgment on the one ethical community, above all, that should have come to the defense of the Jews—the Christian church.

Christian anti-Judaism discloses the dark side of Christian history and identity. It is tragic that a religious movement begun as a sectarian tradition within Judaism should, in breaking off to form a new religious community,

---

1. Rosemary Ruether cites this story from Hitler's *Table Talk* in *Faith and Fratricide* (New York: Seabury, 1979), 223–24.

turn into its mortal enemy. It is tragic that a religious community itself once a minority persecuted tradition should, upon becoming the official religion of the Roman Empire, become a persecuting tradition bent on suppressing Judaism. In embracing the Roman Empire, the church in many ways won the world and lost its soul—it traded its status as an embodiment of an anthropological tradition of transcendence for that of a cosmological tradition of sacred order.

In 313 C.E., the Roman emperor Constantine issued the Edict of Toleration, which for the first time gave Christianity the legal right to exist in the Roman Empire. But it was not until 380 C.E., under Theodosius, the first Christian emperor (Constantine was not baptized until his deathbed), that Christianity was declared the only legal religion of the empire. At that time all pagan traditions were suppressed and forbidden, and Judaism came under severe legal restrictions.

Within that same decade an ominous event set the pattern for the next millennium and a half of Jewish-Christian relations. In 388 the bishop of Callinicum in Mesopotamia led a mob in the burning of a Jewish synagogue. In an attempt to administer justice, Theodosius ordered the bishop to rebuild the synagogue. At this time the emperor's throne was in the city of Milan, and the bishop of Milan was Ambrose, the great church father and teacher of Augustine. Ambrose rebuked Theodosius for his attempt to have the temple rebuilt by the errant Mesopotamian bishop and said that if the opportunity arose he too would be happy to burn any dwelling where Christ is denied. He threatened Theodosius with divine punishment if he forced the restoration of the synagogue. In an effort to compromise, Theodosius then offered to pay for the restoration out of state funds. Still Ambrose refused his approval. Then Ambrose exercised a new and unheard-of power over the emperor, who was, of course, also a member of his congregation. He refused him the sacraments until he acquiesced to his demands.[2]

This event set the pattern for the treatment of Jews in Western civilization from the fourth century onward. The state became an instrument of the church for the suppression of Judaism in particular and "heretics" in general. Behind this event already lay more than three hundred years of theological anti-Judaism in the writings of the church fathers. Justin Martyr (100–165 C.E.) accused the Jews of "killing Christ." Origen (185–254

---

2. Ibid., 193–94.

C.E.) taught that the Jews had committed a crime against the savior of the human race and could never be restored to their "former condition." John Chrysostom (344–407 C.E.), who worried about his Christian flock at Antioch fraternizing with the Jews and attending synagogue services on Jewish holidays, wrote a series of vicious and ugly sermons against the Jews. In these sermons he suggested that God hates and rejects the Jews, who cannot be forgiven for their "crime" and who will remain for all time without a temple or a nation as their just punishment. They are, he suggested, "animals fit for slaughter." According to Edward Flannery, Augustine (354–430 C.E.) was the first to develop the "negative witness" theory to resolve "the Jewish problem," the problem of why God allows Jews to continue to exist at all after the coming of the messiah, Jesus of Nazareth. The sheer continued existence of those who "denied Christ" had to be explained. Augustine's answer was that, as a punishment for killing Christ, God had decreed that they would carry the sign of Cain, condemned to wander the earth forever without a home, as a negative witness to the truth of Christianity.[3]

It is hardly coincidental that the legal status of Jews suffered increasingly as these teachings took hold, first under the Theodosian law code and then later under Justinian's revision of the law code. Justinian's code revoked the legal status that Judaism had enjoyed under the Romans and that Theodosius had continued, with restrictions. In essence, Judaism was no longer afforded any legal rights. As its legal status crumbled, the vulnerability of Jews to prejudice and violence increased: synagogue burnings, Jewish children forcibly taken away from their parents and baptized, expulsions of Jews from country after country, and, especially from the time of the Crusades, repeated mob violence or pogroms with extensive loss of life. Indeed, in the first six months of the First Crusade, between one-quarter and one-third of the Jews of Germany and northern France were slaughtered.[4] Throughout Europe, right into the modern period, Jews lived in fear of their lives every year as holy week came around and the entire history of negative stereotypes about Jews would once more be rehearsed in Christian ritual and sermon.

When Hitler said he was only finishing what the church had started, he knew whereof he spoke. Indeed, as Franklin Littell has pointed out, Hitler

---

3. Edward Flannery, *Anguish of the Jews* (New York: Macmillan, 1965), 49ff.
4. Ibid., 92.

reissued Luther's vicious diatribe *On the Jews and Their Lies* "without gloss or amendment" in order to justify Nazi policies. Moreover, the yellow badge that the Nazis made the Jews wear was adapted from the medieval Catholic church. No wonder Hitler could say in *Mein Kampf*, "I believe that I am acting in accordance with the will of the Almighty Creator: by defending myself against the Jew, I am fighting for the work of the Lord." The historian Lucy Dawidowicz describes Hitler's mental world as apocalyptic and Manichaean.[5] He saw his struggle with the Jews in religious terms, as a cosmic battle between the children of light (the Aryan race) and the children of darkness (the Jews). He saw himself as the messianic figure who would bring this struggle to a successful conclusion on behalf of God's "chosen people"—the German-Aryan race. "Two worlds face one another," said Hitler, "the men of God and men of Satan! The Jew is the anti-man, the creature of another god. He must have come from another root of the human race. I set the Aryan and the Jew over and against each other."[6]

When Hitler identified the Jews as "children of the devil" and "creatures of another god," he was citing a long and popular tradition in Western Christendom, one that can be traced back through Luther and the medieval tradition to church fathers such as John Chrysostom. But the ultimate source is finally biblical: The Gospel of John portrays Jesus as saying to his Jewish audience: "Why do you not understand what I say? It is because you cannot accept my word. You are from your father the devil, and you choose to do your father's desires. He was a murderer from the beginning and does not stand in the truth, because there is no truth in him . . . he is a liar and the father of lies" (John 8:43-44). Whether or not such statements in the New Testament are correctly interpreted as anti-Judaic in terms of their original context, it is a historical fact that such statements have, century after century, incited anti-Judaic prejudice. That is a painful acknowledgment for any Christian to make, and it is an acknowledgment that Christians have been willing to make only after Auschwitz. Auschwitz has

5. The Manichees were a gnostic movement in the early church who taught that there were two gods—one the source of good and the other the source of all things evil.

6. Franklin Littell, *The Crucifixion of the Jews* (New York: Harper & Row, 1975), 104; see Luther, *On the Jews and Their Lies, 1543*, trans. Martin H. Bertram, in vol. 47 of *Luther's Works* (Philadelphia: Fortress, 1971), 121–306. Lucy Dawidowicz, *The War Against the Jews, 1933–1945* (New York: Holt, Rinehart and Winston, 1975), 21, quoting Hitler's *Mein Kampf.*

shaken the foundations of sacred Christian traditions in a way that no previous event in Western history has. It is as if the impact of Auschwitz served to desacralize those anti-Judaic traditions and to make Christians strangers and aliens to their own past. Such a moment, painful as it is, offers up the real possibility that the future might be genuinely utopian, that is, *other* than its past.

THE HOLOCAUST AS HERMENEUTICAL RUPTURE

The Holocaust presents a crisis of faith of cataclysmic proportions for both Jew and Christian. For the Jew the question is whether faith in the God of history is possible after Auschwitz. The victims must wonder how God could allow such an evil to happen. For the Christian, the question is just as challenging but for a different reason. It is not just that a great evil has occurred in history but that the foundations of it were laid by almost two thousand years of Christian anti-Judaism in the form of persecutions, pogroms, and expulsions. Throughout Christian history, as Rosemary Ruether has argued, anti-Judaism has been "the left hand of Christology."[7] Christians, it seems, have found it virtually impossible to affirm Christ without denying the integrity and validity of the ongoing covenant of the Jewish people.

Based on the myth of supersession, which has its roots in the New Testament literature, the Christian claim has been that Christ has brought a "new covenant" that replaces the old (e.g., Hebrews 8). Therefore the people of the Mosaic covenant have no right to exist as God's chosen people. By claiming that election was transferred from the people of Israel to the community of the new covenant, Christians have engaged in a process of spiritual genocide. We have said to the Jew: "You have no right to exist as God's chosen because God has rejected you and chosen us instead. We are the true Israel." The step from such spiritual genocide to physical genocide—from "you have no right to exist as Jews" to "you have no right to exist"—is a step prepared by Christian *religious* anti-Judaism and carried out under Nazi *secular* anti-Semitism.

Both the sacred and the secular in Western civilization, both Christianity and the Enlightenment, prepared the path to Auschwitz. As long as being

7. See Ruether's book *Faith and Fratricide*. For a critical appraisal of her thesis see Alan T. Davies, ed., *AntiSemitism and the Foundations of Christianity* (New York: Paulist, 1979).

a Jew was perceived by the Gentile as a religious claim, the "final solution" to the "Jewish problem" (i.e., the simple fact of their existence) could officially be envisioned as conversion, although the popular response was all too often pogrom and expulsion. Once the secularization process unleashed by the Enlightenment redefined being a Jew in terms of race, however, conversion was no longer a possible solution. Religious anti-Judaism became secular anti-Semitism. Now the "final solution" to the presence of an alien and undesired race came to mean genocide—a solution the Nazis attempted to enact.

A generation after the Holocaust the full weight of what had transpired in Western history began to enter both Jewish and Christian consciousness. For both, the Holocaust has become the occasion for a hermeneutical rupture—a crisis in the interpretation of meaning. Even the search for a way to name this event suggests its challenge to human meaning and understanding. At first the term *Holocaust* gained ascendancy; it is a biblical term for a burnt offering or sacrifice made to God. It revealed a very human need to find meaning in the midst of tragedy. More recently the term *Shoah*, meaning "desolation" or "time of desolation," has come to be widely accepted as more suitable; this term perhaps suggests that such demonic events can have only a negative meaning. Certainly, even when the word *Holocaust* is used, it is now to be understood, at best, as a sacrifice that has no meaning—a meaningless sacrifice. In any case, it has become progressively clear, as the Shoah has permeated our consciousness, that it is no longer possible to interpret and understand what it means to be a Jew or a Christian in the way our ancestors did.

Arthur Cohen, who struggled to find his own name for the Shoah, chose the *Tremendum*. He referred to the hermeneutical rupture that it creates as a *caesura*. It is as if the ground opened up and revealed an abyss that threatens to swallow up all meaning. Even the God of history seems to have disappeared into this abyss. For Richard Rubenstein, the God of history died at Auschwitz. Both the death camps and the emergence of the state of Israel suggest that "the normative theology of history traditionally identified with prophetic and Rabbinic Judaism was effectively demythologized." Religious explanations no longer seem adequate. The messianic coming cannot be used to explain the reestablishment of Israel. Nor can the prophetic tradition be used to explain the atrocity of the Shoah as "a punishment for failing to keep the covenant," as it was used after the fall of the First and Second Temples. That would be asking the tradition to carry more weight than it can bear. Emil Fackenheim has argued that "it was not our Western, agnostic, faithless, and rich but rather the poorest, most pious, and most faithful Jewish communities which were most grievously stricken. . . . Not a single one of the six million died because they had failed to keep the divine-Jewish covenant: they all died because their great-grandparents *had* kept it. . . . Here is the rock on which the 'for our sins we are punished' [theme] suffers total shipwreck." Within Judaism the Shoah seems to be forcing the abandonment of what Rubenstein calls "the myth of history" even as it challenges the very notion of covenant. "Either You are our partner in history, or You are not," says Elie Wiesel, in a dramatic address to God. "If You are, do Your share; if You are not, we consider ourselves free of past commitments. Since You choose to break the covenant, so be it." The caesura is radical. This time it seems as if it is God who has been unfaithful, and this unfaithfulness calls into question the very presence of God in history.[8]

In responding to the Holocaust, Cohen, Rubenstein, and at times Elie Wiesel seem to move away from faith in the God of history and into a mystical faith (although the mysticism of each is quite distinct). Yet hope in the God of history seems to be precisely what Emil Fackenheim refuses to abandon. While others find only the silence and absence of God at Auschwitz, Fackenheim hears a new revelation, a "commanding voice" from Auschwitz. This voice, he argues, forbids Jews to hand Hitler a posthumous victory. Jews "are commanded to survive as Jews, lest the Jewish people perish. They are commanded to remember the victims of Auschwitz lest their memory perish. They are forbidden to despair . . . lest they cooperate in delivering the world over to the forces of Auschwitz."[9] Hence the agonizing dialogue goes on as the Jewish people seek to understand themselves anew after the hermeneutical rupture of the Holocaust. Where it shall all lead is yet to be decided.

Christians too have entered into the agonizing dialogue and have begun to come to grips with the historical complicity of their tradition in establishing the path that led to Auschwitz. Christianity, too, now struggles with

8. See Arthur Cohen, *The Tremendum* (New York: Crossroad, 1981), chap. 1; Richard Rubenstein, *After Auschwitz* (Indianapolis: Bobbs-Merrill, 1966), 69; Emil Fackenheim, *God's Presence in History* (New York: Harper, 1970), 73; Elie Wiesel, *A Jew Today,* trans. Marion Wiesel (New York: Vantage, 1979), 194.

9. Fackenheim, *God's Presence in History,* 84, quoting his own article in *Commentary* (1967), entitled "Jewish Faith and the Holocaust."

the hermeneutical rupture of the Holocaust. The magnitude of this rupture is sending tremors through the very foundations of Christian self-understanding.

One of the paradoxes of the Shoah is that it has caused Jews, for the first time, to question the reality of their covenant just when Christians, for the first time, have become willing to affirm the Jewish covenant. After two thousand years of the "teachings of contempt," undergirded by the myth of supersession and hence a hermeneutic of supersession, the unheard-of and unthinkable happened within Christianity—the admission of the ongoing legitimacy of the Mosaic covenant and the affirmation of the Jewish people as still chosen of God. Although the Vatican II document *Nostra Aetate* is in many ways politically ambivalent, its use of Paul's Letter to the Romans resulted in a radical break with past Christian teachings. This document portrayed the church as a "wild shoot" grafted onto the "well-cultivated olive tree" of Judaism and insisted that God never revokes God's gifts and promises; therefore "the Jews should not be presented as rejected or accursed by God, as if this followed from the Holy Scriptures." This admission of the continuing validity of the Mosaic covenant amounts to a radical desacralization and relativization of the absolute claims made for the "new covenant" in Christ as the "only way to the Father." This admission was a radical break with the entire previous tradition, far more radical than the Catholic church may have realized at the time. Since that Vatican II statement of 1965, numerous official church statements, Catholic and Protestant, have affirmed and expanded upon this revolutionary foundation. In 1973 a joint Protestant-Catholic statement by a study group of the National Council of Churches and the National Council of Catholic Bishops indicated succinctly the dramatic reversal that Christian faith is undergoing in its affirmation: "In Christ the Church shares in Israel's election without superseding it."[10]

I suspect we will be well into the next millennium before the full significance of this radical rupture with the long tradition of the hermeneutic of supersession will fully penetrate Christian consciousness and action. As Nietzsche suggested, in another context, deeds are like astronomical events,

---

10. See Helga Croner, ed., *Stepping Stones to Further Jewish-Christian Relations* (New York: Paulist, 1977), 1–2; see also more recent statements in *More Stepping Stones to Jewish-Christian Relations* (New York: Paulist, 1985); for the statement by the study group see Helga Croner, ed., *Stepping Stones to Further Jewish-Christian Relations*, 152.

such as dying stars—they take time to travel before their effects can be experienced and absorbed. Nevertheless, the direction ahead is probably suggested by Father John Pawlikowski's comment in his survey of recent Christian post-Shoah experiments in Christology: "nearly every Christian scholar [doing post-Shoah theology] . . . has concluded from a serious investigation of the Judaism of Jesus' time that traditional claims for his messiahship must be dropped as unwarranted on the basis of the data at hand."[11] If this be the case, it will mean a rethinking of the very core of Christian faith and identity.

The hermeneutical rupture initiated by the Holocaust and the birth of the state of Israel (after all, part of the myth of supersession was that the Jews should wander homeless till the end of time) forces a radical decentering and relativization of Christian self-understanding. In the end it is bound to have profound effects on the relation of Christians not only to Jews but also to all the other religious communities of the world. For this hermeneutical rupture marks the end of the imperialism of Christian theology. The Shoah has forced upon the Christian tradition the assumption of a humility it has always preached but all too often has not practiced. As Christians absorb the full impact of the Shoah on their tradition they are finding themselves strangers in their own land and strangers to themselves, in need of forging new bonds of friendship and of discovering anew just who they are.

So where are we as Jews and Christians after the Holocaust? Everything has to be rethought and renegotiated. When a Hitler can say: "I believe that I am acting in accordance with the will of the Almighty Creator; by defending myself against the Jew I am fighting for the work of the Lord," and can go on to identify the Jews as "the personification of the devil," and we can trace these themes back through Luther to the Gospel of John (chap. 8), then has not the sacred Christian tradition itself become profane and demonic?

Auschwitz seared the traditional forms of Judaism and Christianity to the core. The question that remains is whether the fires of Auschwitz are the fires of the final destruction or the refining fires of transformation. For

---

11. See Friedrich Nietzsche, *The Gay Science*, in *The Portable Nietzsche*, ed. Walter Kaufmann (New York: Viking, 1968 [1954]), 95–96 (the context is not unrelated, as Nietzsche was speaking of the death of God); see John T. Pawlikowski, *Christ in the Light of Christian-Jewish Dialogue* (New York: Paulist, 1982), 19.

either tradition to go on as if nothing has happened would be to transform living traditions into museum pieces of an age gone by. Faith with integrity is possible after Auschwitz only if we are willing to descend spiritually into those fires, to excavate the abyss of the demonic, to risk destruction while hoping for transformation. To do so is itself a great leap of faith. To fail to do so would be the burial of faith beneath a facade of ahistorical denial.

ON PAUL, JOB, AND THE BURNING CHILDREN

That the Shoah has initiated a hermeneutical rupture in both Judaism and Christianity is clear. With regard to Judaism I can speak about this rupture only from an outsider's point of view. My intention here is to address this rupture from where I stand as a Christian alienated from my tradition by my encounter with Auschwitz. I seek to discover an alternative way to be Christian through a confrontation with the history of my own tradition and through an ongoing dialogue with my companions, Jewish and Christian, on this journey into a post-Shoah world.

Every theologian (Jewish or Christian) who recognizes the Shoah as a hermeneutical rupture has thereby acknowledged the Shoah as a new hermeneutical criterion by which any further interpretation must be measured in some sense. To admit the Shoah as an interpretive criterion leaves quite open in what sense it functions as such. For Richard Rubenstein, within Judaism it functions negatively to mark the death of the God of history and with it Rabbinic Judaism. But for Emil Fackenheim it functions positively as the occasion for a new command from the God of history calling for a renewed Judaism.

Within Christianity, for A. Roy Eckardt it marks the end of faith in the resurrection of Jesus as an already accomplished fact: "That Jewish man from Galilee sleeps now. He sleeps with the other Jewish dead, with all the disconsolate and the shattered ones of the murder camps. . . . Jesus of Nazareth shall be raised. So too shall the small Hungarian children who were burned alive at Auschwitz." Still others, such as Paul van Buren or Clemens Thoma, would reaffirm the resurrection of Jesus but interpret it as an act of God whereby Gentiles might be included to share with the Jews the promises made to Abraham.[12]

---

12. See A. Roy Eckardt, "The Resurrection and the Holocaust" (paper presented to the

Though we are still struggling to understand the full implications, the Shoah clearly forces a rereading and a reinterpretation of the Christian tradition. Whether that revision of Christianity can occur without destroying it remains to be seen. Hermeneutically, the meaning of a text is continually altered by its further implications as they unfold their influence in history. If it is true that "by their fruits you will know them" (Matt. 12:33), then the uses of the New Testament, throughout the history of Christian anti-Judaism, force upon us a violently altered perception of the Christian Scriptures and their meaning for the Christian tradition. It took the Shoah to make us aliens and strangers to our own Scriptures, to force us to read our own Scriptures through the eyes of the Jewish experience. Doing so precipitates a crisis of faith for which one is unlikely to be prepared. Yet I believe this is the path by which Christians must engage in the spiritual descent into the fires of Auschwitz. These fires might just be the refining fires that could restore the integrity of the Christian faith. There may well be a "commanding voice" from Auschwitz addressed to Christians as well as to Jews—for those who have the eyes to see and the ears to hear.

Rereading the Christian Scriptures and the history of Christianity in the light of the desolation of the Shoah profoundly shifts the focus of dominant and recessive elements; in other words, it creates a canon within the canon. We could take as an analogy Luther's tower-room experience and the hermeneutical shift to justification by faith that it produced. Luther's experience caused him to create a new canon within the canon in which he felt free to reject canonical status for certain books, such as the Letter of James, which did not meet the new hermeneutical criterion. Likewise, the Shoah forces the emergence of a new canon within the canon, which, for reasons I shall make clear, revolves around a new reading of Paul's Letter to the Romans and also the book of Job. But the Shoah experience is far more radical than Luther's experience. A better analogy would be the hermeneutical rupture created by the fall of the Temple in 70 C.E. that gave rise to the hermeneutic of supersession. The hermeneutical rupture of the

---

Israel Study Group, New York, March 4, 1978), 13 (quoted by Pawlikowski, *Christ*, 17; this view has since appeared in Eckardt, *Long Night's Journey into Day: Life and Faith After the Holocaust* [Detroit: Wayne State Univ. Press, 1982]; see esp. 128–33); see Paul van Buren, *A Theology of the Jewish-Christian Reality*, vol. 1: *Discerning the Way: A Theology of the Jewish-Christian Reality;* vol. 2: *A Christian Theology of the People Israel;* vol. 3: *Christ in Context* (New York: Seabury, 1980–1988); Clemens Thoma, *A Christian Theology of Judaism* (New York: Paulist, 1980).

Shoah, I am convinced, is bringing about not only a transformation of Luther's understanding of justification by faith but also a subversion of the myth of supersession that has dominated the history of Christian thought since 70 C.E.

Paul and the Apostasy of the Gospel Tradition

Like Marcion (although for very different reasons than those which motivated his anti-Judaic Gnosticism), we may find that everything after Paul is suspect and, at the very least, has to be read and reinterpreted in the light of Paul. Why should Paul's writings be the dividing line? Some have seen him as the main instigator of anti-Judaism. Paul has unquestionably been used that way. This was so, however, because Paul was interpreted in the light of a hermeneutical principle totally alien to him, namely, the myth of supersession. This myth emerged in the New Testament period only after the death of Paul, with the caesura of the fall of the Temple in 70 C.E. The emerging New Testament communities took the fall of the Temple as a sign of God's judgment on the rest of Judaism for its failure to accept Jesus as the messiah. So we are told two or three decades later, in Luke's Gospel, that Jesus wept over Jerusalem and said: "If you, even you, had recognized on this day the things that make for peace! But now they are hidden from your eyes. Indeed, the days will come upon you, when your enemies will set up ramparts around you and surround you, and hem you in on every side. They will crush you to the ground, you and your children within you, and they will not leave within you one stone upon another; because you did not recognize the time of your visitation from God" (Luke 19:42-44). Luke quickly follows this lament of Jesus with the parable of the tenants (found in Mark and Matthew as well), in which the tenant farmers first persecute the messengers sent by the owner of the vineyard to collect his share and finally kill the owner's son. What is the lesson of this parable? "He will come and destroy those tenants and give the vineyard to others" (Luke 20:16). The others, of course, are the followers of his son—the good and faithful servants. The scribes and high priests "realized that he had told this parable against them" (Luke 20:19).

In the light of the Shoah, one has to say that the path to Auschwitz begins here. It may be true that Luke had only the scribes and Pharisees, not the whole of Judaism, in mind, but those fine distinctions were lost on the ears of the Gentiles who came to dominate the movement. As one moves through the Gospels, from Mark (ca. 70 C.E.) to John (ca. 90–100 C.E.), all of which were written after the fall of the Temple, the explicitness of the supersession theme seems to grow stronger and clearer until in John all sympathy and identification with Judaism seems to have dissolved into the nondialectical opposition of "the children of light" against "the children of the devil" (John 8). The metaphor of the Jew as "the child of the devil" then begins to wend its way through the church fathers and the medieval theologians until it finds its way into the writings of Martin Luther and eventually into the speeches of Hitler.

From Marcion to Martin Luther and beyond, Paul's writings seem to have been read as an anti-Judaic vindication of gentile superiority in line with the post-70 C.E. supersessionist hermeneutics. But contemporary scholarship has made it clear that Paul was not a supersessionist, although exactly how to understand his position continues to challenge exegetical ingenuity. It is extremely difficult to recover the frame of reference that existed prior to 70 C.E. The continuing disputes about Paul indicate just how difficult it is to free oneself of the influence of past exegetical traditions, especially Luther's psychological reading of Romans. Thus there is poetic justice in the fact that it is a Lutheran exegete, Krister Stendahl, who has shown us how to read Paul with new eyes and ears. By stripping away the presuppositions with which Luther approached the text and paying attention to the textual location of justification language in Paul, he offers us a reasonable hope of coming closer to seeing and hearing what Paul is saying in his own first-century situation. It is startling to discover that Paul's primary concern in Romans is not whether Jews can be included in a gentile religion but whether Gentiles can be included within the promises made to Jews. It is illuminating to discover that "justification by faith was hammered out by Paul for the very specific and limited purpose of defending the rights of Gentile converts to be full and genuine heirs to the promises of God to Israel" and not to answer the broader question of "on what grounds . . . are we to be saved."[13]

A detailed exegesis of Paul's position in Romans is not my purpose here. Since I am not a professional New Testament scholar, my comments

---

13. Krister Stendahl, *Paul Among Jews and Gentiles* (Philadelphia: Fortress, 1976), 2–3.

can be no more than footnotes on the brilliant new exegetical work on Paul by scholars like Krister Stendahl, E. P. Sanders, and Lloyd Gaston. Nevertheless, I must make a few salient points about my post-Shoah understanding of Paul's Letter to the Romans in the light of this new tradition of exegesis.

Let me begin with an observation made by Jacques Ellul that I consider theologically fundamental. The Letter to the Romans is unique in the body of New Testament literature. I have already noted its historical uniqueness as a document predating the fall of the Temple and the myth of supersession. Ellul's view of its uniqueness has to do with its content and focus. It is the only place in the New Testament where an explicit theology of the relationship between non-Christian Jews and gentile Christians is worked out. It would be a fundamental mistake, Ellul argues, to take fragmentary references to this relationship in the Gospels and other New Testament writings as theologically normative, since they were never written with the intention of giving a full account of this relationship but rather reflect diverse contexts of meaning quite tangential to this issue. Thus, Ellul concludes, Paul's vision is to be taken as normative and all other statements in the New Testament must be reconciled to it.[14]

We have said that Paul is not a supersessionist. Whether Paul has a coherent position on the relation of Jews to gentile Christians is, however, still a matter of debate. E. P. Sanders interprets Paul as a christological exclusivist who cannot envision salvation apart from Christ. He suggests that Paul sacrifices logic in order to hold two irreconcilable convictions: (1) according to God's promise all Israel will be saved, and (2) all salvation is through faith in Christ. Sanders rejects Stendahl's attempt to reconcile these convictions in a two-covenant theology.[15]

Stendahl does not really deny this inconsistency. He responds by noting that Sanders reads Paul as if Paul were a systematic theologian, whereas he reads Paul as being a pastoral theologian who would be far less concerned with logical consistency than Sanders suggests. Sanders describes the difference between himself and Stendahl by saying that election has soteriological significance in his understanding of Paul whereas it does not for Stendahl. My own view is that election does have soteriological significance

14. Jacques Ellul, *Un Chrétien pour Israël* (Monaco: Rocher), 23–24.
15. See E. P. Sanders, *Paul, the Law, and the Jewish People* (Philadelphia: Fortress, 1983), 197–99, 193 (see esp. chap. 6, pp. 171–206).

for Paul, but not the exclusivist significance that Sanders suggests. Sanders treats election through faith in Christ as equivalent to salvation, "the elect" and "the saving remnant" as equivalent to "the saved." But that is to make the mistake that Christians have often stereotypically accused Jews of making, namely, presuming that election or chosenness is a special status (which allows one to take the salvation of the chosen for granted) rather than a special responsibility. But in my view Paul is not guilty of that presumption. Paul's view of election is that it is a call to participate in a remnant that saves not itself but the whole of which it is a part. Election for Paul is vocational and dialectical. It is a matter of becoming part of the remnant (i.e., the hidden righteous) for whose sake God spares the world and showers his mercy, like the rain, on the just and the unjust alike. Finally, Stendahl does not need to make excuses for Paul's inconsistency by appealing to his pastoral style, since once we let go of Luther's reading of Paul and recognize the proper role of election in relation to the concept of the "saving remnant," the alleged inconsistency in Paul disappears.[16]

Both Sanders and Stendahl claim that the goal of their respective interpretations is to recover the meaning of Paul in his own historical context irrespective of contemporary concerns. Yet their interpretations remain at odds. Sanders accuses Stendahl of injecting contemporary Jewish-Christian concerns into his interpretation. I think Stendahl might well accuse Sanders of injecting Luther's understanding of justification by faith into Paul. Stendahl argues persuasively that justification by faith is not the central theme of Paul's thought, as it is for Luther, but a theme restricted to grafting Gentiles into the promises. Stendahl has made a good case for not reading the psychological bias of the Augustinian-Lutheran tradition back into Paul (as I think Sanders still does), for Paul suffers none of the angst of these later figures. As Lloyd Gaston has pointed out, this psychological bias tends to turn justification by faith into a subjective "work" that one must do to be saved.[17]

16. For the details of their dispute see the dialogue between Sanders and Stendahl in *Union Seminary Quarterly Review* 33, nos. 3–4 (Spring and Summer 1978): 175–91.

17. See Lloyd Gaston, *Paul and the Torah* (Vancouver: Univ. of British Columbia Press, 1987), 59. See also Stendahl, *Paul Among Jews and Gentiles,* esp. 23–40 on "Justification Rather Than Forgiveness," and the chapter on "The Apostle Paul and the Introspective Conscience of the West," 78–96. The Reformers avoided turning faith into a work by insisting on the doctrine of predestination, only to end up in double predestination, which makes God seem arbitrary and demonic. Much of contemporary theology and preaching tries to avoid that pitfall by treating faith as a call to personal decision, which, of course, ends up treating faith as a work.

My own reading of Paul is closer to the readings of Krister Stendahl and Lloyd Gaston than to that of Sanders. Gaston argues that for Paul, unlike Luther, salvation occurs not through human faith but through God's gracious faithfulness. Indeed, he is convinced that "the word *pistis* . . . should be translated as 'faithfulness' rather than 'faith,' " and shows that in Romans, the faithfulness that justifies is that of God.[18] Salvation comes not through a subjective human act of faith but through God's promise. Or as Paul puts it quite unambiguously, "it depends not on human will or exertion but on God who shows mercy" (Rom. 9:16).

I believe Stendahl's case, in his dispute with Sanders, can be strengthened by highlighting the dialectical movement of Paul's thought, a movement between Jew and Gentile (in which each is equally balanced in relation to the other) in Paul's understanding of the mystery of the divine plan. Paul's concern in Romans, as Stendahl has argued, is to show that neither Jew nor Gentile has any special advantage in God's sight, and hence neither party has any cause for boasting. In the opening chapters his primary concern is to defuse any Jewish cause for boasting (see chap. 3, especially v. 9), then in Romans 9–11 (see especially 11:25) his concern shifts to defusing any gentile cause for boasting.

In the opening chapters Paul wants to reassure Gentiles that God is the God not only of Jews but also of Gentiles (3:29). The language of "not only . . . but also" is frequently repeated and sets the tone for the letter. Paul's argument is that salvation is not only for the Jew but also for the Gentile. His worry is not that Jews will not be included but that Gentiles may think they cannot be included unless they become Jews. His reassuring message is that "the promise holds true for all Abraham's descendants, not only for those who have the law but for all who have his faith" (4:16). Again, Paul takes for granted the inclusion of those who have the law, and he argues for the inclusion of those outside the law—the Gentiles.

Perhaps Paul thought that Jews who do not accept Jesus as messiah were wrong, but that is probably not the case, since as Lloyd Gaston argues, "*Christos* is for Paul a proper name and is not to be translated 'messiah.' . . . He is neither the climax of history nor the fulfillment of the covenant, and therefore . . . not seen in relation to David or Moses. For Paul, Jesus is the new act of the righteousness of God by which the

18. Gaston, *Paul and the Torah*, 11–14.

Gentiles are included, and therefore he is seen in negative relationship with Adam and positive relationship with Abraham." Indeed, Gaston argues that the real dividing issue, the stone on which the Jews stumbled, was not the question of the messiah but rather accepting that in Jesus God was providing a way for the inclusion of Gentiles, as Gentiles, in the promises.[19] In any case, whatever the stumbling block was, we do not have to wait till Romans 11 to discover that this does not put the Jews outside the divine plan of salvation. For in chapter 3 he asks, "What if some were unfaithful? Will their faithlessness nullify the faithfulness of God? By no means! Although everyone is a liar, let God be proved true" (3:3-4). Paul's confidence rests not on resolving the question of who has faith in Jesus and who does not (a subjective condition), but on God's promises and God's faithfulness (an objective condition not dependent on a believer's subjective consciousness). No matter what persons may do, God does not revoke God's own promises (11:29). Indeed, Paul's conclusion in chapter 11 is that "God has imprisoned all [Jew and Gentile] in disobedience so that he may be merciful to all" (11:32).

This point leads to what I understand as the heart of Paul's position. The core of Paul's argument in Romans 9–11 seems to pivot on a complex dialectical reversal as the underlying structure of God's mysterious plan of salvation. He does not want Gentiles to be ignorant of the mystery, lest they become conceited and think themselves better than the Jews (11:25). That mystery is not simply that "hardening [i.e., blindness] has come upon part of Israel until the full number of Gentiles has come in. And so all Israel will be saved," as Rom. 11:25-26 suggests. It is more complicated than that. According to Paul, God said to Moses: " 'I will have mercy on whom I have mercy, and I will have compassion on whom I have compassion.' So it depends not on human will or exertion, but on God who shows mercy. For the scripture says to Pharaoh, 'I have raised you up for the very purpose of showing my power in you, so that my name may be proclaimed in all the earth.' So then he has mercy on whomever he chooses and he hardens the heart of whomever he chooses" (9:15-17). That is, God hardened the heart of a Gentile, Pharaoh, so that he might elect the Jews, through the Exodus, and make them his own people, that through

19. Ibid., 7, 14, also 129ff. The stumbling block, as I understand it, would not be the inclusion of righteous Gentiles in the "world to come" but rather the inclusion of Gentiles in the "saving remnant" of Israel, the remnant for whose sake God spares the world.

them (and because of Pharaoh's hardness of heart) his name might be spread throughout all the earth. But then God hardened the hearts of the Jews, that "through their stumbling salvation has come to the Gentiles" (11:11). That is, God's plan was that the Jews would reject the message so that Jewish missionaries like himself would be forced to take the message elsewhere, in order to complete the fulfillment of God's purpose—the proclamation of the name of God throughout all the earth. This complex dialectical reversal makes it appear that "as regards the gospel, they [the Jews] are enemies of God" but only "for your [Gentiles] sake." However, "as regards election, they [the Jews] are beloved, for the sake of their ancestors; for the gifts and the calling of God are irrevocable" (11:28-29). It would seem that, for Paul, the status of "enemy" is a dialectical historical role one plays in the divine plan, which in no way affects one's eternal salvation. Indeed, gentile Christians are also described as reconciled with God while still his enemies (5:10).

Paul can remain assured of salvation for all parties, despite their role in the divine strategy, because everything hinges on God's gracious faithfulness, his irrevocable promise. Although God once made Gentiles blind (Pharaoh and the Egyptians) and at another time made Jews blind, his actions are not vindictive or arbitrary. Why? Because "it depends not on human will or exertion but on God who shows mercy" (9:16). For "God has imprisoned all in disobedience that he might be merciful to all" (11:32). Thus Paul can remark: "O the depths of the riches and wisdom and knowledge of God!" (11:33), and conclude, as Krister Stendahl has pointed out, with the only doxology in his writings that is not christological: "For from him and through him and to him are all things. To him be glory forever. Amen" (11:36).[20]

As inclusive as this dialectical vision may be in Paul, one can surely object, as E. P. Sanders has, that it is not fully consistent, since in a number of passages Paul seems to suggest that only a remnant of Israel will be saved. For he says, "at the present time there is a remnant, chosen by grace. . . . the rest were hardened" (11:5-7). Paul also seems to suggest that God has now chosen Gentiles (followers of Christ) in order to make Jews jealous and "save some of them" (11:14). How does one reconcile the emphasis on "some" and "all" in Paul's vision? The answer, I think,

20. Stendahl, *Paul Among Jews and Gentiles*, 4.

lies in Paul's understanding of the saving power of a remnant. For he argues that "if the Lord of hosts had not left survivors [i.e., a remnant] to us, we would have fared like Sodom, and been made like Gomorrah" (9:29). Now what is the lesson of Sodom but that God would have spared the whole city if there had been but a remnant of ten righteous people (Gen. 18:16-33). Paul is thinking like a Jew when he speaks of a saving remnant. As God does not go back on his promises "because of the patriarchs," so in every age God has provided a faithful remnant for whose sake the whole, of which the remnant is a part, is spared. As Gaston says: "That is how the concept of the representative righteous has functioned from Genesis 18 down to the later Jewish concept of the *Lamedvovniks* (thirty-six righteous)."[21] Hence it remains true for Paul that "God has imprisoned all in disobedience so that he may be merciful to all" (Rom. 11:32). The "righteous acts" or "gracious deeds" of God are manifest through the lives of both Abraham and Jesus. God's graciousness is that he always provides a saving remnant who live out of, and witness to, God's faithfulness. This has been true, so that even as there is always a remnant among the Jews who live out of the faithfulness of Abraham, so too now there can be a remnant among the Gentiles who live out of the faithfulness of Jesus. For both Jew and Gentile witness to the same faithfulness, namely, that of the God of Abraham, the God who raised Jesus from the dead (Romans 4, especially v. 24). It is God's faithfulness that justifies or makes righteous.

This witness is historical and dialectical. Who is blind and who can see at any given time is the doing of God, who makes each blind (or "hard of heart") for the sake of the other, so that in the end all can be saved. Thus the fact that some branches have been cut off from the tree of Israel while Gentiles are grafted on is not cause for boasting. For Paul warns the Gentiles: "It is not you that support the root, but the root that supports you" (11:18). Moreover, those "grafted on" and those "cut off," cannot be equated with those "saved" and those "damned," for these terms refer not to eternal salvation but to membership in the saving remnant, by which salvation will be brought to all.

Paul's vision provides a constructive model for post-Shoah Christian theology. It reveals that prior to the fall of the Temple in 70 C.E. there was a radically different vision of the place of Jews and Christians in the divine

21. Gaston, *Paul and the Torah*, 148.

plan of salvation, one that was completely lost to view after the myth of supersession emerged. Paul had a warning about just such a development: "You [Gentiles] will say, 'Branches were broken off that I might be grafted in.' . . . Do not become proud [on that account]" (11:19-20). To be ignorant of the mystery of God's plan is to be conceited (11:25), and for Gentiles to think themselves better than Jews will result in their being "cut off" (11:22). Paul's understanding is precisely the inverse of some Christians who argue that the only "complete Jew" is one who accepts Jesus. For Paul, Jews are complete in their own covenant, for God's election and promise can never be revoked. It is the Gentiles who are incomplete if they do not accept that it is "the root" that makes them holy. Gentiles who in their arrogance refuse to accept their dependent status will be summarily "cut off."[22]

Are we not forced, by the hermeneutical criterion of the Shoah, to reread the history of Christianity from Mark's Gospel in 70 C.E. onward as a history of apostasy? Does not the gospel tradition repeat the sin of Adam, who blamed his transgression on Eve? The rabbis also interpreted the destruction of the Temple as a judgment from God, but they did not try to displace the judgment upon someone else. They did not resort to Adam's tactics, as Christians did. The myth of supersession embedded in the New Testament is the expression of a boasting and a conceit that, according to Paul's criterion, must be said to have resulted in the "cutting off" of these new covenant people. If so, this makes most of Christian history, as a covenant history, null and void very near to its point of origin. We must conclude that Paul's prophetic warning and judgment were fulfilled soon after his death. Once we understand that gentile Christians were "cut off"

---

22. One might imagine Paul's argument in chap. 11 on the analogy of a relay race, in which Israel is a team of two runners in tandem, carrying the baton (symbolizing the carrying of God's name to the nations), passing it on from generation to generation; then toward the end of the race new runners are brought in, the Gentiles, to share in the task (to become one of the runners in tandem) and run the final laps. When the last runner crosses the finish line and the race is won, Gentiles must not think that they won and the Jews lost (i.e., the myth of supersession). On the contrary, Gentiles are partners in the race; they would not be in the race at all if it were not for the Jews. Hence the "root" supports the Gentiles and not vice versa. It would be a sin of pride if the Gentiles were to think that they alone won the race, one which would disqualify them as participants. They have been grafted in and they can be cut out. As I understand Paul's view, both Jews and Christians are on the same team, elected to the common task of carrying God's name to the nations. When the last runner crosses the line, everybody on the team, Jews and Gentiles (including non-Christians) alike, wins—and so does the whole of creation.

from a role in the "saving remnant," then it becomes clear that the entire history of Christian anti-Judaism, especially from Constantine onward, is empirical evidence for the truth of this claim. For one cannot be part of a saving remnant if one has bargained away one's anthropological status as a community of transcendence in order to become a cosmological or sacred society. One cannot be a saving remnant if one has gained the world but lost one's soul.

Job as a Post-Holocaust Parable

The Shoah as hermeneutical principle forces a rereading and reinterpretation not only of the gospel tradition of supersession and its history but also of the post-Holocaust relation of Jews and Christians in the light of that history. Again, transforming the canon within the canon, the book of Job virtually leaps forward as a central text in a post-Shoah world. The Shoah elicits new meanings from this already provocative scripture, meanings that turn it into a post-Shoah parable on the relation of Jews and Christians.

From a Jewish point of view, one of the most salient characteristics of the Job story is the dialectical reversal of the trial metaphor. In the framing story (1:1—2:10 and 42:10-17) Job is put on trial by God, but in the main body of the scripture—the dialogue with the comforters—the roles of God and Job are reversed and Job places God on trial. The comforters wish to make Job guilty so that God does not appear unjust for inflicting or allowing the infliction of suffering upon Job. Job refuses to play that game. He steadfastly insists: "Till I die I will not renounce my integrity. My innocence I maintain, I will not relinquish it" (27:5-6).[23] So Job demands his day in court: "I will say to God: 'Don't condemn me; let me know your case against me' " (10:2). Nevertheless, he is skeptical that he will get a fair hearing: "But how can man be acquitted before God?. . . If I summoned and he answered, I do not believe he would heed me. He would crush me with a tempest" (9:2, 16-17). Having prophesied his own fate, which will come true when God finally appears to him in the whirlwind, still Job persists in his challenge: "Let Shaddai answer me" (31:35).

23. The quotations of the book of Job are from Marvin Pope, *Job*, Anchor Bible 15, 2d ed. (Garden City, N.Y.: Doubleday, 1965). For my interpretation of Job, I owe an intellectual debt to James Williams of Syracuse University, who first taught me to appreciate the dialectical complexity of the book of Job.

Like Abraham before him (arguing with God over Sodom and Go-morrah), who dared to ask: "Shall not the judge of all the earth do what is just?" (Gen. 18:25), Job is not afraid to put God in the judgment seat of the accused. But unlike Abraham, Job is not overconfident that God will answer yes when the question of justice is raised. Job refuses to sacrifice his integrity to make God appear just. Job may well express the spiritual situation of Jews after the Holocaust.

Job is a post-Holocaust parable for the Christian as well, and that is my primary interest here. In this respect it is not the trial of God by Job that interests me but the dialogue between Job and the comforters. The com-forters are the prosecuting attorneys who seek to defend God's honor by making Job appear guilty. So Eliphaz can argue: "What innocent ever perished?" (4:7). Bildad can ask rhetorically: "Does God pervert justice?" (8:3). And Zophar can insist that although "these were your words, you say, 'My doctrine is pure.' You are clean in your own eyes. But would that God might speak, might open his lips against you. He would tell you what is hidden." (11:4-6). The logic of the comforters is clear: God is just, therefore Job must be guilty, and he deserves his suffering.

Is this not precisely the logic Christians have used to explain and justify, and indeed bring about, the sufferings of the Jews throughout Christian history? The Christian apologetic has been that the very suffering of the Jews, as a wandering homeless people, was a negative witness to the truth of Christianity and proof of their guilt before God. If the Jews suffered, it proved the charge that they were guilty of deicide. Of course, the suffering of the Jews was a self-fulfilling prophecy under a Christian majority who so believed.[24]

The point of Job as a post-Shoah parable for Christians lies in the fate of the comforters as portrayed at the close of the tale. In Job's encounter with God in the whirlwind everything Job had predicted about his inability to get a fair hearing from God seems to come true. He predicted that God would not listen to him but "crush him with a tempest" (9:17), and that is exactly what happens. Job is overwhelmed by the mighty power of one

24. For a helpful and fair-minded treatment of the ambivalent history of Christian treatment of the Jews see Pinchas Lapide, *Three Popes and the Jews* (New York: Hawthorn, 1967). The paradox is that, certainly since Gregory the Great, the popes have often been the chief protectors of the Jews against popular hostility while at the same time often promoting this same hostility through their preaching and teaching (see esp. ibid., 51).

who ignores the question of his guilt or innocence and instead roars forth a challenge: "Where were you when I founded the earth?"(38:4). "Would you annul my judgment, condemn me that you may be justified? . . . Can you thunder with a voice like his?" (39:8-9). Job is forced to repent and recant through sheer force of intimidation—"I recant and repent in dust and ashes" (42:6). God wins, but it is a hollow victory, for Job's prophecy is fulfilled and God's arbitrariness is unmasked.

But the story is not yet over. What of the comforters? Here, as in Paul, we encounter a dialectical reversal—one that makes Job the "saving remnant." In the final chapter, God says to Eliphaz the Temanite, "My anger burns against you and your two friends; for you have not spoken truth of me, as did Job, my servant. So now take yourselves seven bullocks and seven rams, and go to Job, my servant, and make a burnt offering for yourselves, and Job, my servant, will pray for you, for I will accept him, so that I may not do anything rash to you; for you have not told truth of me, as did Job, my servant" (42:7-8).

Here we have the paradoxical vindication of Job in his court claim against God. The comforters have been saying, "If you suffer you deserve it, for God is just." Job has steadfastly insisted on his innocence and integrity and therefore questioned the justice of God. Now we find God confirming that Job told the truth and the comforters were lying.

Allegorically transposed by the event of the Shoah, the dialogue of Job and the comforters becomes the historical dialogue between Jews and Christians. Christians have claimed that the historical sufferings of Jews were a divine punishment and a sure sign of Jewish guilt for the rejection and death of the messiah. Jews have steadfastly and rightly maintained their innocence of any such guilt. In a post-Holocaust world, and under the impact of critical historical consciousness, Christians too are now admitting the dubiousness of such charges. They are, perhaps for the first time, ready to hear: "You have not told truth of me, as did . . . my servant."

What is the situation of Jews and Christians, in a post-Shoah world, in the light of this parable? Like Job, Jews find themselves blessed and approved by the God who failed them. Like the comforters, Christians find themselves in the debt of Jews for the reestablishment of their relationship to this God. They must make reparation as did the comforters, and then depend upon the intercession of the Jews as the condition of God's graciousness. The offering of reparation must be nothing less than the reformulation of the Christian gospel on a nonsupersessionist model. This reformulation must be acceptable to the Jewish community, such that they are willing to speak on behalf of Christians to the God whose silent yet commanding voice speaks from Auschwitz. If this voice commands Jews not to grant Hitler a posthumous victory, it also commands Christians to rethink their own self-understanding such that being a Christian is possible only by affirming the authentic integrity of Judaism. Not even the smallest precedent must be afforded any future Hitler for a "final solution to the Jewish problem."

"The Burning Children": A Hermeneutical Criterion

Let me reduce the hermeneutical principle that must guide Christian theology, in its retelling of the Christian story, to a single sentence. The sentence is not mine but Irving Greenberg's: "No statement, theological or otherwise, should be made that would not be credible in the presence of the burning children."[25]

Greenberg reminds us that during the Holocaust the Nazis threw Jewish children alive into the crematoria fires. After Auschwitz, no theologian should ever write a sentence without spiritually descending in sympathy and imagination into those fires to submit his or her writings for the approval of those children. Never again should any theologian write anything that might even remotely reopen the path from supersession to genocide. Here we have the situation of Job and his comforters, where only with Job's approval are their offerings found acceptable by God. This, I believe, is the central hermeneutical principle to be derived from the Holocaust for Christian theologians. With respect to its portrayal of the Jews, no Christian theology is acceptable to God that is not acceptable to his chosen people, the Jews.

BEYOND THE SACRED AND THE SECULAR

Richard Rubenstein maintains that "*the Holocaust was an expression of some of the most significant political, moral, religious and demographic*

---

25. Irving Greenberg, "Cloud of Smoke, Pillar of Fire: Judaism, Christianity, and Modernity after the Holocaust," in *Auschwitz: Beginning of a New Era?* ed. Eva Fleischner (New York: KTAV, 1977), 23.

tendencies of Western civilization in the twentieth century." The Holocaust grew out of the deepest trends of Western civilization, trends that led to modernization and secularization. Drawing on the work of Max Weber and Peter Berger, Rubenstein contends that the emergence of the modern, secular, bureaucratized world was a necessary precondition for the Nazi genocidal project. But more to the point, he argues that such a world is a direct outgrowth of the religious vision of Judaism, which desacralized both nature and society. Begun by Judaism and completed by the Protestant Reformation, this desacralization, once started, could not be stopped. Human existence became more and more defined by scientific and technical-bureaucratic reason. The result is the modern world in which nothing is sacred, not even human life.[26] In such a world of desolation Jewish children are thrown into the crematoria alive to improve on efficiency and save gas.

The great irony of Western history is that this desacralization process, which began with the myth of the God of history who disenchants nature and society, leads finally to the demise of this God in the death camps of a desacralized world. For Rubenstein, the story of Western civilization is the story of the sacred giving way to the profane, the secular, and the demonic. Despite his allusions to Hegelian dialectic (i.e., "the cunning of history"), Rubenstein's vision of secularization seems closer to Comte's (i.e., from myth through metaphysics to science). After Auschwitz, the sacred has been swallowed up by the secular, and Judaism must learn to go on without the God of history. For Rubenstein, the final vindication of his argument is secular Zionist Israel, which has been established after Auschwitz by human secular initiative and in direct contradiction to Orthodox messianic beliefs.[27]

Yet Irving Greenberg draws quite another conclusion from this outcome. Greenberg's understanding of history is neither Comtean nor Hegelian. If there is a dialectic at work in history, it is for him more Kierkegaardian than Hegelian, for it has no synthesis. The Shoah introduces into history an unending dialectic between faith and loss of faith that sears and transforms both the sacred and the secular. The dialectic continually turns back upon itself to negate itself and force the issues of the sacred and the secular to greater and deeper levels of tension.

---

26. Richard Rubenstein, *The Cunning of History: The Holocaust and the American Future*, new ed. (New York: Harper & Row, 1978), 27–31.
27. Richard Rubenstein, *After Auschwitz* (Indianapolis: Bobbs-Merrill, 1966), 69.

According to Greenberg, after the Holocaust the categories of sacred and secular seem to have undergone a reversal. The paradox is that after Auschwitz it is not the most traditional or Orthodox forms of Judaism but Zionism and the secular Israeli state that have come to affirm the sanctity of human life as created in the image of God. While the Orthodox would deny even the right for there to be such a state, the secular Israelis have taken upon themselves the task of welcoming, affirming, and protecting Jews in all their diversity. After Auschwitz, any expression that affirms life is holy and any expression that affirms Jewishness is "orthodox," no matter how "unorthodox" or even secular it seems. In the death camps, no distinction was made between the secular Jew and the Orthodox Jew. Indeed, "in the Holocaust many rabbis ruled that every Jew killed for being Jewish has died for the sanctification of the name of God."[28]

Greenberg is quick to add that one must not deduce from this an unqualified approval of secularism, for that would be to enter into complicity with the very demons of Auschwitz.[29] The radical nature of the Shoah lies in the fact that it demythologizes *both* the sacred and the secular. The sign above the gates that lead to the post-Shoah world of modern civilization should read: "Abandon All Hope in Both the Sacred and the Secular, Ye Who Enter Here." In this world one is forever tossed about in the dialectical whirlwind of hope and despair, of faith and doubt. One is forced, like Job, to use the tradition against the tradition with the desperate hope that a way beyond the contradictions might be found; or if not, a way might be found to live with them. Like Jacob who wrestled with God as with a stranger— a God who refused to give his name and who injured yet blessed him—a post-Shoah faith shall have to wrestle with God as with a stranger (Gen. 32:22-32).

In the post-Shoah world, provided one manages to avoid despair, one seems to be forced into either a mystical silence or a utopian hope against hope. Sometimes, as in Elie Wiesel, one finds both present. Wiesel, who so often turns toward the silence, can also find the voice to say to the God of Israel: "Either You are our partner in history, or You are not. If You are, do Your share; if You are not, we consider ourselves free of past commitments. Since you choose to break the Covenant, so be it. And yet,

---

28. Greenberg, "Cloud of Smoke," 50.
29. Ibid.

and yet . . . we went on believing, hoping, invoking His name. . . . In other words, we did not give up on Him. . . . For this is the essence of being Jewish: never to give up—never to yield to despair. . . . When all hope is gone, Jews invent new hopes." In a mood that echoes Wiesel, Greenberg argues that to succumb to despair is to grant Auschwitz the final word. To be a Jew is to engage in a hope that is "sober, and built on the sands of despair, free from illusions. Yet Jewish history affirms hope."[30]

For both Greenberg and Wiesel, everything depends on a willingness to live out of such an illusionless hope in the midst of the unresolvable tension between the silence of God and the demonic structures of the modern world. Precisely this willingness prevents one from embracing a false hope in either the sacred or the profane. The reality of God, if it is to be found anywhere, is not tied to either the sacred or the profane but, in the tradition of Job, to human dignity wherever it is affirmed. If God is to be God, it cannot be at the expense of human beings; rather it must be the God who says to all false comforters: "You have not told truth of me, as did Job, my servant."

The holiness of God transcends the demonic uses of the sacred and the profane. Where both the sacred and the profane would sacrifice human integrity in the name of some "higher purpose," the holy would affirm human integrity against all such purposes. Remembering that the Nazis proceeded in their atrocities by first denying the humanity of their victims— marking them as "subhuman"—Greenberg, from the midst of the dialectical whirlwind of faith and doubt, would deny the Nazis a final victory by rescuing the image of God as the foundation of human dignity and equality.[31]

If the Shoah as hermeneutical criterion has overturned the categories of sacred and profane with respect to Judaism in a post-Holocaust world, we cannot expect that Christianity will be spared. The hermeneutical principle of the burning children is clear in this matter. If the only way the New Testament tradition can proclaim good news is by denying the integrity of Jewish life and faith through the myth of supersession, then that sacred tradition is demonic. If no interpretation other than the myth of supersession can be derived from the New Testament and embraced in practice by Christians, then Christianity is immoral and obscene.

30. Elie Wiesel, *A Jew Today*, 194, 196; Greenberg, "Cloud of Smoke," 55.
31. Greenberg, "Cloud of Smoke," 28ff. and 40ff.

Some have suggested that the reinterpretation process forced upon Christians by the Shoah may be so radical as to destroy Christianity. It may be that whole segments of the gospel tradition have to be rejected and denied any role in future theology. Would such radical surgery leave anything we would recognize as Christian faith? For example, some theologians suggest that there is neither theological nor historical warrant for identifying Jesus as the messiah. But is Christianity still Christianity if this is denied? The answer, I believe, lies in focusing on the eschatological/apocalyptic theme of the second coming. The second coming is an expectation forced on the New Testament communities by a recognition that despite great diversity in Jewish expectations about the messiah, all agreed that the messiah would bring a new age of peace and justice that did not appear during Jesus' lifetime.

As I read Mark 8:27-33, the title *messiah* is used with reference to Jesus reluctantly, and only after significantly reworking its meaning. In Mark, the Davidic title *messiah* is subordinated in meaning to the apocalyptic title *Son of man*, which is in turn subordinated to the prophetic title *Suffering Servant*. Mark is willing to call the earthly Jesus "messiah" only if one means by messiah first the "Son of man" and only if one's understanding of "Son of man" is modified by the imagery of the "Suffering Servant." Thus he describes Jesus as rebuking Peter for using the term *messiah*. Then Jesus begins to teach instead about the Son of man and how he must suffer. For Mark, Jesus during his lifetime is the Suffering Servant who dies for the sins of the community. Only when he returns in glory, as the Son of man, will he fulfill the messianic prophecies and be "the messiah" who brings a new heaven and a new earth.

The New Testament hope for a second coming reaffirms a Jewish criterion for the term *messiah* and by implication acknowledges that Jesus is at the very least "not yet" messiah. The rule is: no messianic age, then no messiah. Irving Greenberg suggests that from a Jewish point of view Jesus should be understood not as a "false messiah" but rather as a "failed messiah":

A false messiah is one who has the wrong values: one who would teach that death will triumph, that people should oppress each other, that God hates us, or that sin and crime is the proper way. . . . A failed messiah is one who has the right values, upholds the covenant, but who did not attain the final goal. . . . Calling Jesus a failed messiah is in itself a term of irony. In the Jewish tradition, failure is a most ambiguous term. Abraham was a "failure." He dreamt of converting the whole world to Judaism. He ended up barely having one child carrying on the tradition. Even that child he almost lost. Moses was a "failure." He dreamt of taking slaves, making them into a free people and bringing them to the Promised Land. They were hopeless slaves; they died slaves in the desert; neither they nor Moses ever reached the Promised Land. Jeremiah was a "failure." He tried to convince the Jewish people that the temple would be destroyed unless they stopped their morally and politically wrong policies. . . .

All these "failures" are at the heart of divine and Jewish achievements. This concept of a "failed" but true messiah is found in a rabbinic tradition of the Messiah ben Joseph. The Messiah ben David (son of David) is the one who brings the final restoration. In the Messiah ben Joseph idea, you have a messiah who comes and fails, indeed is put to death, but this messiah paves the way for the final redemption. In fact, Christians also sense that Jesus did not exhaust the achievements of the final messiah. Despite Christian claims that Jesus was a total success . . . even Christians spoke of a Second Coming.[32]

Greenberg offers a useful perspective for Christian theological reflection. As the Pauline Letter to the Ephesians suggests, in Jesus we Gentiles who "were strangers to the covenant and its promise . . . without hope and without God . . . [are] now in Christ Jesus . . . brought near" (Eph. 2:12-13). And "this means that you are strangers and aliens no longer" (Eph. 2:19). What is accomplished in the first coming of Jesus is that Gentiles are grafted into the messianic hope to share in the messianic task, in which, as Greenberg suggests, both Jews and Christians are called to "recover the true role of Israel/Jacob who struggles with God and with humans, for the sake of God and of humanity."[33]

The New Testament does not witness to two comings of the messiah—only two comings of Jesus. The purpose of the second coming is precisely to bring the messianic age. Thus Christians, just as much as Jews, still await the coming of "the messiah." Christians, unlike Jews, may feel confident that when the messiah comes it will be Jesus of Nazareth. But lest we be tempted to take this confidence as an excuse for arrogance, we

---

32. Greenberg, "The Relationship of Judaism and Christianity: Toward a New Organic Model," *Quarterly Review* 4, no. 4 (Winter 1984): 10–11, in the reprint of this article in *Perspectives* published by the National Jewish Center for Learning and Leadership, 421 Seventh Avenue, New York, NY 10001.

33. Ibid.

should remember that to welcome the stranger is to welcome the messiah (Matt. 25:35). Indeed, as the book of Revelation insists, when the messiah comes he will appear as a stranger bearing a "new name" (Rev. 3:12). The Christian declaration of Jesus as messiah must remain a statement of faith and hope about the future. A careless use of the term *messiah* transforms a confession of faith and hope about the future into a supposedly already accomplished fact.

I do not believe this interpretation does violence to New Testament faith. On the contrary, it is more attuned to the gospel than the careless and triumphalist proclamation of Jesus as messiah as an already accomplished fact. Christians need not radically rewrite the Scriptures, as Marcion was inclined to do. All that is required is a faithful response to the hermeneutical shift to a new canonical core, a shift brought about by a theological and ethical confrontation with the reality of Auschwitz in the light of the history of Christian anti-Judaism.

If Luther's tower-room experience could force a reinterpretation of Christian faith that altered our understanding of the core of the gospel, then how much more so the Shoah. If Luther could reject everything in the Scriptures (Old Testament and New Testament) that did not teach justification by faith in Christ, then surely the burning children can forge for us a new canon, in which nothing is the word of God that does not teach the irrevocable election and integrity of the Jewish people. By implication, nothing is the word of God that teaches or in any way implies the supersession of Jews by Christians. Ironically, this new canon within the canon would include not only the book of Job but also (like Luther's canon) Paul's Letter to the Romans. But our post-Shoah reading of Romans would be a desacralized one, a reading no longer subject to the hubris of the supersession myth imposed on it after the fall of the Temple.

The new hermeneutical work on Paul presents us with a model that relativizes both Judaism and Christianity as sacred religions. The sacred always forces a dualism (i.e., sacred-profane) that separates the included from the excluded, or one's own from those who are strangers. In the dialectical Pauline vision of history, however, those who are strangers to each other (Jew and Gentile) only take on the appearance of being enemies and only for each other's sake, while before God (the Holy) they stand as equals in the divine promises (Rom. 11:28-29). Where the sacred divides, the holy reveals unity in diversity. As the work of Stendahl and Gaston suggests, God's act of justification or making righteous through Jesus is not primarily a psychological event of inner faith but a sociological event that establishes a right relationship between two communities of faith, Jews and Gentiles. (And the witness of these two communities as a saving remnant reconciles God and the whole human race.) This is accomplished when the sacrifice of Jesus overcomes the hostility toward the law on the part of Gentiles who, being outside the law, felt excluded from God's promises.[34] As the Letter to the Ephesians puts it, in the blood of Christ, those who had no part in the promises are now included as Gentiles, and this brings the hostility between Jews and Gentiles to an end (Eph. 2:11-22). It is a tragic irony that what was intended as an act of reconciliation became interpreted as a cause for pride. This led to supersessionist claims on the part of Gentiles who refused to allow that God could accept Jews and Christians as different and therefore insisted all must become the same—namely, Christian.

Reading Paul in the light of Job as a post-Shoah parable, should not Christians now be prepared to bring a desacralized and demythologized gospel story before the God of Israel with the hope of Jewish intercession on their behalf? The test of this new faith will be its commitment to the integrity of the Jewish people as an autonomous covenant community of faith and a commitment to the secular state of Israel as an essential component of that autonomy. Moreover, this test extends beyond the Jewish people to the protection of human dignity wherever it is threatened by the genocidal tendencies of our age. For it is not those who say "Lord, Lord" who shall enter the kingdom of God, but those who comfort and protect the afflicted and the stranger. It is not those who would rob the stranger of his or her dignity in order to make God appear just who will be speaking the truth about God, but those who by their words and deeds save all future children from the fires of any future Holocaust.

---

34. The "burden of the law," if I understand Gaston rightly, reflects not a Jewish attitude to the law but the attitude of gentile Judaizers who, not understanding the covenant as gracious election, think that the key to being saved is obedience to the law.

CHAPTER TWO

ETHICS AFTER AUSCHWITZ

CHRISTIANS AND THE JEWISH NARRATIVE TRADITION OF CHUTZPAH

UNQUESTIONING OBEDIENCE AND ICONOCLASTIC AUDACITY

The problem of faith after Auschwitz is different for Jews than it is for Christians. For Jews, it is God's credibility, as well as belief in the goodness of human beings, that is in question. How can one go on believing and trusting in either the God of history or in other human beings after Auschwitz? For Christians, it is their own credibility that is in question. How could those who claim to be followers of the messiah be the bearers of so much hatred and destruction? How could they who were taught to love their neighbor, and indeed even their enemy, stand by so passively while Jews were slaughtered? How could they who were called to be in the world but not of it be so completely conformed to the demonic and destructive world of Hitler's Germany?

For Christians the Shoah presents a moral problem that forces a rethinking of the meaning of their faith. Once Christians face the historical links between Christian anti-Judaism and the Shoah, they are confronted with a moral imperative not to repeat the sins of their ancestors. Moral integrity demands that Christians rethink and reshape the way they tell the gospel story. Having suggested the hermeneutical core of this reshaping process, I must now address the question of Christian ethics in the light of the Shoah. Quite apart from the obvious need to root out the teachings of supersession and contempt and to rethink the messianic and christological claims of Christianity, there is a fundamental weakness in the Christian understanding of faith that helps to account for the ethical weakness of Christians in their failure to stand with their Jewish brothers and sisters during the Shoah.

The hypothesis I wish to explore in the aftermath of the Shoah is that different models of faith have different ethical consequences. How is it possible that, in spite of more than two thousand years of oppression and persecution, Jews have remained faithful to their tradition? Why did Christians, who in the beginning were also persecuted, become persecutors and abandon the central gospel injunction to love one's neighbor, even one's enemy, as oneself? Life and history are more complex than the answer I wish to propose here. But I propose it simply and starkly, in order to highlight what I take to be an important factor in any more complex accounting for moral courage and moral failure during the Holocaust. My hypothesis is that the dominant model of faith in Judaism is more complex than that which achieved dominance in Christianity. That complexity has been a training ground in the courage of ethical resistance to evil, and its absence in Christianity accounts, in large part, for the Christian propensity to compromise and to accommodate Christian morality to political and social orders whose own inherent ethic runs directly counter to the love of neighbor and enemy.

Christianity's break from Judaism seems to have diminished the idea of faith as found in the biblical tradition and continued in Rabbinic and Hasidic Judaism. The covenantal understanding of faith as a dialogue in which the Jew was expected not only to trust and obey God but was also allowed to question (and even call into question) the behavior of God seems to have virtually disappeared in Christianity. The complex dialectic of faith as trust *and* questioning came to be reduced in Christianity to a very different understanding of faith as unquestioning trust and obedience. This dialectic of trust and questioning seems to provide post-Shoah Judaism with the thread of continuity that enables it to go on, even as the absence of this dialectic helps to explain the moral failure of the ethical traditions of Christianity during the Shoah—a failure that leaves Christian faith and ethics standing at a dead end and in need of a fundamental reformulation.

WRESTLING WITH GOD

Chutzpah in Pre-Shoah Judaism

Anson Laytner argues that, while obedience to the God who commands plays a central role in Judaism, as it does in Christianity and Islam, "yet, on the other hand [unlike Christianity and Islam], there has existed alongside this mainstream tradition another expression of the covenantal relationship. . . . According to this view of the Covenant, it is as though God and the Jewish people grew up together and so treat each other with the familiarity common to old friends or lovers."[1] This understanding of the divine-human relationship gives rise to the uniquely Jewish narrative tradition of chutzpah.

According to Belden Lane, there is in the Jewish tradition,

> an audacious faith, almost bordering on insolence, that stalks the high country of belief and disbelief. It seems especially prevalent in the rarefied air above Mt. Sinai. Rooted deeply in the human experience of adversity and anguish, it opens onto a landscape where God and human beings walk as friends. *Hutzpah k'lapei shamaya'* it is called in the Jewish tradition—a boldness with regard to heaven. From Moses, the Psalmist, and Jeremiah to such rabbinical figures as Honi the Circle Drawer in the first century B.C.E.— from Levi-Yitzhaq of Berditchev in the Hasidic world of Eastern Europe to the pain-soaked novels of Elie Wiesel—it echoes through the Jewish past with a stubborn insistence.[2]

Judaism understands covenant as a personal and communal relationship that is essentially a two-way street. It is a dialogue between God and God's people grounded in a set of mutual expectations. The formula "I will be your God and you will be my people" is understood as an ethical contract of love and commitment obligating *both* parties. Jews are obligated to live by the commandments but God also has obligations: to be with his people, to guide them, and to protect them. Although the term *chutzpah* has rather lighthearted connotations in American Jewish culture, the Israeli scholar Mordechai Rotenberg points out that it has a weightier meaning in the talmudic tradition and is the most appropriate term for this contractual relationship "according to which God as a dynamic 'personality' allows man to influence him. . . . [Indeed, chutzpah is] a symbol for man's capacity to affect God and change his decrees and consequently man's future by his actions and justified complaints."[3] Within the covenant one

---

1. Anson Laytner, *Arguing with God: A Jewish Tradition* (Northvale, N.J.: Jason Aronson, 1990), xvi–xvii.

2. Belden Lane, *"Hutzpa K'lapei Shamaya:* A Christian Response to the Jewish Tradition of Arguing with God," *Journal of Ecumenical Studies* 23 no. 4 (Fall 1986): 567–68.

3. Mordechai Rotenberg, *Dialogue with Deviance: The Hasidic Ethic and the Theory of Social Contraction* (Philadelphia: Institute for the Study of Human Issues, 1983), 14.

is permitted to call God into question in the name of the covenant promises whenever human dignity (i.e., one's being created in the image of God), especially the dignity of the stranger, is violated or threatened.

As the patriarch of Judaism, Abraham is held up as a model of faith, as one who exemplifies both aspects of Judaism—obedience to the will of God and at the same time audacity or chutzpah. Faith expresses itself as a wrestling with God in a mutually limiting dialectic of obedience and audacity. Contrary to the typical Christian interpretation of Abraham, the Judaic model of Abraham as a man of faith balances the obedient Abraham of the *Akedah* (Genesis 22) with the Abraham who has the chutzpah to call God into question in defense of the stranger. In his confrontation with God over the fate of Sodom and Gomorrah (Gen. 18:16-33), Abraham protests the potential taking of innocent lives by reminding God: "Shall not the judge of all the earth do what is just?" (18:25).[4]

Judaism sees faith, as exemplified in the stories of Abraham, to be a dialogical and dialectical tension of trust and questioning. Trust does not preclude the challenging and questioning of God; trust is not a Kierkegaardian unquestioning obedience (expressed in a "teleological suspension of the ethical") but rather a confidence that the two-way street of the covenant relationship both permits and demands this kind of honesty between God and the person of faith. The element of chutzpah in this dialogical covenant relationship is most prominent precisely when the tragedies of life seem to call into question the very justice of God. Perhaps no other book in the Tanakh (the Jewish Bible corresponding to the Christian Old Testament) speaks to the theme of faith as chutzpah more profoundly than the book of Job. As we have observed, unlike the pious Job of the ancient folk tale contained in the framing story (chaps. 1–2; 42:10-17), the Job who is introduced in chapter 3 is angry and defiant. This is a Job who has the chutzpah to reverse the roles, to put God on trial and win (42:7-9).

4. Ronald Green has pointed out that, contrary to the typical modern Christian/Kierkegaardian interpretation, namely, that God can give commands that "suspend the ethical," "Jewish thinkers refused to relinquish a moral conception of God." Green's point is that a Kierkegaardian interpretation violated the rabbinic sense of who God is and so they appealed to a variety of midrashic stories to circumvent such an interpretation. See Ronald Green, "Abraham, Isaac and the Jewish Tradition: An Ethical Reappraisal," *Journal of Religious Ethics* 10, no. 1 (Spring 1982): 17; cf. p. 9. See also idem, *Religion and Moral Reason* (New York: Oxford Univ. Press, 1988), chaps. 4 and 5, which survey, respectively, Jewish and Christian exegeses of the Akedah. Here Green points out that, prior to Kierkegaard, Christian exegesis also circumvented the Kierkegaardian conclusion of a religious suspension of the ethical.

Alongside the book of Job, however, a particular narrative in the book of Genesis is equally important. It is the biblical story of Jacob wrestling with a stranger (Gen. 32:22-32).

This naming story of Israel as a people defines the community of faith as those who wrestle with God and humans and prevail. Faith in the tradition of Abraham and Job, faith as a dialectic of trust and chutzpah, is the faith of Israel. This communal, dialogical, and dialectical tradition of wrestling with God was preserved in postbiblical talmudic and Hasidic Judaism but was largely lost to the history of Christianity. Where the Christian tradition tended to focus on answers formulated as doctrine, the talmudic tradition focused on questions and the vigorous debate over, and with, God's Word.

The talmudic tradition, says Jacob Neusner, sanctifies the capacity to doubt and to criticize. "The wonder of the Talmud is its tough-minded claims on behalf of the intellect, not in search, but in the service, of God." God is found in the "thrust and parry of argument." Talmudic debate is in fact a ritual for experiencing God through the questions. Although the talmudic scholar is vigorous and bold in his or her questions, such questioning cannot be divorced from the mythic context in which it takes place. The Talmud is constructed on a dialectic of trust and questioning that is foundational to faith as an expression of chutzpah. According to one talmudic story, Rabbi Eliezer ben Hyrcanos began to prove his interpretations of the Talmud by working miracles. Other scholars challenged and chided him for such tactics and invited him instead to "wrestle with us over the text." Finally Rabbi Eliezer called on heaven to vindicate his interpretation, and a heavenly voice responded: "What do you want already with Rabbi Eliezer? The *Halakah* is always as he says." Rabbi Yoshua cried out: " 'The Torah says not even to trust voices from heaven!' and Rabbi Yirma added, 'You, Yourself God, told us on Mt. Sinai to follow the community of those who agree on the truth.' " After this God was silent. Later the prophet Elijah was asked to interpret that silence and "he smiled . . . and said, 'My children have defeated me. My children have defeated me!' "[5] The meaning of the halakah is not to be determined by miracles or even by the voice of God. Even God is bound to accept the meaning that the

5. Jacob Neusner, *Invitation to the Talmud* (New York: Harper & Row, 1973), xviii; the talmudic story is from the Babylonian Talmud, *Baba Metzia* 59b (cited by Raphael Patai, *Gates to the Old City* [New York: Avon, 1980], 244-45, and quoted in Belden Lane, "Hutzpa," 568).

rabbis come to understand through wrestling with the Word. The talmudic way is the art of wrestling with God and with others and winning.

This same understanding of faith as chutzpah is embodied in the mystical-Hasidic traditions of Judaism as well. The Hasidic master Rabbi Levi-Yitzhaq of Berditchev, it is said, one day asked a poor tailor to speak of the argument he had had with God that day in his prayers. The tailor responded:

> I told the Master of the Universe, . . . today is the Day of Judgment. One must repent. But I didn't sin much. I took a little left-over cloth from the rich. I once drank a glass of brandy and ate some bread without washing my hands. These are all my transgressions. But *You*, Master of the Universe, how many are *Your* transgressions? You have taken away small children who had not sinned. From others you have taken away the mothers of such children. But, Master of the Universe, I shall forgive You Your transgressions, and may You forgive mine, and let us drink *L'Hayyim* [to life]!" That year Reb Levi-Yitzhaq proclaimed that it was this tailor with his argument who had saved the Jews. "Ah," he added, "but if I had been in his place, I would not have forgiven the Master of the World such great sins in return for a little leftover cloth. While I had Him, I would have asked that He send us His Messiah to redeem the World!"[6]

Faith as chutzpah has a long and continuous history in Judaism prior to the Shoah.[7] What is important to note, however, is the power that this tradition has to make being a Jew possible even after the Shoah. In the post-Shoah era, this tradition offers Jews not only a powerful understanding of faith but one that binds their past and future into a unity. Moreover, it is extremely suggestive for a post-Shoah ethic.

Chutzpah in Post-Shoah Jewish Theology

If Judaism's faith was grounded in answers, the Shoah might well have meant the end of Judaism. But the faith of Jews is not grounded in answers to metaphysical questions but in a covenant relationship of ongoing dialogue and debate, a continuous wrestling with God. More than any other factor, this one provides the foundation for post-Shoah Jewish theology. Thus

---

6. The story is recounted in Lane, "Hutzpa," 581.
7. For an extensive treatment of the history of faith as chutzpah, see Anson Laytner, *Arguing with God.*

Eliezer Berkovits states: "After the Holocaust Israel's first religious responsibility is to 'reason' with God and—if need be—to wrestle with Him. . . . Faith, because it is trust in God, demands justice of God." Like Abraham and Job, "in our generation, Job's brother, if he wishes to be true to his God-given heritage, 'reasons' with God in believing rebellion and rebellious belief."[8] Berkovits's description fits not only his own post-Shoah theological work but also that of other leading authors such as Emil Fackenheim, Elie Wiesel, and Irving Greenberg.

As we have seen, Emil Fackenheim has raised the fundamental question: Where was God at Auschwitz? Like virtually all other Jewish authors on this subject, he rejects the pious traditions that accounted for misfortune by suggesting that it is punishment for sins, for the Jews who died in the death camps were overwhelmingly Jews from the most pious and observant communities in Europe. God cannot be let off that easily. But then where was God? How can one continue to be Jewish in the face of God's seeming abandonment of the Jewish people in the death camps? Fackenheim responds to these questions:

> There is a kind of faith which will accept all things and renounce every protest. There is also a kind of protest which has despaired of faith. In Judaism there has always been protest which *stays within* the sphere of faith. Abraham remonstrates with God. So do Jeremiah and Job. So does, in modern times, the Hasidic Rabbi Levi Yitzhak of Berdiczev. He once interrupted the sacred Yom Kippur service in order to protest that, whereas kings of flesh and blood protected their peoples, Israel was unprotected by her King in heaven. Yet having made his protest, he recited the Kaddish, which begins with these words: "Extolled and hallowed be the name of God throughout the world. . . ."
>
> Can Jewish protest today remain within the sphere of faith? . . . In faithfulness to the victims we must refuse comfort; and in faithfulness to Judaism we must refuse to disconnect God from the holocaust. Thus, in our case, protest threatens to escalate into a totally destructive conflict between the faith of the past and faithfulness to the present.[9]

In spite of this, the Jewish theologian does not have to invent an answer to the question, How is faith possible after the Shoah? It is more a matter of observing that an answer has emerged in Jewish experience.

8. Eliezer Berkovitz, *Faith after the Holocaust* (New York: KTAV, 1973), 68–69.
9. Emil Fackenheim, *God's Presence in History* (New York: Harper & Row, 1970), 73, 76.

After Auschwitz, the Jew has no haven in either the sacred or the secular. Jews were rounded up and taken to the death camps whether they thought of themselves as religious or not. Assimilation into the secular world proved to be no more protection than the affirmation of religiousness. What has spontaneously emerged, however, is a movement beyond the distinction of sacred and secular. Today, whether they think of themselves as religious or not, Jews refuse to grant a posthumous victory to Hitler by abandoning their Jewishness. Even the secularist Jew proudly and defiantly continues to affirm Jewish identity. Today, says Fackenheim, Jews are united by a commanding Voice that speaks from Auschwitz, forbidding them to despair of either God or humanity "lest they cooperate in delivering the world over to the forces of Auschwitz."[10] Jews have instinctively responded with audacity (chutzpah). Wrestling with God and humanity, they continue to prevail.

Like Emil Fackenheim, Elie Wiesel also seeks to discover a path for post-Shoah Judaism. As a voice out of the Shoah itself, Wiesel speaks with a unique authority. More than any other author, Wiesel deserves to be seen as the bearer of the tradition of chutzpah in our post-Shoah world. Wiesel tells us: To be a Jew "means to serve God by espousing man's cause, to plead for man while recognizing his need of God. I remember my Master . . . telling me, 'Only the Jew knows that he may oppose God as long as he does so in defense of His creation.' " Or again, "Judaism teaches man to overcome despair. What is Jewish history if not an endless quarrel with God?"[11]

Standing like Job in the dialectical and dialogical tradition of chutzpah, Wiesel chooses to put God on trial and call him to account. This persistent theme throughout his writings culminates in his play *The Trial of God*. The play is set on the eve of Purim in 1649 in a small town that has just been decimated by a pogrom. The innkeeper Berish and his daughter Hanna survive to put God on trial. But before the trial can be concluded it is interrupted by an impending second pogrom. The village priest urges them to flee or, if they wish, to convert. Berish responds, "My sons and my fathers perished without betraying their faith; I can do no less." Though

---

10. Ibid., 84.
11. Elie Wiesel, *A Jew Today*, trans. Marion Wiesel (New York: Vantage, 1979), 6, 193.

he is prepared to die for his faith, he is not ready to forgive God and bring the trial to an end: "The trial will go on. . . . I lived as a Jew, and it is as a Jew that I shall die—and it is as a Jew that, with my last breath, I shall shout my protest to God! And because the end is near, I shall shout louder. Because the end is near, I'll tell him that he's more guilty than ever!"[12]

The Trial of God embodies the paradox of Jewish faith, the paradox of trust and chutzpah. But it is more than a work of the imagination. It is based on an experience Wiesel had in the death camps, where he witnessed three rabbis who "decided one winter evening to indict God for allowing his children to be massacred." When the trial was over and God was found guilty, the rabbis realized it was time for prayers and so they bowed their heads to pray.[13] The dialectical and dialogical faith of trust and chutzpah is not the fictive invention of post-Shoah theologians. It is a lived faith, a tradition of faith reaffirmed in the very bowels of the death camps.

Irving Greenberg also appeals to the tradition of chutzpah. Greenberg's treatment of this theme is most valuable for its ethical implications. Greenberg takes issue with Richard Rubenstein's belief that God died at Auschwitz. In response to Rubenstein's declaration that "Jewish history has written the *final chapter* in the terrible story of the God of History. . . . The world will *forever* remain a place of pain . . . and *ultimate defeat*," Greenberg says: "After the Holocaust, there should be no final solutions, not even theological ones."[14] What Greenberg finds unsatisfactory in Rubenstein's response to the Shoah is his definitiveness. Rubenstein has broken with the paradoxical dialectic of Jewish existence—the dialectic of trust and chutzpah. Rubenstein has abandoned the talmudic-Hasidic path of questioning existence and settled for a definitive answer. He does not wrestle with the unnamed God.

Greenberg chooses to wrestle with this God, however, and so spells out his own understanding of Jewish existence after the Shoah. Like Fack-

---

12. Elie Wiesel, *The Trial of God* (New York: Schocken, 1979), 154, 161.
13. Ibid., from the introduction entitled *The Scene*. See also Robert McAfee Brown, *Elie Wiesel: Messenger to All Humanity* (Notre Dame: Univ. of Notre Dame Press, 1983), 154.
14. See Richard Rubenstein, "Homeland and Holocaust," in The *Religious Situation 1968* (Boston: Beacon, 1969), 39–111, quoted in Irving Greenberg, "Cloud of Smoke, Pillar of Fire: Judaism, Christianity, and Modernity after the Holocaust," in *Auschwitz: Beginning of a New Era?* ed. Eva Fleischner (New York: KTAV, 1977), 26.

enheim and Wiesel, but in his own way, he suggests that the line between believer and unbeliever, religious and secular, has been eliminated. After Auschwitz, faith for the Jew is a dialectical faith of moments. There are moments when one has faith and moments when faith is overwhelmed by the immensity of the Shoah. If the Shoah sometimes overwhelms the faith of a Jew and leads him or her to ask, where was God? it also at times overwhelms a Jew and leads to the question, where was humanity—secular, enlightened, and scientifically sophisticated humanity? The Shoah has relativized and demythologized our confidence in both the sacred and the secular. One can have no absolute hope in either. If God seems to have abandoned the Jew, so have human beings with their politics, science, technology, history, and all other vehicles of secular hope.

The ethical implication of this dialectical and momentary faith, which tosses the Jew to and fro between the sacred and the secular, is that one should be skeptical of all movements, religious or secular, whether of the left or of the right. "Nothing dare evoke our absolute, unquestioning loyalty, not even our God, for this leads to possibilities of SS loyalties." At this point, Greenberg appeals to the writings of Elie Wiesel and the tradition of chutzpah. God needs to be accused for betrayal of the covenant, and this too is part of the dialectic of momentary faith. "Wiesel teaches us that in the very anger and controversy itself is the first stage of a new relationship, perhaps the only kind of relationship possible with God at this point in history."[15]

If the line between sacred and secular, and between belief and unbelief, has blurred, a new line separates faith from unfaith—the deed. After Auschwitz, actions speak louder than words. An ethic of chutzpah or utopian audacity challenges all appeals to God and religion that serve to denigrate human dignity and violate the image of God in which we are created. The ethic of chutzpah appeals to God against God in the name of God's creation. An ethic of chutzpah is the proof of authentic faith. It shows itself in actions that refuse to accept the Nazi strategy of legitimating genocide by classifying Jews and others as *untermensch*, as less than human, as animals. Genocide begins by defining the human so as to exclude its victims from the privileged circle.

15. Greenberg, ibid., 38, 40.

Authentic faith, after Auschwitz, reveals itself in actions that deny this option and protect human dignity and equality against every form of dehumanization. Actions, not words, tell us who has experienced the reality of God. Thus Greenberg points out that during the 1967 war against Israel it was Sartre, the atheist, who spoke out against potential genocide and Pope Paul VI who was silent. After Auschwitz, Greenberg concludes, it is Sartre, not the pope, who has shown himself to be a man of faith, one who has experienced the reality of God and God's image in every human being. Or again, he argues that in Israel today it is the secular Israelis, not the Orthodox Jews, who represent authentic faith. For it is the secular Israelis, not the Orthodox Jews, who insist on the admission of all Jews to Israel; some Orthodox Jews, even after the Shoah, would turn their backs on Jews who do not meet their "religious" standards. Here the final paradox of the tradition of chutzpah reveals itself. The tradition that calls God into question is the tradition that calls human beings into question as well—in the name of the image of God in all creatures. It is the paradox of appealing to God against God (and against other human beings) on behalf of God's creation. Wherever human freedom, dignity, equality, and interdependence are affirmed, there the reality of God is affirmed.[16]

THE ETHICAL FAILURE OF CHRISTIANITY

What Went Wrong?

What went wrong with Christianity during the Shoah? Why did the majority of Christians, and especially clergy, either actively or passively support Hitler and his "final solution to the Jewish problem?" As Franklin Littell sums it up: "The truth is that the church struggle was fought out within the institutions themselves, not between 'insiders' and 'outsiders,' that most church constituents apostasized and only a small percentage remained faithful." For the most part the church struggle focused on the question of the institutional autonomy of the church and largely ignored the Jewish question, except in cases of baptized Jewish converts, who of course "belonged to the church" and therefore were an issue of church autonomy. Even the famous Barmen Declaration of the Confessing Church did not raise the issue of the treatment of the Jews. The leading figure in the

16. Ibid., 47, 49ff.

formulation of that declaration, Karl Barth, later indicated: "I have long felt guilty that I did not make this problem central, in any case not in public, for instance in the two Barmen declarations of 1934 which I had composed. . . . There is no excuse that I did not fight properly for this cause."[17]

Some suggest that the church was powerless to do anything under the totalitarian rule of Hitler. But there is strong evidence to indicate otherwise. In a comprehensive study, Helen Fein does a country-by-country analysis to try to understand who did and who did not resist Hitler and aid the Jews, and why. She observes that "German instigation and organization of extermination usually succeeded because of the lack of counterauthorities resisting their plans, not because of their repression of such resistance."[18]

Fein argues that the church was the ideal institution to lead such a resistance because its membership spanned all social classes; its leaders were spread throughout the state; and it had access to ruling elites, resources for hiding Jews, and the prestige to significantly legitimate or delegitimate state policies. Fein's data suggest that the church could have made a decisive difference, as indeed it did on a few occasions:

Where both state and church refused to sanction discrimination—as in Denmark—internal resistance was highest. Where the state or native administrative bureaucracy began to cooperate, church resistance was critical in inhibiting obedience to authority, legitimating subversion and/or checking collaboration directly. Church protest proved to be the single element present in every instance in which state collaboration was arrested—as in Bulgaria, France, and Rumania. Church protest was absent in virtually all cases in which state cooperation was not arrested. Church protest was also the intervening variable most highly related to the immediacy of social defense movements that enabled Jews successfully to evade deportation. The majority of Jews avoided deportation in every state occupied by or allied with Germany in which the head of the dominant church spoke out *publicly* against deportation before or as soon as it began. . . . The greater the church resistance, the fewer Jews became victims. . . . By contrast, states in the colonial zone with high Jewish victimization are states in which the dominant church was actively antagonistic toward Jews.[19]

17. Franklin Littell, *The Crucifixion of the Jews* (New York: Harper & Row, 1975), 44; Barth cited on 46. The quote is from a letter to Eberhard Bethge reported in *Evangelische Theologie* 28 (1968): 10:555.
18. Helen Fein, *Accounting for Genocide* (Chicago: Univ. of Chicago Press, 1979), 90.
19. Ibid., 71, 67.

The failure of the church during the Shoah was primarily a failure of leadership. As Sarah Gordon notes, "very few Catholic leaders preached against racial persecution [and] even fewer Protestants did." Among those who did resist the Nazis and aid Jews, the preponderance were ordinary laypersons, acting on their own.[20]

Franklin Littell puts the number of Protestant pastors who remained faithful to the Confessing church at approximately 20 percent, and only a minority of these directly addressed the issue of the treatment of Jews. William Allen states: "The most ironic statistic of the Third Reich . . . was that more Catholic priests and Protestant ministers died in the German army than were put into concentration camps: from an actuarial point of view it was safer to oppose Hitler than to support him." Indeed, according to Fein, "outside the SS zone, no German sanctions have been reported against clergy for protest alone. No churches protested in the SS zone." But, as Sarah Gordon says, the greatest shame of the church was "the tendency for all church-going Catholics and Protestants to be more anti-Semitic than were those who no longer attended services regularly."[21]

On reviewing the history of the church during the Shoah we must sadly conclude that the church was tested and found wanting. The church was not a leaven in the world speaking and acting on behalf of the human dignity of all persons, most especially Jews. The church did not witness to the truth of the sanctity of the life of all persons created in the image of God. The church did not strive to transform the world but became obediently conformed to the Nazi world. One should not take anything away from the exceptional heroes of the rank and file in the church who did act courageously, but it is sad that they had to do so with little encouragement and almost in spite of church leadership. What went wrong? The simple answer would be to say that the church substituted the state for Christ as its Lord. But it is more complicated than that. Christian faith came to be defined as requiring (in varying degrees) obedience to the state as an aspect of obedience to Christ. Therein lies the heart of the problem.

20. Sarah Gordon, *Hitler, the Germans and the Jewish Question* (Princeton: Princeton Univ. Press, 1984), 255. See esp. chap. 8, "The Attitudes of the Churches."

21. Littell, *Crucifixion*, 50; William Sheridan Allen, "Objective and Subjective Inhibitants in the German Resistance to Hitler," in *The German Church Struggle and the Holocaust*, ed. Franklin Littell and Hubert Locke (Detroit: Wayne State Univ. Press, 1974), 122; Fein, *Accounting*, 94–95; Gordon, *Hitler*, 260.

Faith as Unquestioning Obedience

Somewhere along the way, as Christianity separated itself from its roots in Judaism, the dialectical and dialogical understanding of faith as a paradoxical unity of trust and audacity or chutzpah was lost. The gospel tradition primarily portrayed the life of Jesus as a model of unquestioning trust and obedience. Even in the Garden of Gethsemane, on the night before his crucifixion, when the Gospels depict Jesus as directing some questions to God about whether his suffering and death are necessary, he concludes with "not my will but yours be done" (Luke 22:42). Christians are enjoined to follow Jesus, to emulate his obedience even unto death on the cross (Phil. 2:1-8).

Now faith as a fierce and unquestioning loyalty to the will of God revealed in Christ could be an ethically powerful force for good in the world were the will of God confined to the message of love of neighbor, and even of one's enemies, as oneself. But when the message of God in Christ is taken to include the theme of supersession and the requirement of obedience to the state, the implications become ominous. Even if the Nazis had invented anti-Semitism instead of simply adapting the church's traditions of anti-Judaism, the church would probably still have gone along with the Nazis because of its teaching of faith as unquestioning obedience, especially in its Lutheran form.

The gospel tradition, of course, has elements in it that sharply oppose the state, as the book of Revelation and, many would say, the Sermon on the Mount attest. But another strand is embodied in the teachings of Hellenistic diaspora Jewish followers of Jesus, like Paul of Tarsus, himself proudly a Roman citizen. Such missionaries were anxious to establish good relations between the Christian community and the ruling order of Gentiles, to become all things to all people in order to convert some of them. As the postbiblical period set in and the apologetic movement of the gentile Christian *logos* theologians was set in motion, there was an even greater anxiousness to show that Christianity was no threat to Rome and that Christians could be good citizens.

When Christianity went from being a minority and sometimes persecuted religion to being first the favored religion under the Roman emperor Constantine (313 C.E.) and finally the only legal religion of the empire under the emperor Theodosius (381 C.E.), Christians of the fourth century were extremely impressed by this reversal of fortunes. Men such as Eusebius of Caesarea, author of the first history of the church, and Augustine, perhaps the most influential theologian in the shaping of Western Christianity, took this amazing victory of the church over the empire as a sign of God's will and God's favor. The emergence of the Roman Empire came to be seen as the will of God for the establishment of a universal order of peace to facilitate the spread of the gospel. It was a mutually beneficial interpretation. The empire gained stability from a new legitimating religion and Catholic Christianity gained a favored and protected ascendancy over its Christian and non-Christian rivals.

At least since the time of the Reformation, the alignment of the church and state has been seen by some (Anabaptist traditions and their late medieval precursors, and since then by outside sympathizers) to be the greatest fundamental mistake of the church in its entire history. But the Anabaptists themselves were a persecuted minority within the church precisely because they rejected the authority of both the state and the institutional church. By contrast, both the Catholic and the main strands of the Protestant Reformation (Lutheran and Calvinist) accepted this alliance as proper and necessary. With the acceptance of the linkage between church and state as providential came the implication that unquestioning obedience to Christ requires obedience to the state. To be sure there were various qualifications on this obedience. For instance, both Aquinas and Calvin allowed for revolt against unjust rulers under very specific conditions. Luther took the most extreme position, however, by suggesting that under virtually no conditions is revolt permissible. That extreme ethic of obedience goes a long way toward explaining the cooperation of the churches with the Nazis. But even in its less extreme Catholic and Calvinist forms the presumption is still on the side of obedience to the state.

The key scripture which seems to have promoted this ethic occurs in Paul's Letter to the Romans:

> Let every person be subject to the governing authorities; for there is no authority except from God, and those authorities that exist have been instituted by God. Therefore whoever resists authority resists what God has appointed, and those who resist will incur judgment. For rulers are not a terror to good conduct, but to bad. Do you wish to have no fear of the authority? Then do what is good, and you will receive its approval; for it is God's servant for your good. But if you do what is wrong, you should be afraid, for the authority does not bear the sword in vain! It is the servant

of God to execute wrath on the wrongdoer. Therefore one must be subject, not only because of wrath but also because of conscience. For the same reason you also pay taxes, for the authorities are God's servants, busy with this very thing. Pay to all what is due them—taxes to whom taxes are due, revenue to whom revenue is due, respect to whom respect is due, honor to whom honor is due.

(Rom. 13:1-7)

Such a statement, carrying the weight of scriptural status, especially from one as prominent in the Christian tradition as Paul, naturally promoted an identification between obedience to God in Christ and obedience to Caesar, that is, the state. It is to this statement that Luther appealed in formulating his extreme position in response to the peasant revolts of his time. The peasants responded favorably to Luther's message of the freedom, equality, and dignity they had in Christ. They felt encouraged by it to revolt against the nobility, whom they believed abused and ignored their dignity and equality. Luther was then forced to clarify his position on the two kingdoms through which God rules the world: the spiritual inner kingdom of God expressed through the lives of the faithful in the church and the outer physical kingdoms of the world expressed through established rulers. Through the first God rules with the right hand of grace and compassion and through the second God rules with the left hand of justice and wrath.[22] The freedom of the gospel, it seems, is only an inner spiritual freedom. The equality of all in Christ is only to be realized in the next life. Here in this world there can never be equality. God acts through the state to establish order, and everyone must learn to accept their assigned place in that social order. Only God can establish rulers and only God can remove rulers. It is not permissible for human beings to revolt, even against a vicious and unjust ruler.

The need to be obedient to the rule of God through both the right and the left hand led Luther to formulate an ethic of paradox. One must live in the world with the knowledge that one is always, at the same time, both a saint and a sinner. Even a Christian society of saints would remain a

---

22. In *The Ethics of Martin Luther,* trans. Robert C. Schultz (Philadelphia: Fortress, 1972), Paul Althaus makes the point that, according to Luther, God's grace and wrath are present in both kingdoms (see chap. 3, esp. pp. 53–54 and 81). But the subtle ways in which that is true seem not to have undermined Luther's basic insistence on unquestioning obedience to secular authority.

society of sinners in need of both God's gracious compassion and just wrath. For Luther, one must clearly distinguish between one's personal life, which is under the rule of God's right hand, and one's public life, which is under the rule of God's left hand. While one should be loving and forgiving in one's personal life, one may also have to perform harsh acts of justice for the good of others in the public realm. The paradox of the ethical life is that one can be both a loving and forgiving Christian and at the same time perform the role of public executioner or hangman, for example, without inconsistency or moral culpability. In fact, while the medieval Catholic tradition required the executioner to do penance, Luther insisted that no such penance was necessary, since God takes the life, not the executioner, who acts only in obedience to his duty and hence accrues no personal guilt.[23] In both realms one is carrying out the will of God. It is on the basis of this ethic of paradox in relation to the divinely sanctioned order of society that Luther felt compelled to order the German princes to slay the peasants without mercy when rebellion broke out.

Luther did express some sympathy for the plight of the peasants, and he considered the German princes to be corrupt. In *Admonition to Peace*, addressed to the German bishops and princes, he declared: "As temporal rulers you do nothing but cheat and rob the people so that you may lead a life of luxury and extravagance." Yet he did not think it permissible for the peasants to seek to overthrow these authorities established by God. When the revolt began he issued another pamphlet, *Against the Robbing and Murdering Hordes of Peasants*, which reminded the German princes that they were to be the instruments of God's wrath; thus he counseled them that "anyone who can be proved to be a seditious person is an outlaw before God and the emperor; and whoever is the first to put him to death does right and well. . . . For rebellion is not just simple murder. . . . It makes widows and orphans and turns everything upside down, like the worst disaster. Therefore let every one who can, smite, slay, stab, secretly or openly, remembering that nothing can be more poisonous, hurtful, or devilish than a rebel. It is just as when one must kill a mad dog; if you do not strike him, he will strike you, and a whole land with you."[24] This infamous event confirms the underlying conservatism of Luther's gospel,

23. Ibid., 74, 137.
24. *Luther's Works*, American Edition, vol. 46, (Philadelphia: Fortress, 1967), 19, 50.

which set the tone of church-state relations in the history of Germany. The model of faith as obedience to God and to the rulers of this world that emerged here set the church on a dead-end path, a path in which Christian faith and ethics self-destruct in the death camps.

A full account of the propensity to affirm the duty and obligation of obedience to the state in Germany would have to include more than an appeal to this tradition of interpretation of Christian faith and ethics. One would have to deal with the history of Germany and the European conspiracy to keep Germany divided and weak since the time of the Protestant-Catholic wars in the aftermath of the Reformation. Then there are the psychological repercussions from the Napoleonic conquest and ignominious defeat in World War I, as well as the burgeoning nationalism that was emerging in the nineteenth century as Germany belatedly struggled for the status of a nation-state with an almost obsessive need to compensate for its previous history of humiliation, etc.

Fein's study also indicates that variables other than religion can hinder or promote obedience or rebellion with respect to the state. For instance, resistance to Hitler was greatest in states that had existed the longest, especially those with strong democratic traditions. One of the most dramatic examples occurred in Denmark. In this case, geographical distance from Germany, the lateness of the German campaign against the Jews of Denmark, the small number of Jews in Denmark, and the long history of democratic institutions as compared to Germany are undoubtedly all important factors. What is remarkable is that the dominant church in Denmark was Lutheran, as it was in Germany; yet the results, because of these other factors, were quite the opposite. Clearly the church in Denmark rose above its Lutheran anti-Jewish heritage. Even before the war the Danish Lutheran church resisted anti-Semitic interpretations of the gospel and rejected Luther's anti-Semitic writings.[25] Nevertheless, Denmark is the exception that proves the rule, for the total level of church resistance throughout Europe was so low and the total complicity so high that the Christian ethic of obedience must be seen as a major variable. I do not want to suggest a one-factor explanation of history, especially of this specific slice of history. But I do want to isolate an important factor in that history—the role of religion. I do want to know why the church failed, and I want to learn what the church needs to do differently.

25. See Fein, *Accounting,* 114–20, 144–52.

Genocide as Sublimated Deicide

In addition to the factors of the myth of supersession, the teachings of contempt, and the reduction of faith to unquestioning obedience, the religious dimension of Christian apostasy during the Shoah has at least one other component. Christian faith has not only been an unquestioning faith but it has assumed that it somehow has exclusive rights to God. It is as if the doctrine of the incarnation (i.e., the Word of God became flesh in the person of Jesus) somehow gave exclusive ownership of God to Christians. In this claim Christians have shown themselves to be, in some important and fundamental respects, one with their pagan forebears in the history of anti-Semitism.

It is common to divide anti-Semitism into two types: sociological and religious. The first is thought to be due to the clash of cultures in which Judaism insists on retaining its distinctive culture and traditions that the larger culture takes as an offense to its assumptions of superiority. This is supposed to typify pagan, especially Hellenistic, anti-Semitism. The second, religious anti-Semitism, is said to be due to the specific christological religious claims of Christianity and to be tied to the myth of supersession. While there are important differences among them, the anti-Judaism of pre-Christian pagans, that of Christians, and that of neo-pagan/neo-Christian Nazis are all fundamentally religious and as such exhibit similar sociological characteristics. All three examples exhibit a fundamental rage at the sheer existence of the Jew as one who is other, an alien or a stranger who does not conform to their world.

In the premodern world Jews refused to assimilate and be conformed to the world around them. The refusal of Jews to assimilate led pagans and Christians alike to a violent rage against Jews, because the otherness of Jews reminded them that what is truly holy or transcendent cannot be owned by them. God cannot be domesticated. The existence of Jews has reminded pagans and Christians alike that God's ways are not the same as their ways. The existence of Jews reminded the Hellenists, the Christians, and the Nazis that perhaps their truth, their values, their way of life was not final and unquestionable. The very existence of Jews called their values and way of life into question and hinted at a God who might very well call them into question. In the world of the Shoah, the existence of Jews was a burdening reminder of "faithfulness" to the Christian conscience for those who preached the value of not being conformed to the world but practiced conformity to the world of Nazi values—a reminder that Christians were only too happy to have out of sight and out of mind.

In the Nazi period this rage against the Jewish witness to transcendence escalated to a point of no return. The religious rage masked itself in the myth of race, which made assimilation as a "final solution" impossible. Hence the Nazis turned to genocide. But make no mistake about it, the rage against the Jews (whether pagan, Christian, or Nazi) is a scarcely disguised rage against the transcendence of God, the God who cannot be used to legitimate Christian hegemony or Nazi hegemony, the God who cannot be owned or used for the political and ideological purposes of the will to power, the God who is the limit of all conformity to this world. The attempted genocide of the Jews is a thinly disguised attempt at deicide, in which the perpetrators have all too typically projected their own motives onto the victims as a justification for their own actions.

The focus of this analysis has been on the ethical failure of Christianity, but the Shoah witnesses to more than the failure of Christianity. It reveals a massive failure of Western civilization as a whole—a failure of the sacred but also of the secular. Germany after all was the home of the greatest of the Enlightenment philosophical ethicists, Immanuel Kant. Kant urged Germans (and all human beings) to embrace the autonomy of reason in order to discern the universal moral obligations and duties that human beings owe to each other—especially the duty never to treat each other as means only, but always first and foremost as ends. Nevertheless, the call of rational and moral autonomy was apparently not heard as clearly as the call to obligation or duty. Once universal humanity was reduced to the category of the German *Volk*, the call to duty no longer required either autonomous reason or universal moral obligations but only reason in unquestioning service of the Reich and moral obligations only toward members of the pure Aryan race.[26]

26. According to Hannah Arendt, during his trial Adolf Eichmann "declared with great emphasis that he had lived his whole life according to Kant's moral precepts, and especially according to a Kantian definition of duty. This was outrageous, on the face of it, and also incomprehensible, since Kant's moral philosophy is closely bound up with man's faculty of judgment, which rules out blind obedience. . . . To the surprise of everybody, Eichmann came up with an approximately correct definition of the categorical imperative: 'I meant by my remark about Kant that the principle of my will must always be such that it can become the principle of general laws'. . . . He had not simply dismissed the Kantian formula as no longer applicable, he had distorted it to read: Act as if the Principle of your actions were the same as that of the legislator or of the laws of the land—or, in Hans Frank's formulation of

Christianity was not the only moral resource of Western civilization. An enlightened secular age thought that humanity could place its hope in philosophy, education, science, technology, professional responsibility, etc. But all these secular resources failed, just as surely as did Christianity. All these resources, which can be potential vectors of transcendence, were rendered subservient to the cosmological myth of the pure Aryan race. With respect to universities and university professors, Alice Gallin concludes: "I found cells of resistance in the army, the intelligence circles, the labor unions, and the churches, but none in the universities," with one exception in Munich.[27]

"When barbarism came to twentieth-century Europe," George Steiner has observed, "the arts faculties in more than one university offered very little moral resistance, and this is not a trivial or local accident." What troubles him is that "literary values and the utmost of hideous inhumanity could coexist in the same community, in the same individual sensibility, . . . that bestiality was at times enforced and refined by individuals educated in the culture of traditional humanism. Knowledge of Goethe, a delight in the poetry of Rilke, seemed no bar to personal and institutionalized sadism." "I find myself," he says,

> unable to assert confidently that the humanities humanize. . . . It is at least
> conceivable that the . . . substance of our training and pursuit, diminishes
> the sharpness and readiness of our actual moral response. Because we are
> trained to give psychological and moral credence to the imaginary, to the

'the categorical imperative in the Third Reich,' which Eichmann might have known: 'Act in such a way that the Führer, if he knew your action, would approve it' *(Die Tecnik des Staates,* 1942, pp. 15–16). Kant, to be sure, had never intended to say anything of the sort. . . . All that is left of Kant's spirit is the demand that a man do more than obey the law, that he go beyond the mere call of obedience and identify his own will with the principle behind the law—the source from which the law sprang. In Kant's philosophy, that source was practical reason; in Eichmann's household use of him, it was the will of the Führer. . . . There is not the slightest doubt that in one respect Eichmann did indeed follow Kant's precepts: a law was a law, there could be no exceptions. . . . This uncompromising attitude toward the performance of his murderous duties damned him in the eyes of the judges more than anything else . . . but in his own eyes it was precisely what justified him. . . . No exceptions—this was the proof that he had always acted against his 'inclinations,' whether they were sentimental or inspired by interest, he had always done his 'duty.' " See Hannah Arendt, *Eichmann in Jerusalem: A Report on the Banality of Evil* (New York: Penguin Books, 1963, 1964), 135–37.

27. Alice Gallin, *Midwives to Nazism: University Professors in Weimar Germany 1925–1933* (Macon: Mercer Univ. Press, 1986), 4. See also idem, *German Resistance to Hitler: Ethical and Religious Factors* (Washington: Catholic Univ. of America Press, 1961).

character in a play or a novel, . . . we may find it more difficult to identify with the real world. . . . The cry in the poem may come to sound louder, more urgent, more real than the cry in the street outside. . . . Thus there may be a covert betraying link between the cultivation of aesthetic response and the potential of personal inhumanity.[28]

If the liberal arts failed to live up to their moral calling, so did science, technology, and the professions. The death camps were planned and run by Ph.D.'s and M.D.'s, by "technological barbarians" as Franklin Littell calls them.[29] In his brilliant study of the Nazi doctors, Robert Jay Lifton demonstrates in detail that the biological-racial vision of the Nazis provided the context for the "medicalization" of the "final solution." Why were the *selections* (of those Jews who would immediately be gassed and those who would be interred in the camps for slave labor, medical experiments, etc.) required to be done by M.D.'s? His answer is that a biomedical metaphor underlay the "final solution"—the metaphor of the Jews as a malignant intrusion into the healthy body of the German *Volk* that must be removed to restore the body to health. By requiring a physician to make the selections, the Nazis used the scientific, technical, and professional status of the medical doctor and researcher to legitimate their "final solution" to the "Jewish problem." The Nazi physician found himself or herself in the paradoxical role of the professional who had to kill in order to heal.[30]

On the basis of the godlessness of the modern world the churches would have predicted the failure of the secular. That Christians failed, however, is something the churches need to confront. Christians need not have been so deeply implicated in the Nazi "final solution" of genocide against the Jews. Christians should have stood firmly against Hitler and with the Jews. But given that Christians were in fact deeply implicated, one must address the question: What needs to be changed in Christianity so as to prevent that kind of complicity with evil from occurring again? This analysis of the history of two kinds of faith and ethics embodied in the histories of Judaism and Christianity is meant to suggest where the problem lies in the

28. George Steiner, *Language and Silence: Essays on Language, Literature and the Inhuman* (New York: Atheneum, 1970), 61.
29. Littell, *Crucifixion*, 13–14.
30. Robert Jay Lifton, *The Nazi Doctors: Medical Killing and the Psychology of Genocide* (New York: Basic Books, 1986), esp. 30ff.

Christian tradition and why, and what Christians might learn from Jews about faith and ethics so as to better live up to our own ideals. In a post-Shoah world there is a need for a chastened Christian community to link arms with a determined Jewish people and all secular sympathizers in a common strategy to defeat the powers of darkness that threaten to bring down a final apocalyptic desolation upon us all.

A NARRATIVE ETHIC OF AUDACITY

The Need for a New Beginning

Hitler has been defeated, but like the beast in the book of Revelation that seemed to be slain but was not and so reappeared, new Hitlers could appear once more. We live in a world, as the recent history of Cambodia indicates, in which new Hitlers are possible. Still, the defeat of Hitler is a reprieve; Christians have been given a chance to repent of their past, a chance to make a new beginning. Once more Christians are offered the choice—life or death—and encouraged to choose life (see Deut. 30:19).

But unlike Jews, who have found a strand of continuity with their past through the tradition of chutzpah, which gives them life and enables them to go on, we Christians have not fully faced up to the moral problem of continuity with pre-Shoah Christianity. Pre-Shoah supersessionist Christianity is an obscenity. Full continuity with that tradition is fundamentally immoral. The understanding of Christian faith and ethics grounded in unquestioning obedience must be reexamined and reformulated in the light of the lessons of history. Christians, too, ought to hear a commanding voice from Auschwitz, a voice of judgment demanding a *metanoia* (i.e., a change of heart, a conversion, a "turning around").

In the light of the Christian apostasy at the time of the Shoah, I do not see any way to go back to the Christian understanding of faith as unquestioning trust and obedience. That option has proved itself spiritually and morally bankrupt. From faith as obedience came an ethic of obedience to Caesar as if to God, and from that came a loss of self-transcendence. The Christian came to be conformed to the world and a negative witness to the transcendence of God. The irony is that the church, which developed the theory that Jews were, by their homeless wandering, a negative witness to the truth of Christianity, turns out to have grasped the truth in reverse.

It is the Jews who have been in but not of the world and Christians who have become the embodiment of the negative witness.

What is required of Christians is a little humility. Christians must be willing to learn from their Jewish brothers and sisters—to learn the full meaning of faith in the biblical tradition, faith as a living covenant, a dialectical and dialogical covenant characterized by the paradoxical tension of trust and chutzpah. I am convinced that, had the life of faith among Christians been shaped by the narrative tradition of chutzpah, the number of apostasizing Christians during the Shoah would have been far fewer. Christians who have, historically, all too often taken faith to be an unquestioning trust in and obedience to both the sacred (the god of Christendom) and the secular (the state) would have been prepared to question both and to act on behalf of God's creation and against Hitler and the god of the Deutsch Christians.

The world can no longer afford the luxury of unquestioning faith, which is pagan faith and a nearly universal characteristic of religion. Virtually all forms of religion have asked followers to sacrifice their will and to surrender themselves to a higher reality. All faith that asks for a total surrender of will is finally not only pagan but demonic, even if it is faith in Jesus or the God of Jesus. For such faith is a training ground in fanaticism that blurs the distinction between God and the state and leads to the dehumanization of the chosen victims of the state. The only authentic faith is a questioning faith, a faith prepared to call even God into question. The difference between God and idols is that idols will brook no dissent. The test of authentic faith is the possibility of dissent against all authority in the name of human dignity. Such audacity demonstrates an authentic transcendence, one which reflects the utopianism of being created in the image of a God without image and enables one to struggle to make the world anew.

Starting Over

"Whether, once . . . Christians begin to learn from . . . Jews," says Franklin Littell, "this dimension of great, living faith [i.e., chutzpah] can be built into Christian religious life remains to be seen. . . . Christians have not usually been trained to wrestle with the angel, to question what happens under God's sovereignty. Christian mystics, like Muslim faithful, have raised obedience, submission, and acceptance of one's fate . . . to religious virtues." To incorporate the tradition of chutzpah or utopian audacity into Christian faith could give new meaning to the symbolism of the cross. As John Howard Yoder points out, the cross of the Christian should be assumed as the price for not being conformed to the world. "It is not, like Luther's or Thomas Müntzer's or Zinzendorf's or Kierkegaard's cross or *Anfechtung*, an inward wrestling of the sensitive soul with self and sin; it is the social reality of representing in an unwilling world the Order to come."[31]

The way back to authentic faith, for Christians, is difficult, because it is not ethically possible to embrace much of the pre-Shoah traditions of Christianity. For example, if the gospel itself teaches a faith of unquestioning obedience, how can Christians legitimately embrace an understanding of faith as chutzpah without abandoning their identity as Christians?

The answer to that question is threefold. First, the Christian who would seek to preserve his or her identity will lose it, whereas the Christian who is prepared to lose his or her identity, for Christ's sake, shall find it (Matt. 16:25).

Second, in the Gospel stories of Jesus we still have an echo of the tradition of chutzpah, even though, for the most part, it seems to have been suppressed as Christianity left the Jewish and entered the gentile world. Two parables in Luke's Gospel suggest that chutzpah was part of the tradition of the teachings of Jesus. In Luke 11:1-13, Jesus tells a parable about a man who knocks on a friend's door in the middle of the night and asks for a loaf of bread and refuses to leave until he gets it. The lesson of this parable is that one should pray to God with unrelenting persistence and demand that God listen. If one is demanding enough, God will hear and respond. In a similar parable in 18:1-8, Jesus tells of a widow who took her case before an uncaring judge and won by wearing the judge down with persistence, for the judge reasoned: "I am going to settle in her favor or she will end by doing me violence." The lesson Jesus draws from this is: "Will not God then do justice to his chosen who call out to him day and night?" One could also turn to Jesus' dying words on the cross as reported in Mark and Matthew—"My God, My God, why have you forsaken me?" (Mark 15:34, Matt. 27:46). This is not a submissive Jesus,

---

31. Littell, *Crucifixion*, 127; John Howard Yoder, *The Politics of Jesus* (Grand Rapids: Eerdmans, 1972), 97.

but a Jesus who, like Job, challenges God and calls God into question. Nevertheless, the tradition of chutzpah in the Gospels is such a slender thread that I doubt it can bear the whole weight of what is required.

Third, the appropriation of the tradition of faith as chutzpah can succeed only as long as Christians continue to reject the paganizing and gnostic teachings of Marcion, who, in the early church, tried to reject the teachings of the Tanakh (Old Testament) and base Christianity on edited selections from Luke and Paul. The gnostic tradition sought to oppose the savior God of the gentile Christians to the creator God of the Jews; the latter was the source of evil while the former was the source of good. Early Christianity rejected those teachings as heresy and insisted that the creator God and the savior God are one and the same, that the God of Abraham and the God of Jesus are the same. The tradition of faith as chutzpah is available to Christians because they share a common heritage with the Jews. The Deutsch Christians wanted to reject that common heritage in favor of an Aryan Jesus. A post-Shoah Christian faith will see the glaring error of that strategy and will learn to reaffirm the unity of tradition between Jews and Christians, but with the humility, this time, to allow that perhaps Jews have a better understanding of that common tradition since it is theirs first. An exclusively New Testament faith is not a Christian faith but a gnostic and paganizing faith. As Krister Stendahl puts it, the Tanakh is a book for the "long haul."[32] Without it, the faith of the New Testament becomes truncated and shortsighted. A New Testament faith is inadequate. Only a biblical faith will do. If that is the case, then Jews do indeed have something to teach Christians about the paradoxical complexity of faith as a dialectic and dialogue of trust and chutzpah.

Chutzpah as the Foundation

While the theme of wrestling with God has not been predominant in the Christian understanding of faith, it has not been entirely absent. However, the way it has been used typically tends to subvert rather than to utilize the ethical potential of this theme. The response of chutzpah is not just a new theological idea to be experimented with. It is an instinctive response

---

32. Krister Stendahl, "The Jewish People in Christian Preaching: A Protestant Perspective," in *The Jewish People in Christian Preaching*, ed. Darrell J. Fasching (New York and Toronto: Edwin Mellen, 1984), 73.

rooted in a compassion for one's neighbor, for the stranger, and even for one's enemy; it is so strong and compelling that one is willing to wrestle with God in order to demand justice. Such a response can emerge only out of an authentic experience of the transcendent dignity of the humanity of the other. Simply appealing to "the idea" of faith as wrestling with God does not guarantee that it will result in an ethic of chutzpah or utopian audacity. In fact, one should take it as an axiom of Christian ethics that if an ethical norm can be subverted it will be. Thus in order to identify authentic experiences of transcendence it is useful to point out two deformations of chutzpah or utopian audacity and then to suggest what I believe to be a genuine utopian use of chutzpah—a mean between these extremes which can truly have a transforming effect on the world. The typical forms of deformation are psychological individualism and political collectivism.

Authentic wrestling with God occurs within the context of a community and tradition that promotes individuality and ethical autonomy. Such a community stands in tension with the wider society, yet is committed to the dignity of all human beings, within and beyond that community, so much so that it is prepared to call God into question in the name of God's creation and the image of God in all persons, especially the stranger. The abuse of the wrestling theme occurs when the tense link (i.e., being in but not of this society) between the community and the larger world is replaced by a conjunction between individualism and collectivism that makes the collective norms of society final and ultimate. These contrasting options will be explored in the remainder of this chapter.

Luther's Psychological Individualism

The most common use of the theme of wrestling with God in Christianity is probably in the literature on spirituality and the inner life. Here wrestling with God is typically reduced to a psychological inner struggle between God and the inner self or soul almost to the exclusion of concern for and commitment to the well-being of the whole of creation beyond the self. It is appropriate to our subject matter to use Martin Luther as an example here. Luther's thought and experience have had a profound impact on the Western philosophical-psychological tradition, both religious and secular. He stands in a venerable tradition that can be traced from Plato through Augustine and beyond Luther himself to culminate in the work of Kierkegaard. From Augustine's *Confessions* onward, this tradition sees God as seeking out the individual and acting upon him or her inwardly through the emotions. Augustine interprets the inner struggle of his life as a kind of wrestling and quarreling with God. He feels torn between God and the world, in which he is drawn first toward one and then the other. The struggle is finally over when he surrenders his will to God and is turned around (*conversio*), away from the world and toward God. Conversion occurs at the moment of the surrender of self when God is the victor. Thus Augustine can say: "You [God] were always with me, angered against me in your mercy, scattering the most bitter discontent over all my illicit pleasures . . . you, who shape sorrow to be an instructor, who give wounds in order to heal, who kill us lest we shall die away from you."[33]

In this tradition, God can appear as the enemy who attacks the self but only for the purpose of bringing about a conversion, a transformation, a surrender of will—at which point God the enemy reveals himself as God the redeemer. In Luther these two sides of the God experience virtually split in two. At times Luther's volatile psychological experience seems to border on a Manichaean Gnosticism that replaces one God with two—one of wrath and the other of love. I say virtually, because I think Luther does hold these two sides together, but barely so. For Luther, the paradox of faith begins with the hiddenness of God and the two sides of God that are revealed through contrary appearances. Thus he tells us:

> Faith has to do with things which are not seen [Heb. 11:1]. Thus that there may be room for faith, everything which is believed must be concealed; but it cannot be more deeply concealed than under the contrary appearance, sensation and experience. Thus when God brings to life, he does it by killing; when he justifies, he does it by making guilty; when he exalts to heaven, he does it by leading to hell. . . . Thus he conceals his eternal goodness and mercy under eternal anger, his righteousness under unrighteousness. . . . The outward appearance of grace is as though it were pure anger, so deeply is it concealed. . . . Thus even to ourselves it always seems as though God wishes to abandon us and not keep his word, and that he is beginning to be a liar in our hearts. And finally, God cannot be God unless the first becomes a devil and we cannot go to heaven unless we first go into

---

33. Augustine *Confessions,* trans. Rex Warner (New York: A Mentor-Omega Book published by The New American Library, 1963), 2.2 (p. 42). For a general treatment of Augustine's conversion experience, see my article, "Mythic Story and the Formation of Personal Identity in Augustine's *Confessions, Florida Speech Communication Journal* 15, no. 1 (1987): 39–59.

hell, and cannot become the children of God, unless we first become the Devil's children. . . . But the world's lies in their turn cannot become lies unless they first become the truth, and the godless do not go down into hell, unless they have first been to heaven, and do not become the Devil's children unless they have first been the children of God. And finally the Devil becomes and is no Devil, unless he has first been God. . . . We have spoken in extreme terms of this, and we must understand what is just as startling, that God's grace and truth, or his goodness and faithfulness, rule over us and demand our obedience. . . . For a little while I must accord divinity to the Devil, and consider our God to be the Devil. But this does not mean that the evening lasts for the whole day. Ultimately, his steadfast love and faithfulness are over us [Ps. 117:2].[34]

This is a very powerful statement of religious experience. But in the context of the total structure of Luther's theology it is clear that this kind of wrestling with God is a form of psychological individualism, whose purpose, as in Augustine, is finally to bring the individual into submission to the will of God. In this wrestling match the outcome is the opposite of the story of Jacob's wrestling (Gen. 32:22-32), for it is God who is the victor, God who prevails, and the individual person who comes to surrender his or her will to the one who "rule[s] over us and demand[s] our obedience." It is precisely with the exegetical reversal of this story that an ethic of audacity (chutzpah) is transformed into an ethic of obedience.

When Luther's psychological individualism is placed within the context of Luther's two-kingdom theology, which forbids the individual to intervene in the social order, even when rulers are unjust, it is clear that this kind of wrestling with God will not give rise to the audacity to question authority, sacred or secular. Its final outcome will be submission to the will of the God who rules over the world with his left-handed wrathful side and over the church with his right-handed compassionate and forgiving side. God's will must finally be respected and obeyed as it is expressed through both "hands"—through both the state and the church. In this model wrestling with God has been reduced to psychological individualism and does not allow for the possibility of championing the world against God. On the contrary, one can safely ignore the world and concentrate on one's individual relationship to God and one's individual salvation. The ethic implied in

34. Quotations from Luther's collected works cited by Gerhard Ebeling in *Luther: An Introduction to His Thought,* trans. R. A. Wilson (Philadelphia: Fortress, 1970), 236–37.

this model of faith leads to quietism and conservatism in the social realm, and to an ethic of duty as unquestioning obedience to the responsibilities of one's station in life.

Emmanuel Hirsch's Political Collectivism

Individualism and collectivism are two sides of the same coin. A nation of individuals, a nation having no intermediate communities with distinctive traditions and values mediating between the individual and the state, is a collectivist society in which the criterion of dignity and equality is sameness. In such societies the primary crime will be differentness—the differentness of a community with an alternative scale of values that refuses to be assimilated. Such communities function as a limit on the authority of the state and represent a threat to the security of the collectivist identity. As a result collectivist societies will always try to control, suppress, and, if possible, eliminate such communities. Psychological individualism and political collectivism are mutually reinforcing identity structures that relate in the manner of Descartes' two worlds of unextended and extended substances or Kant's noumenal and phenomenal worlds, or in the manner described by Luther's two-kingdom theology. That is, they function as two correlated but mutually unobstructive worlds. Again, Luther's example of the executioner is relevant: it is possible for a Christian to be both a hangman, expressing God's judging wrath in society by executing its criminals, and at the same time a loving, forgiving, and compassionate Christian in one's personal life.[35] These two realms are structured to guarantee that they will not interfere with each other. They only reinforce each other. They break apart and enervate the tense unity in diversity of life that is held together by an ethic of audacity or chutzpah rooted in compassion for the created world and the image of God in all persons. In a collectivist society, those who are not the same (e.g., Aryan, in Nazi collectivist society) are considered not human but less than human (e.g., *untermensch*, "subhumans," as the Nazis called Jews). All who are defined as outside the human community are therefore outside the community of ethical obligation. In such a world it is possible to spend one's days fulfilling one's obligation to society in an unquestioning ethic of duty—gassing Jews and

---

35. See Paul Althaus, *Ethics of Martin Luther*, esp. chap. 4, "The Two Kingdoms and the Two Governments" (43–82). The example of the hangman is found on p. 74.

other aliens who are different—and return home to be a loving father or mother to one's children and a concerned neighbor and citizen among those who are the same.

Thus the theology of Emmanuel Hirsch (1888–1972), a leading theologian of the Nazi sympathizing Deutsch Christians, with its Aryan collectivist tendencies, fits very well with the Lutheran ethos of Nazi Germany and with the private psychological angst of Luther's subjectivist piety. In 1933 "Hitler named Chaplain Ludwig Müller (1883–1945) as his special 'Plenipotentiary for questions on the Protestant Churches.' Hirsch immediately became a major backer and adviser to Müller and remained so through the struggles of the months ahead."[36] Hirsch became a leading spokesman for the Deutsch Christian movement and against the Confessing Church, in which Karl Barth was a major figure and his chief opponent. During his years of teaching he was considered the leading scholar on Kierkegaard and he produced a classic work on his thought. In 1937 he became an official member of the Nazi party. For six years, during Nazi rule, he was dean of the theological faculty at the University of Göttingen. After the war, at age 57 he was forced into retirement because of his associations with the Nazi party.

As Hirsch developed his theology from the onset of World War I through his forced retirement in 1945, the concept of *Volk* played an important and integrating role. He distrusted all ecumenical internationalism as artificial and found the German *Volk* to be the natural and proper vehicle for the church and the gospel. The gospel and belief in God "sharpens in our conscience the law and the duty to do and to suffer everything for our own *Volk* and our own state, without regard for our own person." In good Lutheran (and Catholic) fashion he argued that the church provides the moral order that the state needs, and the state provides the political order needed for the spread of the gospel. The Jews are a foreign race with a foreign history who tried to disguise their differences and infiltrate the German *Volk*. Judaism is the legalistic religion of an alien people. Only Christianity is a religion founded upon a free, personal, and individual relationship to God. Indeed, since Jesus came from Galilee, "according

---

36. Robert P. Ericksen, *Theologians under Hitler: Gerhard Kittel, Paul Althaus and Emmanuel Hirsch* (New Haven: Yale Univ. Press, 1985), 147. Chapter 4 (pp. 120–97) is an illuminating discussion of Hirsch's life and thought, to which I am indebted for the characterization of Hirsch's theology.

to all the rules of scientific probability, Jesus was of non-Jewish blood" and his teachings were not Jewish teachings. All this fits well with Hirsch's insistence that the ethic of obedience in Christianity fits naturally with the hierarchical ethos of the German *Volk* (Hirsch distrusted the artificial equality that democratic regimes try to create) and the natural destiny of the white or Aryan races to rule history. Hirsch saw Hitler's coming to power as a fateful and providential moment in this history. He was grateful to the Nazis for bringing to an end the seemingly never-ending questions and debate that plagued modern Enlightenment culture. In response to Freiderich Gogarten, who maintained that " 'the final word allowed in religion is the question,' Hirsch insists that his theology and his concept of ethics and conscience are based upon *knowledge*." Faith, it seems, is an absolute affirmation of a god who is beyond all for questions and questioning, for "where the invisible is grasped by conscience, there grows an obedience which is ready courageously and unselfishly to wander the long, toilsome path of suffering resistance, which alone can lead our Volk again up to the heights."[37]

All of this is what we might expect from a Nazi or Deutsch Christian. But what has it to do with our theme of wrestling with God and the ethics of chutzpah? The answer is that, as early as 1914, Hirsch did allow one kind of questioning. In the early days of World War I, Hirsch preached a sermon on Genesis 32:22-32, Jacob wrestling with the stranger. This sermon depicted war as an unavoidable part of history used by God for God's purposes. "All the sacrifices of possessions and blood are nothing but the attempt to force from God a decision in our favor; [if] we do not leave him alone, then he will bless us."[38]

Six years later, Hirsch returned to this theme in *Deutschlands Schicksal*, where he described war as a "question to God." The "God of history . . . blesses only those . . . who set all their power and will on their freedom and their life goals. He does not listen to a Volk which questions only half-heartedly, which does not struggle for its life seriously and to

37. Emmanuel Hirsch, *Deutschlands Schicksal*, 2d ed. (Göttingen, 1922), 153 (quoted in Ericksen, *Theologians*, 139); Hirsch, *Das Wesen des Christentums* (Weimar, 1939), 158 (quoted in Ericksen, Theologians, 164); Hirsch, *Deutschlands Schicksal*, 163 (quoted in Ericksen, *Theologians*, 140); 166 (quoted in Ericksen, *Theologians*, 141).
38. See Hirsch's sermon in Jens Hoger Schjorring, *Theologrische Gewissenethik und politische Wirklichkeit: Das Beispiel Eduard Geismars und Emanuel Hirschs* (Göttingen, 1979), 58 (quoted in Ericksen, *Theologians*, 125).

the ultimate degree." Moreover, "if war truly is a question to God, yes, a struggle with God, which strikes investigatively at the main pillars of the national being, then it is an inconceivably hazardous undertaking. One can only justify it if one carries it through to the end, if one does not leave God alone until he gives his blessing. Fighting a lukewarm war, without the will to do and sacrifice everything, seems to me to be also a religious crime."[39]

Here we have it—the other end of the spectrum of the Christian use of the theme of wrestling and chutzpah. If Luther subjectivized it, Hirsch objectivized it and turned it into a political-collectivist parable for the legitimation of war as an expression of the will to power on the part of nation-states in general and of the German state in particular. Unlike Luther's wrestling with God, Hirsch's wrestling does issue in an ethic of chutzpah, but it is a counterfeit ethic. It is not an ethic arising out of compassion for the suffering of God's creation to challenge God in the name of God. It is not an ethic defending the image of God in every person. It is rather a collectivist ethic for the justification of the ascendancy of the Aryan *Volk* over and against all others, but especially over and against the Jews. This ethic is not a demand for justice but a thinly veiled disguise for the will to power. Hirsch's definition of faith as wrestling with God is counterfeit because he is not wrestling with the God who is the limit to every state but rather with a god who has been domesticated for the purposes of legitimating the German *Volk*. Hirsch's god is not the God of transcendence but a negative witness to transcendence.

Beyond Individualism and Collectivism

Both the psychological-individualist and the political-collectivist interpretations deviate from the authentic use of chutzpah because they fail to hold individuality and community in a tense, paradoxical unity in diversity. Both functionally collapse a two-kingdom ethic into the one-kingdom morality of a cosmological sacred society that values neither individuality nor differentness. In most times and places throughout history humans have lived within sacred societies, which understand religion and society as a unity that expresses the sacred order of the cosmos. A "holy" community (as

39. Hirsch, *Deutschlands Schicksal,* 108–9 (quoted in Ericksen, *Theologians,* 135–36).

the Hebrew *kadosh* suggests) is a community "separated" from society. It is an alternate community with its own traditions whose values stand in tension with the larger society.

A sacred society sacralizes its own finite order and requires conformity of all human selves to their divinely ordained place in that order, which inevitably identifies some as more human than others. By contrast, a holy community sees all selves as having an irreducible dignity that stems from being radically open to the infinite. Because the self is seen as mirroring the infinite it cannot be defined and confined to any dehumanizing definitions, and hence all selves are equal by virtue of their indefinability. (Both the Judaic understanding of the self created in the image of a God without image and the Buddhist understanding of no-self would be examples.) Holy communities oppose the cosmological ethic of a sacred society with an anthropological ethic that makes human dignity the measure of a just society—provided that the measure of the human is the infinite.

Because they are open to the infinite, such communities have an inherently utopian dimension; that is, they have the capacity to desacralize the status quo and keep self and society open to their infinite possibilities. They have the capacity to transform the sacred order of every society in the name of a higher justice that protects human dignity. In so doing they inevitably produce an ethic of two kingdoms or two realms by juxtaposing their own ethic against that of the larger society. The holy community calls the larger social order into question in the name of a "wholly other" order of values that the community seeks to embody. The point of the alternative ethic is not so much to replace the cosmological ethic of society (since that would result only in the production of another sacred order) as it is to desacralize its sacred order so as to protect human dignity, especially that of the stranger. Every society needs the continuing counterpresence of alternative communities if human dignity is to be recognized and respected.

Holy communities emerged independently only twice in the history of religions: in the Jewish synagogue and in the Buddhist *sangha*. It is significant that in both cases they gave birth to an ethic of welcoming the stranger and the outcast in such a way as to defy the sacred order of the surrounding societies. A sacred society (even if it claims to be secular) has its center within itself and defines being human in terms of sameness even as it abhors difference. By contrast, a holy community has its center outside itself, in a transcendence whose social analogue is the stranger. Thus a holy community defines the human in terms of an otherness that gives birth to an ethic of hospitality.

One becomes an individual, able to separate the self from collective identity, by virtue of belonging to such an alternate community. Compassion binds the individual within the holy community to the individuals in the society beyond its borders. In the biblical tradition, one encounters God, as Jacob did, through the encounter with the stranger—the one who is alien or other than oneself and one's religion or culture. Biblical ethics is rooted in the command to welcome the stranger, which appears "thirty-six times in the Torah, far more than any other mitzvah."[40] This command appeals to our capacity to identify with the stranger. "You shall not oppress a resident alien; you know the heart of an alien, for you were aliens in the land of Egypt" (Exod. 23:9). Knowing how the stranger feels one must "love the stranger, for you were strangers in the land of Egypt" (Deut. 10:19). In encountering the stranger, one encounters a witness to the transcendence of God, one who, like God, cannot be domesticated in order to legitimate one's life, religion, or cultural-national identity—one who by his or her very differentness or otherness calls one's identity into question. Respect for the dignity of the stranger is an implicit recognition of the image of the God who is Wholly Other (and without image) in the *otherness* of the stranger. Such compassion compels one to call into question all authority, sacred (i.e., the god of one's nation) or secular (i.e., the state), that would abuse that transcendent dignity.

Nechama Tec's study of Christian rescuers of Jews in Nazi-occupied Poland indicates that those rare Christians who risked their lives to help Jews did so out of a sense of alienation that enabled them to identify with the stranger. "Only a minority of those saved reported having been saved by friends. Many reported approaching friends first, being turned down and then being aided by strangers. More than half simply said they were protected by strangers."[41] The common characteristic of these helpers was not class, political affiliation, religious institutional affiliation, or even friendship but alienation, a psychological or sociological sense of being

40. Richard H. Schwartz, *Judaism and Global Survival* (New York: Atara, 1987), 13.
41. Nechama Tec, *When Light Pierced the Darkness* (New York: Oxford Univ. Press, 1986), 129. See esp. chap. 10.

marginal and hence different or separate in some way. This sense of "set-apartness" (should we not say holiness?) permitted them to act with autonomy, even audacity (chutzpah). They did not succumb to the social pressure to conform to their anti-Semitic environment. Moreover, because they experienced themselves as strangers, they seemed able to identify spontaneously with the suffering of the Jews as human beings who were, like themselves, aliens. As a result their actions on behalf of Jews were typically spontaneous rather than the result of a long inner debate. Virtually without exception these rescuers reported that they "had no choice" but to help—someone was in need. Their actions expressed their character, the kind of people they were, for they had histories of being compassionate helpers that predated the war. Moreover, their character was shaped not so much by the larger culture and the institutional church, which, for the most part, expressed collective cultural values, but by a subculture of significant others in their lives. This subculture was their true "holy community" (even in the case of secular or nonreligious individuals) that enabled them to call into question and to transcend the sacred and the profanely secular—a community defined by its openness to doubting and questioning all "sacred" values and to welcoming the stranger. Such individuals were most certainly among the hidden righteous, the saving remnant, for whose sake God spares the world.

For the most part, the Polish church offered these rescuers no message of audacity on behalf of the stranger. Still, in some cases, Christian rescuers reported that their personal understanding of the gospel message of love gave them the audacity to transcend all the negative teachings about Jews that they were getting from the pulpit. Churchgoers who defied the anti-Semitism being preached in the churches were typically strangers within their own tradition who "were very independent." They insisted on their own "personal brand of religiosity" instead of conforming to the official message. One rescuer, who shrugged off a sermon where he was told that his "official duty" was to turn in Jews, had the chutzpah to explain: "the devil finds his way even into the church."[42] The church as an institution failed during the Shoah. Were it not for a saving remnant, it would have no future. The church had the necessary resources within its tradition but failed to draw upon them and live up to them. Modeled on the Judaic

42. Ibid., 146, 137.

synagogue, the church began as a holy community and shared in the narrative traditions of welcoming the stranger. Yet only a remnant seemed to have heard this message. This ethic of welcoming the stranger is clearly present in the New Testament traditions. It is presented in the parable of the Good Samaritan (Luke 10:25-37), where the command to love one's neighbor is illustrated by the story of a Samaritan who finds a stranger injured by the roadside and proceeds to arrange for his care. As the parable illustrates, compassion for the stranger is to be extended even to one's enemy (a view also affirmed in the Sermon on the Mount, Matt. 5:43-48). Compassion for the stranger is also communicated in the parable of final judgment (Matt. 25:31-46), in which those who fed and clothed the stranger are welcomed into the kingdom as those who, in welcoming the stranger, were in fact unknowingly welcoming Christ (25:35).

Alternate communities that nurture audacity on behalf of the stranger have to be communities oriented beyond both the secular and the sacred— as alternatives not only to society but to the prevailing religious community that has conformed itself to society. An authentic ethic of audacity or chutzpah is nurtured in the experience of alternate communities as the context for the promotion and sustaining of unique individuality, which comes to expression in the compassion for the other—the alien or stranger. When Christianity separated itself from Judaism and became the religion of the Holy Roman Empire, it seems to have lost its capacity to accept the alien or the stranger as different. The stranger could only be welcomed as a potential convert to sameness. The stranger who remained a stranger within Christendom was like a nagging reminder, an implicit question, as to whether one could have a monopoly on God. The stranger, if one accepted him or her as an image of God, would require one to affirm that God really is transcendent and does not belong to one's *Volk*. The stranger is a reminder that God cannot be domesticated. The ascendancy of Christianity over the Roman Empire from Constantine (313 C.E.) to Theodosius (381 C.E.) was marked by a movement from tolerance to intolerance of the stranger. From the time of Theodosius Christianity became the only legal religion of the empire. Henceforth there were to be no strangers in the land.

There could be no ethic of chutzpah in pre-Shoah supersessionist Christianity because Christendom had no place for the stranger. That kind of Christianity could only be a negative witness to the transcendence of God. The whole of Deutsch Christianity and of the Nazi program of the Shoah is such a negative witness, a witness to the bestiality of human beings who are incapable of chutzpah because they are incapable of recognizing the image of God in anyone, even themselves, and hence are incapable of the compassion and moral outrage necessary for an ethic of chutzpah. When humans no longer live in awe of their being created in the image of the God who is without image, they resort to defining the indefinable. Instead of awe and questions before the wonder of the human, the Nazis and the Deutsch Christians knew what the human was and clearly defined it—the human is the same as Aryan. They knew that those who were not Aryan, those who were different, were not human and therefore were beyond the realm of moral obligation. They also knew who God was—"god with us," the Aryan Jesus. As Hirsch's theology suggests, the Nazi Deutsch Christians preferred a theology of answers to a faith rooted in transcendence and questioning. They preferred a theology of unquestioning obedience and surrender of will to the Aryan Christ and his messianic precursor, Hitler. Most sadly, even the Christians of the Confessing Church who stood in opposition to the Deutsch Christians had more in common with them than they should have. The whole history of Christianity has too much in common with the Deutsch Christians. Not enough of Marcion's gnostic heresy was rejected and far too much was retained.

The burning question remains: Can Christianity be de-paganized? Can it abandon the religiosity of unquestioning obedience and surrender of will? Can it return to its roots in Judaism to relearn the meaning of faith as trust and chutzpah, of faith as an affirmation of transcendence? The point of identifying audacity or chutzpah as a fundamental ethical option should not be read as recommending a certain set of ideas from which ethical action flows but rather as attempting to identify authentic transcendence so as to critique our various pale excuses for faith. Chutzpah cannot be manufactured upon demand; it flows out of a certain experience of transcendence and must be nurtured with an alternate or holy community. Christians need to face up to the fact that the test of faith is welcoming the stranger as "other"; anything short of that is masquerading as faith and is pure ideology. Christians will know they have recovered authentic faith when, in their teaching and preaching, and especially in their actions, they are able to affirm the continuing presence of their Jewish brothers and sisters (and indeed other strangers in the land) as other than themselves and a true witness to God's transcending presence. Christian ethics will express genuine chutzpah when the stranger or alien is finally welcomed as a neighbor to be loved as oneself. For it is out of that compassion that the ethic of chutzpah will emerge as a common ethic of Jews and Christians, and other strangers and aliens, against the dark forces that would lure humanity into yet another and even more engulfing apocalyptic time of desolation.

CHAPTER THREE

THE CHALLENGE OF AUSCHWITZ

RETHINKING CHRISTIAN NARRATIVE ETHICS

NARRATIVE AS A MODE OF ETHICAL REFLECTION

As far back as we can see into the misty recesses of time and the human adventure, human beings have told stories; although, to be sure, the particular stories they tell are quite diverse. Human beings are not just storytellers, they are story dwellers. Stories are not external to human identity but the very substance of it. The choices we make, even the options we think we have, are governed by the kind of story we think we are in and the role we see ourselves playing in it. It is significant that prior to the modern period, all peoples everywhere conveyed their stories in song, drama, and dance—that is, in mythic and ritual enactment. Their stories coursed through their veins and sinews and lived in their every gesture and movement. By dwelling in the story, by living through the narrative, one became human. To be human is to be like the gods or God or to do as the sacred ancestors did. That is why, in primal (oral) cultures the right way to do anything is the ritual way. For ritual is the archetypal repetition of those actions through which the right order of the world was created. It is significant that both the words *right* and *rite* are derived from the Sanskrit term (*rita*) for sacred cosmic order. Morality in such a world takes the form of a cosmological ethic, in which Is = Ought. Ritual conforms human action to the way things are as established in the beginning.

Modern human beings, existing after the fall into sociohistorical consciousness (in the nineteenth century), no longer understand themselves as living in a normative cosmos. They "know" that such cosmic stories are cultural fictions. Human beings are now historically self-conscious and "enlightened" creatures who can do without stories—or so the story goes. Such stories, it is thought, belong to the childhood and adolescence of the human race. Having reached the enlightened adulthood of the modern situation, contemporary individuals have put aside these childish stories. But as Stanley Hauerwas, the leading theological proponent of narrative ethics, has argued, the modern person is still living out a story, one that is meant to put an end to all stories. The form of the story is modeled on the mystical vision of Joachim of Fiore, a monk of the late Middle Ages who imagined history as made up of three successive ages—that of the Father, the Son, and the Spirit. In the apocalyptic last age of the Spirit, the human race would reach maturity and institutions would no longer be needed (not even the church), as all would be guided inwardly by the Spirit and live in spontaneous harmony. In its later secularized forms, this narrative vision came to form the foundational myth of the Enlightenment and modernization. In its modern versions it drew on Lessing from the eighteenth century and Comte (the father of sociology) in the nineteenth century to suggest a story of the three ages of the human race in which the age of myth (i.e., story) is superseded by the age of metaphysics, which in turn is superseded by our own rational age of science.[1]

In the story to end all stories we are told that we no longer need stories—only universal human reason. In what Hauerwas describes as the "standard account" of post-Enlightenment or modern ethics, the entire focus is on removing the person from his or her concrete, particular historical and narrative context. The moral point of view is said to require an "objectivity" that can come about only by removing the decision maker from the perspective of one who is involved so that he or she views the ethical situation as if a "disinterested observer" who is uninfluenced by the "subjective beliefs, wants and stories of the agent who makes them." This "standard account . . . has the distressing effect of making alienation the central moral virtue. We are moral exactly to the extent that we learn to view our desires, interests and passions as if they could belong to anyone. The moral point of view, whether it is construed in a deontological or teleological

---

1. See Stanley Hauerwas, Richard Bondi, and David B. Burrell, *Truthfulness and Tragedy: Further Investigations in Christian Ethics* (Notre Dame: Univ. of Notre Dame Press, 1977), 25ff.

manner, requires that we view our own life as if we were outside observers."[2] Moral reason gains its legitimacy by demonstrating that it is applicable to all persons everywhere, regardless of time, place, or social relationship. Not only ethical agents but also ethical issues are stripped of their histories and geographical locations and reduced to "case histories," which are mostly cases (quandaries) with very little history. These cases focus on isolated "moments of decision"—Is it morally permissible to have an abortion? Can feeding tubes be withdrawn from hopelessly comatose patients?—and so on.

Alasdair MacIntyre, the leading philosophical proponent of narrative ethics, has argued that the Enlightenment quest for a universal rational ethic has collapsed into ethical relativism and emotivism. MacIntyre presents our situation most vividly by telling the following story or parable:

> Imagine that the natural sciences were to suffer the effects of a catastrophe. A series of environmental disasters are blamed by the general public on the scientists. Widespread riots occur, laboratories are burnt down, physicists are lynched, books and instruments are destroyed. Finally a Know-Nothing political movement takes power and successfully abolishes science teaching in schools and universities, imprisoning and executing the remaining scientists. Later still there is a reaction against this destructive movement and enlightened people seek to revive science, although they have largely forgotten what it was. But all that they possess are fragments: a knowledge of experiments detached from any knowledge of the theoretical context which gave them significance. . . . None the less all these fragments are reembodied in a set of practices which go under the revived names of physics, chemistry and biology. Adults argue with each other about the respective merits of relativity theory, evolutionary theory and phlogiston theory, although they possess only a very partial knowledge of each. . . . Nobody, or almost nobody, realises that what they are doing is not natural science in any proper sense at all. For everything that they do and say conforms to certain canons of consistency and coherence and those contexts which would be needed to make sense of what they are doing have been lost, perhaps irretrievably.
>
> In such a culture . . . what would appear to be rival and competing premises for which no further argument could be given would abound.[3]

---

2. Ibid., 16, 23.

3. Alasdair MacIntyre, *After Virtue: A Study in Moral Theory* (Notre Dame: Univ. of Notre Dame Press, 1981), 1–2. Contra the claims of behaviorists, MacIntyre denies that any action can be known and understood apart from some story or interpretive context. I may observe someone who appears to be striking someone else, only to discover upon questioning him that he was not attacking this other person but killing a mosquito. Thus that person's actions were interpreted incorrectly as a certain behavior because I used the wrong interpretive story to make sense out of that person's actions. Every action demands an interpretive context in order for it to be understood as an intelligible behavior. See ibid., chap. 15, 190–209.

In this situation, contemporary philosophy would be of no help. Analytical philosophy would be unable to discover the disorder, and neither existentialism nor phenomenology would be aware that anything was wrong— for all these approaches are descriptive, not normative. The world MacIntyre is describing is produced by what Bernard Lonergan calls the "longer cycle of decline," in which knowledge is reduced to common sense (i.e., what everybody knows), hence no further questions need be raised.[4] In such a world, by default, the way things are is viewed as the way things ought to be, since no one seems able to imagine otherwise. The point MacIntyre is making, of course, is not about science but about ethics. "The language of morality is in the same state of grave disorder as the language of natural science in the imaginary world which I described."[5]

According to MacIntyre, the quest for a universal rational ethic that philosophers have been pursuing since Kant and the Enlightenment has been a dismal failure.[6] This is so because such a quest is historically naive in that it fails to recognize the sociohistorical and narrative context (in myth, epic, and story) of every ethic. As a result, ethicists have tried to construct an ethic by stripping the narratives from different ethical traditions and by lifting various theoretical components out of their diverse sociohistorical and narrative contexts in order to fit them together, as if they were all from the same jigsaw puzzle. Modern ethicists have tried to construct a "storyless" rational ethic from these theoretical fragments but the pieces do not fit. As a result, we live in a world of ethical quandaries in which our best philosophical minds cannot come to agreement because they are arguing from arbitrary and incommensurate first principles that have no coherent narrative to make sense of them. Faced with such storyless

---

4. Although I think MacIntyre is essentially correct in this judgment, I would qualify it by saying that existentialism is at least aware that something is wrong. It is essentially a philosophy of protest against scientific positivism. Nevertheless, MacIntyre is still right in that existentialism lacks the theoretical resources to really correct the situation since it chooses to embrace the irrational rather than link reason with self-transcendence, as, for instance, Bernard Lonergan has done in *Insight: A Study of Human Understanding*, (London: Darton, Longman, and Todd; New York: Philosophical Library, 1957), 226ff.; and also *Method in Theology* (New York: Herder and Herder, 1972).

5. MacIntyre, 2.

6. This claim should not go entirely unchallenged. Ronald Green has produced impressive arguments on behalf of the universal, cross-cultural applicability of Kant's understanding of moral reason. But Green does argue that this universal reason is purely formal and can function within a variety of different narratives offering a variety of different norms. See his *Religious Reason* (New York: Oxford Univ. Press, 1978); idem, *Religion and Moral Reason* (New York: Oxford Univ. Press, 1988).

first principles, we have no rational way of adjudicating their rival and contrary claims. Thus, unintentionally, ethical theories that argue from duty, utility, etc., are reduced to diverse expressions of ethical emotivism or relativism. Unable to advance good reasons for first principles, my claim that I "ought" to do *x* becomes the equivalent of *I feel strongly about x* or *I prefer x*. As a result, without anyone intending it, the Enlightenment quest for universally valid reasons has collapsed into a pervasive ethical relativism.

Following the lead of MacIntyre, Hauerwas contends that Christian ethical claims are substantive and not merely emotivist expressions of preference. However, the substance they have can be recovered only within a narrative context. The more Christian ethicists do ethics on the "standard account" the harder it is to tell what is Christian about the ethics they do. Apart from theological reflection on the ethical implications of the Christian story, Christians have no ethical wisdom to offer either each other or the world. It is not just that stories are often the best way of communicating ethical values and lessons. Hauerwas makes a much stronger claim, namely, that narrative shapes our very understanding of what good and evil are; thus, apart from certain narratives, important ethical insights are unavailable to us. Narrative ethics is more than a means of communication—it is a distinctive, powerful, and indispensable mode of ethical reflection in its own right. Story is so essential to Christian ethics that when a Christian ethicist relegates the Christian story to an addendum of the "standard account" of ethics, he or she risks ceasing to be a Christian ethicist at all.

According to Hauerwas, narrative is the connected description of contingent events and human sufferings that captures the drama of human life in a plot. The plot explains to us just what that drama is and thus what kinds of responses might be appropriate. Stories have the power to draw us emotionally into their way of seeing the world. Narrative is the mode of moral reflection that illuminates the lived texture of human existence in all its complexity and ambiguity with a degree of particularity and nuance that no abstract ethic of rules and reasons can ever approach.

"It is exactly the category of narrative," says Hauerwas, "that helps us to see that we are not forced to choose between some universal standpoint and the subjectivistic appeals to our own experience. For our experiences always come in the form of narratives. . . . I cannot make my behavior mean anything I want it to mean, for I have learned to understand my life from the stories I have learned from others." The language of ethical reflection is not "mine" but "ours." The "I" that decides is not an individualistic "I" but a narrative "I." Character is formed within families and communities shaped by narrative traditions. Character is rooted in story. One cannot communicate the truth of someone's character except by telling stories that reveal the kind of person they are. "The kind of decisions we confront, indeed the very way we describe a situation, is a function of the kind of character we have. . . . Character, inasmuch as it is displayed by a narrative, . . . provides the context necessary to pose the terms of a decision, or to determine whether a decision should be made at all."[7] Contrary to quandary ethics, most of our life is not spent making rationally calculated decisions. Rather than choosing to do this or that, we do what we do because of the kind of person we are—because of our character.

Stories have the power to seduce us into new ways of seeing the world. Unlike purely rational arguments, stories unite reason and emotion so as to move not only the mind but the heart. When they are successful, their seductiveness can bring about a conversion in our understanding of ourselves, our world, and our destiny. The seductive power of the story reaches down into the unconscious and transforms our way of seeing and our willingness to act on our new insights. The kinds of stories that have this power are not those allegorical stories whose meaning can be summarized "in other words." Rather, they are those mythic stories (political, social, religious) that have no point beyond themselves but give meaning and intelligibility to everything else. For Hauerwas, the gospel is such a story, one that gives the Christian a way of being in the world. The Christian story changes the world by changing the self. The gospel story is utopian, it does not simply mirror the world (as in cosmological ethics) but seeks to transform it. "The truth of religious convictions at least involves how the self is formed to rightly know the world as it should be but is not, except as it is subject to divine and human agency."[8]

All religious traditions communicate through story and narrative, but only in the biblical tradition is story the central metaphor for religious experience. Unlike the primal religions and the religions of Asia, the biblical traditions imagine life not as a drama structured in relation to the cyclical

7. Hauerwas et al., *Truthfulness and Tragedy*, 21, 20.
8. Ibid., 74.

rhythms of nature (e.g., the myths of eternal return, the yin/yang of the Tao, or the wheel of Samsara) but as a drama in which even the cosmos itself is more like a story with a beginning and an end. The Bible views the drama of life as history, that is, his-story (or "her-story")—a story told by the divine storyteller. "In the beginning" God speaks, and the story of creation begins and will continue until the story is completed. The Bible presents us with the story of a people's journey with God through time. Christians know who they are when they are able to place their own life stories within "God's story." "This is the basis for the extraordinary Christian claim that we participate morally in God's life." In such a story Christians come to see themselves as God's creatures who receive their existence in this world as a gift. To know who God is and who we are is to know the stories of "God's continuing faithfulness to the Jews and the ingathering of a people to the church." This narrative helps Christians to see the world "correctly," as a place of crucifixion, a tragic world. Moreover, it helps Christians to identify themselves as "crucifiers," as sinners who contribute to the tragedy of the world. The essence of sin is self-deception, whereby we attempt "to live as if we are or can be the authors of our own stories. Our sin is, thus, a challenge to God's authorship and a denial that we are characters in the drama of the kingdom."[9] Christian ethics is about conversion to a story that enables Christians to see themselves truthfully, so that what we do will flow out of our character, out of who we are. Thus conversion requires participation in a Christian community in which the stories are told and our character is shaped by this truthful self-understanding.

Since Christian ethics is rooted in the Christian story, Christian ethics must not be confused with some general ethic for all human beings. On the contrary, it is ethics for a particular holy community with a particular covenant obligation and call. But "that does not mean Christian convictions are of significance only for the church, for Christians claim that by learning to find our lives within the story of God we learn to see the world truthfully. Christians must attempt to be nothing less than a people whose ethic shines as a beacon to others illumining how life should be lived well."[10]

9. Hauerwas, *The Peaceable Kingdom,* (Notre Dame: Univ. of Notre Dame Press, 1983), 27, 28, 31.
10. Ibid., 34.

To recommend the Christian story, however, implies that we can distinguish between stories that are true and false, better and worse. If, as Hauerwas and Burrell claim, "all our notions are narrative-dependent, including the notion of rationality," then, contrary to the Comtean myth of secularization and universal reason, there is no neutral vantage point from which to judge between stories. "There is no story of stories, i.e., an account that is literal and that thus provides a criterion to say which stories are true or false. All we can do is compare stories to see what they ask of us and the world which we inhabit."[11] This view, of course, raises the problem of determining the truth and value of our stories, and with it, the specter of ethical relativism. It is at this point that Hauerwas and the narrative ethics approach are weakest. Hauerwas seems to have rescued Christian ethics from the vacuous, storyless "standard account" of ethics and given to Christian ethics its own unique perspective and content. But in the process he has had to claim that all ethical traditions are rooted in particular stories and communities and thus no universal ethic is possible. If even our understandings of rationality are "narrative-dependent," then it seems difficult to imagine how we can talk of the truth of a story or about some stories being more morally praiseworthy than others.

Hauerwas does attempt to answer this challenge. While his answer is not entirely satisfactory, it can be amended in ways that make it viable.

A true story must be one that helps me to go on, for, as Wittgenstein suggested, to understand is exactly to know how to go on. For when we do not understand, we are afraid, and we tell ourselves stories that protect ourselves from the unknown and the foreign. . . . Thus a true story is one that helps me to uncover the true path that is also the path for me through the unknown and foreign. It is important to note in this sense that I cannot make the story true by how I use it, but the story must make me true to its own demands of how the world should be. . . . A story that is true must . . . demand that we be true and provide us with the skills to yank us out of our self-deceptions, the main one of which is that we wish to know the truth.[12]

Thus the central ethical criterion of a true story is that it shape "actual lives and actual communities" and result in "truthful lives"[13] and lives open to the foreign—to strangers and their stories.

11. Hauerwas et al., *Truthfulness and Tragedy*, 21; Hauerwas, *Peaceable Kingdom*, 78–79.

12. Hauerwas, *Peaceable Kingdom*, 80.

13. See ibid., 80–81.

"Our only hope," says Hauerwas, "is the presence of the other, through which God makes present the kingdom in which we are invited to find our lives." In welcoming the stranger, we are welcoming God, "the ultimate stranger," into our lives. "God is such a stranger to us because we have chosen to live as if we were our own masters. God thus comes challenging our fears of the other by forcing us to patiently wait while others tell us their story." The church ought to be that form of community in which we "learn to make others' histories our own."[14]

ALBERT SPEER'S SELF-DECEPTION

Hauerwas and David Burrell explore the problem of the relationship of narrative to truthfulness in two autobiographies. They use Augustine's *Confessions* to illustrate the process and criteria whereby one comes to embrace a "true story" and Albert Speer's *Inside the Third Reich* to illustrate the ethical bankruptcy of the person who has succumbed to the myth of the "storyless person" and fallen into self-deception. We shall examine Speer's autobiography first, and then later raise the question of whether Hauerwas and Burrell's interpretation of Augustine meets the challenge of articulating the criteria for a "true story" that their analysis of Speer's autobiography raises.

Their essay, "Self-Deception and Autobiography: Reflections on Speer's *Inside the Third Reich*," is useful to us not only because it attempts to explore the lessons of the Shoah for doing Christian ethics but also because in the process it illuminates the peculiar challenges that professional role and identity present to the assuming of personal responsibility in a technical civilization. In this essay, they explore "the challenge of Auschwitz for persons who intend to be Christian" by addressing the relationship between "self-deception and cooperation with murder" in the life of Albert Speer.

---

14. Hauerwas, *Peaceable Kingdom,* 144; idem, *Against the Nations* (Minneapolis: Winston, 1985), 197. If there is a significant difference in the way Alasdair MacIntyre and Stanley Hauerwas approach narrative ethics, it seems to be that MacIntyre bewails the Babel of the ethical pluralism of diverse stories and prepares for the new dark ages by settling into the one story that he wishes were universal, whereas Hauerwas does not settle for the particularity of his Christian narrative tradition but rejoices in its particularity while insisting that other narrative traditions may have something to teach us as well. The difference may be the result of Hauerwas's strong emphasis on the biblical ethic of welcoming the stranger.

Auschwitz stands as a symbol of one extreme to which our self-deception can lead. For the complicity of Christians with Auschwitz did not begin with their failure to object to the first slightly anti-Semitic laws and actions. It rather began when Christians assumed that they could be the heirs and carriers for the symbols of the faith without sacrifice and suffering. It began when the very language of revelation became an expression of status rather than an instrument for bringing our lives gradually under the sway of "the love that moves the sun and the other stars . . . 'The conditions of self-deception that created Auschwitz still prevail in our souls. . . . We cannot afford to ignore Auschwitz, for to overlook it sets the stage for yet further self-deception."[15]

Self-deception is a profoundly common and debilitating moral condition that involves not only engaging in contradictory beliefs and actions but doing so without being fully aware of doing so, so that one is helpless to extricate oneself from this condition. "I can be conscious of what I am doing without perceiving myself doing it, and I can be aware of what I am up to yet fail to take it into account." It is a mistake to equate consciousness with "taking a look," for it is "more like an ability to say than the power to see." Indeed, the ethical life depends on our ability to spell out for ourselves what we are doing. Self-deception is compounded not only by our avoiding becoming conscious of our actions but also "avoid[ing] becoming explicitly conscious that we are avoiding it. . . . To bring certain things to consciousness requires the moral stamina to endure the pain that such explicit knowledge cannot help but bring."[16]

Hauerwas and Burrell argue that the very nature of self-deception requires that it be practiced as a consistent policy, as an expression of one's character, for to let up for even one moment would be to come face-to-face with precisely that which cannot be faced. Self-deception feeds on our desire to be sincere. The cynic has no need for self-deception. Self-deception feeds the illusions we need to keep us "sane," that is, to sustain the sense of identity we cling to as sincere, decent, and responsible individuals. "Societal roles provide a ready vehicle for self-deception, since we can easily identify with them without any need to spell out what we are doing. The role is accepted into our identity. It may define our identity." Thus we hide behind our identity as a company man or a public servant

15. Hauerwas et al., *Truthfulness and Tragedy*, 82, 83.
16. Ibid., 85.

who sometimes has to make difficult and ugly decisions in order to accomplish some greater good.

> Self-deception is correlative with trying to exist in this life without a story sufficiently substantive and rich to sustain us in the unavoidable challenges that confront the self. . . . To live bravely is to be willing to risk our present lives in pursuing the consequences of the commitments we have made. A policy of fidelity cannot help but challenge the story we currently hold about ourselves. We can afford to let go of our current story, however, only to the extent that we are convinced that it does not hold the key to our individual identity. So we will remain subject to those propensities which lead to a state of self-deception as long as we feel ourself to be constituted either by the conventional roles we have assumed or by the level of awareness we have been able to articulate. Alternatively, we will have some leverage on these powers in the measure that we believe ourself to be constituted by a story given to us by a power beyond our will or imagination. . . . If it is to counter our propensity to self-deception, the story that sustains our life must give us the ability to spell out in advance the limits of the various roles we will undertake in our lives. . . . To lack such a story, as we shall see in the case of Speer, is to be deprived of the skills necessary to recognize or challenge the demonic. And to be bereft of those skills is to fall prey to these powers. That much we can now say, after Auschwitz.[17]

Hauerwas and Burrell are convinced that the lack of such a "master story" explains Albert Speer's involvement in the aims of Hitler. The source of their observations is Speer's autobiography, *Inside the Third Reich*, which I am drawing upon here in addition to their essay.[18] Speer's story is of interest not only for what it says about conditions in Nazi Germany but for the broader lesson we can derive from it about the unique ethical dangers that surround bureaucratic and professional roles in a modern technical civilization.

Speer was seduced into ethical blindness and self-deception by implicit stories, dancing in his head, of professional glory and success. He was a well-educated young man from a prosperous and liberal German family, and when the time came for him to choose a career, he says, "I . . . decided, to my father's delight, to become an architect, like him and his

17. Ibid., 87–88.
18. Albert Speer, *Inside the Third Reich*, trans. Richard and Clara Winston (New York: Macmillan, 1970).

father before him."[19] A skilled architect, Speer considered himself above politics. He was never a fervent Nazi. He married and had six children and was apparently a loving father.

Of his education he says:

> We were being educated in terms of a conservative bourgeois view of the world. In spite of the Revolution which had brought in the Weimar Republic, it was still impressed upon us that the distribution of power in society and the traditional authorities were part of the God-given order of things. . . . In school, there could be no criticism of courses or subject matter, let alone of the ruling powers in the state. Unconditional faith in the authority of the school was required. It never even occurred to us to doubt the order of things, for as students we were subjected to the dictates of a virtually absolutist system. Moreover, there were no subjects such as sociology which might have sharpened our political judgments.[20]

At home, even though his father was a liberal, politics was never discussed. Looking back, Speer feels that there was little in his upbringing to prepare him for critical, autonomous, political and ethical judgment.

Speer was drawn into Hitler's National Socialist Party (NSDAP) when, in 1930, he heard Hitler speak to the faculty and students of the University of Berlin and of the Institute of Technology, at which he held the equivalent of a graduate assistant appointment. He was impressed by the number of professors in attendance and the enthusiasm with which both students and faculty greeted Hitler. But Speer was most impressed by Hitler's appearance and demeanor. "On posters and in caricatures I had seen him in military tunic, with shoulder straps, swastika armband, and hair flapping over his forehead. But here he was wearing a well-fitted blue suit and looking markedly respectable. . . . Then . . . he began a kind of historical lecture rather than a speech. To me there was something engaging about it—all the more so since it ran counter to everything the propaganda of his opponents had led me to expect. . . . The mood he cast was much deeper than the speech itself, most of which I did not remember for long. . . . [Afterward,] shaken, I drove off into the night, . . . stopped in a pine forest near the Havel, and went for a long walk. Here, it seemed to me, was hope. Here were new ideals." Hitler promised the defeat of communism

19. Ibid., 9.
20. Ibid., 7–8.

and economic recovery, and "mentioned the Jewish problem only peripherally. But such remarks did not worry me, although I was not an anti-Semite." In January of 1931 he joined the party. Quite unknown to him at the time his mother also joined the party, after seeing an SA (storm troopers) parade. "The sight of discipline in a time of chaos, the impression of energy in an atmosphere of universal hopelessness, seems to have won her over also. . . . Both of us seem to have felt this decision to be a breach with a liberal family tradition. In any case, we concealed it from one another and from my father."[21]

Speer says that he joined the party purely out of response to Hitler's personality. He did not read the party literature, he did not even read *Mein Kampf*. Thus he reflects that self-deception was part of the process from the beginning. "At this initial stage my guilt was as grave as, at the end, my work for Hitler. For being in a position to know and nevertheless shunning knowledge creates direct responsibility for the consequences—from the very beginning."[22]

Speer was drawn into deeper and deeper involvement with Hitler by the promise of professional opportunity. He had completed his architectural training as Hitler and the National Socialist Party were coming to power. It was a time of severe economic chaos with ridiculous levels of inflation. As he opened his own architectural office, opportunities were scarce. But then his party affiliation began to get him opportunities to do redecorating and rebuilding for various party offices and buildings. Very shortly he came to the attention of Hitler, who, Speer discovered, had an intense interest in architecture. Hitler seems to have viewed architecture as his missed calling and identified the young Speer as an embodiment of his own youthful ambitions. Hitler took Speer under his wing and gradually increased his responsibilities until it was clear to Speer that he was to be "Germany's architect," rebuilding its cities in magnificence. It was the opportunity of a lifetime, to design the great public buildings that would immortalize Germany in its emerging golden time of glory under Hitler. Indeed, Hitler seems to have seen Speer as his guarantee of immortality, for later he wrote him: "I was looking for an architect to whom I could entrust my building plans. I wanted someone young; for as you know these

21. Ibid., 15–16, 18.
22. Ibid., 19.

plans extend far into the future. I need someone who will be able to continue after my death with the authority I have conferred on him. I saw you as that man." Speer reflects that "after years of frustrated efforts I was wild to accomplish things—and twenty-eight years old. For the commission to do a great building, I would have sold my soul like Faust. Now I had found my Mephistopheles."[23]

"In responding to this challenge," says Speer, "I gave up the real center of my life: my family. Completely under the sway of Hitler, I was henceforth possessed by my work. Nothing else mattered. . . . My position as Hitler's architect had soon become indispensable to me. . . . The intensity with which I went at my work repressed problems that I ought to have faced. . . . I so rarely—in fact almost never—found the time to reflect about myself or my own activities. . . . Today, in retrospect, I often have the feeling that something swooped me up off the ground at the time, wrenched me from all my roots, and beamed a host of alien forces upon me." What troubled him at the time was not what was happening to Jews, Social Democrats, or Jehovah's Witnesses but the direction he was taking as an architect. As long as he was not directly involved in decisions regarding the mistreatment of others, he did not, at that time, feel responsible. Moreover:

> The ordinary party member was being taught that grand policy was much too complex for him to judge it. Consequently, one felt one was being represented, never called upon to take personal responsibility. *The whole structure of the system was aimed at preventing conflicts of conscience from even arising.* . . .
> Worse still was the restriction of responsibility to one's own field. . . . Everyone kept to his own group—of architects, physicians, jurists, technicians, soldiers, or farmers. The professional organizations to which everyone had to belong were called chambers . . . , and this term aptly described the way people were immured in isolated, closed-off areas of life. The longer Hitler's system lasted, the more people's minds moved within such isolated chambers. . . . What eventually developed was a society of totally isolated individuals. . . .
> . . . We had derived our principles from the *Obrigkeitsstaat,* the authoritarian though not totalitarian state of Imperial Germany. Moreover, we had learned those principles in wartime, when the state's authoritarian character had been further intensified. Perhaps the background had prepared us

---

23. Ibid., 31.

like soldiers for the kind of thinking we encountered once again in Hitler's system. Tight public order was in our blood; the liberalism of the Weimar Republic seemed to us by comparison lax, dubious, and in no way desirable.[24]

Hitler was so impressed by Speer's organizational and managerial skills that when the war escalated he asked him to step out of his architectural role and assume the position of Minister of Armaments. It has been estimated that his skill in this position may have lengthened the war by as much as two years. In this position he allowed the use of slave labor in Germany's factories and mines. He had no direct connection with the extermination of the Jews; "conveniently" he chose to ignore the existence of the death camps. "Hitler's hatred for the Jews seemed to me so much a matter of course that I gave it no serious thought. I felt myself to be Hitler's architect. Political events did not concern me. . . . Today it seems to me that I was trying to compartmentalize my mind. . . . It is . . . true that the habit of thinking within the limits of my own field provided me, both as architect and as Armaments Minister, with many opportunities for evasion. . . . But in the final analysis I myself determined the degree of my isolation, the extremity of my evasions, and the extent of my ignorance."[25]

Speer was an intelligent, impressive, one might even say conscientious and sincere young man. According to Trevor H. R. Roper, "in Hitler's court Albert Speer was morally and intellectually alone. . . . As an administrator, he was undoubtedly a genius. He regarded the rest of the court with dignified contempt. His ambitions were peaceful and constructive: he wished to rebuild Berlin and Nuremberg, and had planned to make them the greatest cities in the world. Nevertheless, in a political sense, Speer is the real criminal of Nazi Germany, for . . . he did nothing." He did nothing until the very end when he saw that his own work and hopes for Germany were being totally destroyed by Nazi policy. Then he defied Hitler and, according to Hauerwas and Burrell, "almost single-handedly, and with great courage, stayed the execution of Hitler's scorched-earth policy against Germany."[26]

24. Ibid., 32–33 (emphasis added).
25. Ibid., 112–13.
26. H. R. Trevor-Roper, *The Last Days of Hitler* (New York: Macmillan, 1947), 240–41, quoted in Hauerwas et al., *Truthfulness and Tragedy*, 94; Hauerwas et al., *Truthfulness and Tragedy*, 90.

"What staggers us," says Hauerwas, "is not what Arendt . . . called the banality of evil, but the reality of a good man serving such masters. . . . He is reminding us that integrity and sincerity in themselves are not sufficient safeguards against the seduction of evil." The young Speer symbolizes "the pure technician, the classless bright young man without background, with no other original aim than to make his way in the world and no other means than his technical and managerial ability." Speer is the archetypal model for the "technological barbarian" of which Franklin Littell speaks. Speer himself remarked during his final speech at the Nuremberg trials: "Hitler's dictatorship was the first dictatorship of an industrial state in this age of modern technology. . . . Dictatorship of the past needed assistants of high quality in the lower ranks of the leadership also—men who could think and act independently. The authoritarian system in the age of technology can do without such men. The means of communication alone enable it to mechanize the work of the lower leadership. Thus the type of uncritical receiver of orders is created."[27]

Reflecting on his ethical failure, Speer says: "I did not see any moral ground outside the system where I should have taken my stand."[28] Hauerwas and Burrell suggest that this is due to his lack of a master story. "Our ability to 'step-back' from our deceptions is dependent on the dominant story, the master image, that we have embodied in our character." Speer presumed that the "images and symbols . . . offered by conventional roles" could give coherence to his life and that he needed nothing else. What he needed however was a "true story," one which was "continually discomforting" and thus able to check the tendency to self-deception. "We need a story that allows us to recognize the evil we do and enables us to accept responsibility for it in a nondestructive way. . . . Christians claim to find the skill to confess the evil that we do in the history of Jesus Christ. It is a history of suffering and death that must be made our own if we are to mine its significance. The saints formed by this story testify to its efficacy in purging the self of all deception as it forces the acceptance of a new self mirrored in the cross. Moreover, this story has given the saints a way to go on as they become disciples of the way—the way of learning to deal

---

27. Hauerwas et al., *Truthfulness and Tragedy*, 89–90; Speer, *Inside the Third Reich*, 344–45 (quoting *The Observer*, April 9, 1944); Franklin Littell, *The Crucifixion of the Jews* (New York: Harper & Row, 1975), chap. 1; Speer, *Inside the Third Reich*, 520–21.
28. Speer, *Inside the Third Reich*, 375.

with evil without paying back in kind. The stories that produce truthful lives are those that provide the skills to step back and survey the limits of our engagements."[29]

THE SHOAH, THE GOSPEL STORY, AND SELF-DECEPTION

The first thing that ought to strike us about Hauerwas's and Burrell's critique of Speer's ethical bankruptcy and the proposed solution of a return to a Christian narrative ethic is that after Auschwitz this solution seems highly implausible. If the ethical test of a narrative tradition is its ability to produce truthful lives and truthful communities, then the Christian narrative tradition is in deep trouble. For after two thousand years of anti-Judaism in the Christian tradition (as I argued in chap. 1) we Christians find ourselves, like Job's comforters, guilty of not having spoken the truth. This history reveals that the Christian story has produced a serious form of self-deception, the myth of supersession—one that legitimated its spiritual genocide of the Jewish people by claiming a direct authorization from God through the Christian story. Hauerwas's and Burrell's criterion of a story's truth (truthful communities and truthful lives that avoid self-deception and are open to the foreign and strange) serves only to corroborate my argument that shortly after Paul, through the sin of pride, Christianity cut itself off from the covenant story into which it had been grafted.

Hauerwas is aware of the problem of Christian anti-Judaism. "If it can be shown that the Holocaust lies at the heart of Christian claims about the kind of life required to be a disciple of Jesus, it would surely provide strong evidence that Christianity is a false and perverse faith." "I have always assumed," he says,

> that the Holocaust, and Christian complicity in the Holocaust, is a decisive test case for anyone attempting to think ethically as a Christian. That may seem an odd claim since I have seldom directly discussed the Holocaust. But it seems odder still, since I have been one of the few persons working in contemporary religious ethics who has called for Christian ethics to be unapologetically Christian. I have emphasized those aspects of the moral

29. Hauerwas et al., *Truthfulness and Tragedy*, 95, 96, 98.

life—character, narrative, the separateness of the church—that make Christian convictions about Jesus morally intelligible and significant. . . . Even more shocking, I am said to assert that "the notion of a common morality is an illusion; believers and non-believers simply have their stories through which their characters are shaped." This characterization is essentially correct. . . . From the perspective of many, and especially those concerned with Auschwitz, this reassertion of the particularity of Christian ethics cannot but appear as a dangerous new tribalism.[30]

Hauerwas's position seems to many to be devoid of the universal ethic needed to challenge the narrow loyalties of the Nazis. But as anyone familiar with his work might expect, Hauerwas sees the problem from just the opposite angle. He is convinced that the problem of the failure of Christian ethics during the Holocaust has to do not with a failure to assume its proper universality but with its failure to accept its unique particularity.

Hauerwas agrees with Eliezer Berkovits that Christian imperialism began with Constantine, when Christianity became the official religion of the Roman Empire under the conviction that it had the universal message that must be brought to, and accepted by, all of humanity. The victory of Christianity over the empire seemed to Christians like a divine affirmation of exactly such an understanding. But quite the contrary, Hauerwas argues; this was a false universalism that ended up identifying Christianity with the state and in the process sanctioning state violence against all who choose not to conform to "universal Christian values." If, as Berkovits contends, we now live in a "post-Christian" era, still, Hauerwas argues, Constantinianism has not disappeared but only "shifted to a new key. No longer able or willing to try to control the governmental apparatus itself, Christians seek to form societies that embody their values on the assumption that those values are universal."[31] To the degree that they make this assumption, Christians are in danger of continuing the same mistake that led them to brand the Jews as unwelcome strangers in the Europe of the Nazi period. For as long as Christians continue to think in universalist terms they will feel compelled in conscience to convert all who are different to universal sameness, and this compulsion leads not only to violence toward the stranger but also conformity to the collective sacred order of society.

30. Hauerwas, *Against the Nations*, 65–66, 63–64.
31. Ibid., 71. See Eliezer Berkovits, *Faith After the Holocaust* (New York: KTAV, 1973), 37ff.

Thus if Christians wish to prevent another Holocaust they must learn to accept the particularity of their faith and to resist all attempts to create a universal ethic, Christian or otherwise, for all forms of a universal ethic have violence built into them.

The lesson of Jewish experience in Europe is explicit—whether sacred or secular, universalism is deadly. Not only under Christian universalism did the Jews experience prejudice and violence, but also under secular Enlightenment universalism. Enlightenment universalism promised to free humanity from the last frontier of "religious particularity and prejudice" and therefore to emancipate Jews to be full members of European society. Jews who wanted to be members of this "universal" community as Jews, however, and not just as storyless universal human beings, found that the secular Enlightenment world turned against the Jewish world even more viciously than had Christendom. Hauerwas is surely right to argue that "philosophical liberalism provided the theoretical basis for emancipation, but at the same time suggested the basis for this transition from religious to nationalist anti-Semitism." This same "enlightened" attitude now makes it seem "from any universally humanistic framework, [that] the destruction of European Jewry is one notable chapter in the long record of man's inhumanity against man." For universalistic humanism does not value memory of the particular, of tradition and its stories, and it is only within the traditions of the biblical story that the Holocaust stands out among these atrocities as an attack not only on the Jews but on the God of the Jews, which is to say the God of the whole human race. Universalism

not only results in cultural and social imperialism, but it also distorts the nature of faith itself. For . . . in order to sustain the presumed universality of our convictions, the convictions are transformed into general truths about "being human" for which "Christ" becomes a handy symbol. Our universalism is not based on assumed commonalities about mankind; rather it is based on the belief that the God who has made us his own through Jesus Christ is the God of all people. . . . When the universality of humanity is substituted for our faith in the God of Abraham, Isaac, and Jacob, the eschatological dimension of our faith is lost. Christian social ethics then becomes the attempt to do ethics for all people rather than being first of all an ethic for God's eschatological people.[32]

32. Hauerwas, *Against the Nations*, 71–72, 73, 76–77.

Hauerwas finds the true ethical power of Christianity in its diaspora status as a holy community. "I am trying to suggest that Christianity . . . must always be a diaspora religion. But we have hardly begun to think through the social implications of that claim." "The great social challenge for Christians is learning how to remember the history of the Jews, as part of and as essential to our history, . . . learning that the Jews are our partners in discerning God's way in the world. To learn to remember in this manner is a radical political act in that it must of necessity change our understanding of the Christian community and its relationship to our world."[33]

While Hauerwas is surely right in his critique of both Christian and Enlightenment universalisms, he ignores the fact that the Nazi onslaught against the Jews was rooted in a Romantic reaction to Enlightenment universalism. For the Nazis (including the Deutsch Christians), the problem with the Jews was not that they were not truly universal but that they were the wrong particularity—they were Jewish, not Aryan. Accepting one's particularity is not in itself a redeeming quality. It is so only if one's particular community can accept the presence of those who are different and so welcome the stranger. Moreover, Hauerwas's position leaves the most crucial issue unaddressed—the relation of the gospel stories to the history of Christian anti-Judaism. Only twice in this essay does he touch on that issue. Once, in passing, he mentions that Christian ethics should be founded on the "particularity of Jesus" in order to assess adequately the Christian failure during the Holocaust. At another point he mentions, also in passing, that in contrast to Berkovits's focusing on the fourth century, Rosemary Ruether has made "a more compelling case against Christian anti-Semitism by tracing Christian persecution of the Jews to the Gospel itself."[34] But then he moves on with the argument I have reviewed here and never returns to the far more devastating problem: whether the Christian story is inherently anti-Judaic. For if it is, how can it provide the "master story" that Hauerwas identified as missing from the life of Albert Speer? What is even worse, it may be that Christianity provides a master story that produces not an Albert Speer, a "decent" man without ethical resources, but an Adolf Hitler, who thinks that by ridding the world of Jews he is "doing the work of the Lord."

33. Ibid., 77, 75.
34. Ibid., 66, 69.

The Shoah reveals the limits and weaknesses of narrative ethics. If one's master story is the final norm of good and evil and it authorizes the notion of the Jews as a rejected people, then one has no recourse but to accept and to act on that story. If there is no narrative independent form of rationality through which to assess one's story, then how can one escape a pure ethical relativism? How do we tell a divine from a demonic story? Hauerwas suggests that the *Confessions* of Augustine offer a model for discerning true and false stories, for Augustine's life story is a story of how he went from story to story until he found a "true story."

AUGUSTINE'S *CONFESSIONS* AS A MODEL FOR NARRATIVE TRUTH

If there is no narrative independent rationality and no meta-story by which to judge all stories, "how can stories themselves [be used to] develop a capacity for judging among alternatives?" To answer this question Hauerwas and Burrell turn to the *Confessions* of Augustine. For "a complete account of the way narrative functions . . . would be a narrative recounting how he [i.e., anyone] came to judge certain stories better than others. . . . Augustine's *Confessions* offer just such an account by showing how Augustine's many relationships, all patterned on available stories, were gradually relativized to one overriding and ordering relationship with God revealing himself in Jesus." One of the advantages of this narrative model is that "we would have a vantage for judgment beyond the intrinsic merit of the narrative itself, in the perceived character of its author."[35] By this I take Hauerwas and Burrell to mean that if an important criterion of narrative is that it produces truthful lives, then Augustine's own life and character are a further criterion for judging his own master story.

Writing ten years after his conversion to Christian faith, Augustine looked back over his life and recounted his quest to find a true story that would answer two critical questions: (1) How to account for evil? and (2) How to conceive of God? The pear tree incident, in his youth, raised the first question for him. Stealing pears is a relatively trivial incident. Upon reading Augustine's account one's first response is likely to be that his reaction to this incident is excessive, out of proportion. But what horrified

35. Hauerwas et al., *Truthfulness and Tragedy,* 30, 31.

Augustine is precisely the triviality of the incident. The pears offered no sufficient motive for the act; there was nothing to be gained by stealing them. Indeed, once stolen, he discarded them. Since the pears were hardly valuable, Augustine concluded that he stole them for the pure love of stealing, a love for the evil itself. From this incident Hauerwas and Burrell draw the lesson that "what makes an action evil is not so much a reason as the lack of one. So we would be misled to attribute evil to the creator who orders all things, since ordering and giving reasons belong together." They suggest that insight into this fact led Augustine to break with the Manichees, who attributed human evil to a metaphysical cause, an evil deity. He realized that only human freedom allows us to act for no reason at all. "Since explanations offer reasons, and evil turns on the lack of reasons, some form other than a causal explanation must be called for. The only form which can exhibit an action without pretending to explain it is the very one he adopted for the book itself: narrative."[36]

"We cannot give up . . . looking for an explanation unless our very horizon shifts. . . . Yet horizons form the stable background for inquiry, so normally we cannot allow them to shift. In Augustine's case, as in many, it only occurred to him to seek elsewhere after repeated attempts at explaining proved fruitless." The shift away from explanatory modes to narrative, which is just such a shifting of horizons, led Augustine to reconceive divinity as well. For to the degree that he accepted responsibility for his own acts, Augustine felt a need to confess them, which led him to develop a language of inwardness by which to judge his actions in response to an inner demand for truthfulness. The language of inwardness was facilitated by his discovery of the Platonists, but what he did not find in the Platonists were the "tears of confession." As Hauerwas and Burrell explain, "they [Platonists] do not tell us how to do what we find ourselves unable to do: to set our hearts aright."[37] This power of conversion, of turning around, Hauerwas and Burrell find only in the seductive power of biblically inspired stories. Indeed, the actual moment of Augustine's conversion is preceded by stories told to him of the conversion of others.

Augustine's conversion is worth looking at more closely. As he tells it, it was through the power of stories that God seduced him. The moment

36. Ibid., 33, 32.
37. Ibid., 32, 33.

of crisis that led to his turning around and his embracing the biblical story was precipitated by a series of stories. On the verge of embracing the Christian story, he was unable to make the decision and he sought the advice of someone wiser. He visited Simplicianus, the man who had been responsible for the conversion of Ambrose. Simplicianus told him a story about the conversion of Victorinus, a Platonic scholar who had translated some of the Neoplatonic writings Augustine had read and who taught rhetoric in Rome. His situation was therefore directly parallel to Augustine's in Milan. Augustine admired this man very much, and now Simplicianus was telling him the story of how Victorinus had become a Christian and given up his teaching post in order to serve the church. When he heard the story, Augustine said, "I was on fire to be like him, and this, of course, is why he had told me the story" (8.5.10).[38] At this point he longed to emulate Victorinus, but he was still held back, he said, by the "iron bondage" of his will.

Shortly after this, Augustine had a visit from a stranger, a fellow North African who had heard that Augustine and his friends were from his homeland. The young man, Ponticianus, found Augustine reading from Paul's letters. He took the occasion to indicate that he was a Christian, and then he began to tell Augustine the story of the conversion of St. Antony. He went on to tell another story about men living together in a monastery near Milan and how two friends of his, who were Roman civil servants (just as Augustine was), recently came upon this monastery. There the monks told them the story of Antony's conversion, and these friends were so moved that they gave up their jobs, broke their engagements to be married (Augustine's own engagement offered yet another "coincidence"), and became Christian monks.

Now as Ponticianus was speaking, says Augustine, "You Lord . . . were turning me around so that I could see myself; you took me from behind my own back . . . and you set me in front of my own face" (8.7.16). Augustine implied that God was seducing him through the power of the story. Here, as he was being turned around, we find a characteristic Augustinian theme—knowledge of God occurs through self-knowledge. That is, "turning around" is a turning toward God that occurs through a turning

38. All quotations from the *Confessions* are from Rex Warner's translation (New York: a Mentor-Omega Book, New American Library, 1963).

inward to search the memories of one's life, discovering the "footprints" of God in the remembered events of one's life. That is why Augustine abruptly ended his autobiography with his conversion in chapters 8 and 9 and then turned to a discussion of memory and time in chapters 10 and 11. He was showing what it means to turn inward and to explore the self through its narrative history, to search for God in the times and memories of his life.

As he was being turned around by the power of the story, Augustine was being torn apart by inner conflict. "Great indeed was the quarrel which I had started with my soul in that bedroom of my heart which we shared together" (8.8.19). Here Augustine combined a metaphorical wrestling with God with the sexual metaphor of a lover's quarrel. The previous decade or more of seduction and counterseduction in which he had been torn between God and the world was now interpreted as a lover's quarrel in the intimacy of the bedroom.

Augustine was in a state of turmoil. All he had to do was will to "turn around" (it was, he said, as if God were standing behind him) and he would be where he wanted to go—namely, in God's presence—but he could not. Why? Because his will, he said, was divided. Part of him wanted to surrender to the seductiveness of the world and part of him wanted to surrender to the seductiveness of God. As a result his will was divided against itself and he was unable to choose. Augustine had come a long way from his Manichaean days when he would have appealed to two different selves created by two different creators to explain the war within him. Now he saw only one self and one creator of the cosmos, and he interpreted evil as the product of a divided will. "It was I who willed it [to surrender to God], and it was I who was unwilling. It was the same 'I' throughout" (8.10.22).

In desperation Augustine then cried out, "Now, now, let it be now!" Still he "hesitated to die to death and to live to life," to tear himself away and to turn. But as he began to turn, he says, "I could see the chaste dignity of Continence; she was calm and serene, . . . and . . . she was enticing me to come to her without hesitation, stretching out to receive and to embrace me." She speaks to him: "Why do you try and stand by yourself, and so not stand at all? Let him support you" (8.11.27). The misery of his whole life passed before him as he got up, flung himself desperately at the foot of a fig tree, and repeated to himself, "How long,

O Lord, how long." Then suddenly he heard the voice of a young boy or girl (he could not tell which) repeating in a kind of singsong: "Take it and read it. Take it and read it." He took these words as a command from God, got up, opened the letters of Paul that he had been reading, and read the first passage his eyes fell upon: "Not in rioting and drunkenness, not in chambering and wantonness, not in strife and envying: but put ye on the Lord Jesus Christ, and make not provision for the flesh in concupiscence." Immediately he felt himself to be "filled with a light of confidence and all the shadows of . . . doubt were swept away" (8.12.28 and 29).

The effect of the stories that turned Augustine around, Hauerwas and Burrell argue, "is to insinuate a shift in grammar tantamount to the shift from explanation to narrative. . . . [This way of understanding his life] is not a new way, for it consciously imitates the biblical manner of displaying God's great deeds in behalf of his people. Without ceasing to be the story of Israel, the tales of the Bible present the story of God. Similarly, without ceasing to be autobiography, Augustine's *Confessions* offer an account of God's way with him. The language of will and struggle is replaced by that of the heart. . . . So the answer to his shaping questions is finally received rather than formulated, and that reception is displayed in the narrative."[39]

Augustine's move beyond the explanatory story of the Manichees to embrace eventually the Platonic story, they insist, is different from his move beyond the Platonic story to the gospel.

> This second step moves beyond philosophical therapy to a judgment of truth. That is why recognizable arguments surround the first step, but not this one. Assent involves more subtle movements than clarification . . . assent of this sort . . . is not an assent *to* evidence but an assent *of* faith. . . .
>
> Accepting a story as normative by allowing it to shape one's own story in effect reinforces the categorial preference for story over explanation as a vehicle of understanding. Augustine adumbrates the way one step leads into the other towards the beginning of Book 6:
>
>> From now on I began to prefer the Catholic teaching. The Church demanded that certain things should be believed even though they could not be proved. . . . I thought that the Church was entirely honest in this and far less pretentious than the Manichees, who laughed at people who took things on faith, made rash promises of scientific knowledge, and then put forward a whole system of preposterous

39. Hauerwas et al., *Truthfulness and Tragedy*, 34.

inventions which they expected their followers to believe on trust because they could not be proved.[40]

Finally, Hauerwas and Burrell insist that it is in books 8, 9, and 10 that the various ways

> for discriminating among stories is developed. It is less a matter of weighing arguments than of displaying how adopting different stories will lead us to become different sorts of persons. The test of each story is the sort of person it shapes. . . . The choices we make display in turn our own grasp of the *humanum*. . . .
>
> The criteria for judging among stories, then, will most probably not pass an impartial inspection. . . . Yet we can certainly formulate a list of working criteria. . . .
>
> Any story which we adopt, or allow to adopt us, will have to display:
>
> (1) power to release us from destructive alternatives;
> (2) ways of seeing through current distortions;
> (3) room to keep us from having to resort to violence;
> (4) a sense for the tragic: how meaning transcends power.[41]

It is not a matter of finding these features "in the story," we are told. Rather, they should be found in the effects that the story has on someone whose life is shaped by it. What is curious about this list is how little Hauerwas and Burrell's account of the *Confessions* prepares us for it. With imagination we might make our own connections to the first two points, but the last two points seem to call for connections that are not even alluded to in their account of the *Confessions*. One suspects that this list preceded rather than followed from the *Confessions*.

While these criteria might well help us to judge master stories and therefore the ethical implications of Christian stories, it is not clear that they can be derived from the *Confessions* as a narrative model for separating true from false stories. One can guess that Hauerwas and Burrell would hold that these criteria can be derived from the gospel stories themselves, but in any case the narrative context of these criteria remains unexplicated here.

40. Ibid., 34.
41. Ibid., 35.

DOUBT: THE ESCHATOLOGICAL NORM
OF NARRATIVE TRUTH

The point I wish to make, however, is that Hauerwas and Burrell have completely overlooked a normative criterion for separating true from false stories at work in the *Confessions*, a criterion that I believe can pass impartial inspection of believer and unbeliever alike. To discover this criterion, we need to return to Augustine's dispute with the Manichees and to reflect on it in the light of his awakening passion for wisdom that occurred on reading Cicero's *Hortensius* at age nineteen. This was, I believe, the decisive turning point in his life. It was the beginning of the turning around (i.e., conversion) that set him on the path that took him from story to story until he finally embraced the Christian story.

In the *Confessions*, Augustine tells us that up until the age of nineteen he was seduced by the pleasures of the world (4.1.1), but then he began to be seduced by the desire for wisdom. About the time he was completing his studies in Carthage, he came across Cicero's *Hortensius*. It was, he says, a book on wisdom. This book set him on fire with a new kind of desire—the desire for wisdom. "I was not encouraged by this work of Cicero's to join this or that sect; instead I was urged on and inflamed with a passionate zeal to love and seek and obtain and embrace and hold fast wisdom itself, whatever it might be" (3.4.8). The awakening of the desire for wisdom represented the appearance of a new kind of seductive power in Augustine's life. That it is a seduction is evident in the way he spoke of this event. He did not say that the *Hortensius* changed his thinking but that it "altered my way of feeling . . . and gave me different ambitions and desires" (3.4.7). For more than a decade, from the time of his reading of the *Hortensius* until his conversion to Christian faith, Augustine experienced his life as a war between two selves grounded in opposing patterns of emotion. One self, present since birth, was driven by *cupiditas* or self-love and was constellated by the seductive power of the world with its offers of fame, power, and pleasure. Then the reading of the *Hortensius* evoked a second self driven by a new emotion, *caritas* or the surrender of selfless love, and was constellated by the seductive but hidden power of the infinite God manifest through the passion for wisdom. The worldly emotions that constellated the first self seduced him away from self-transcendence and left him wandering and disoriented. But not all emotion was disorienting. The reading of the *Hortensius* set him ablaze with the desire for wisdom, sent him panting after truth, and caused him to surrender himself to the questions no matter where they led. This new passion for wisdom carried him beyond himself and, though he was not fully aware of it at the time, seduced him into an openness to the infinite.

Augustine came to see the hand of God at work in all his emotions. As he looked back on his life, it seemed that God had acted on him even through his more selfish emotions, "dragging" him away to Rome, as he put it, "by the force of my own desires" (5.8.15), where he sought fame and fortune. Even the discontent and depression he experienced in his youth, which left him restless and seeking for something more, he interpreted as the work of God, hidden in the events and emotions of his life, "using even sorrow to be an instructor" (2.2.4), and preparing him for the awakening experience of the *Hortensius*.

Augustine's own first act of faith was a surrender to the questions, a surrender to the passion for wisdom. It was an implicit conversion that led to his explicit or self-conscious conversion. This surrender was the key turning point in his life because it set him on the path of self-transcendence, it opened him to the infinite. Like Abraham, Augustine set out on a journey without knowing where he was going but implicitly trusting God to lead the way (Heb. 11:8). Like Jacob (Gen. 32:22-32), who wrestled with the stranger who refused to identify himself, Augustine wrestled with himself and his questions and only later concluded that in doing so he had wrestled with God. After his conversion to Christianity, he came to identify the passion for wisdom revealed in his surrender to the questions with the Logos who is Christ, the Wisdom of God (e.g., 11.9.11). Thus, for Augustine, the awakening of faith was expressed in a surrender to doubt as a surrender to the self-questioning Logos. This Logos is the Wisdom of the trinitarian God who sought him out and initiated his quest even before he knew who or what he was seeking. As I read the *Confessions*, this experience provides the guiding norm as Augustine goes from story to story in search of a true story. That is, a true story is one that welcomes questions and encourages us to follow them wherever they lead. A false story is one that either avoids or forbids the raising of questions.

This normative criterion is missing from Hauerwas' and Burrell's account of Augustine's quest, especially from their account of Augustine's encounter with the Manichees. Almost immediately after his *Hortensius* experience Augustine fell in with the Manichaean movement, for it seemed to offer him the wisdom he was seeking. The Manichaean Psalmbook promised him the "sweet taste" of wisdom: "Wisdom invites you that you may eat with your Spirit."[42] Nevertheless, certain questions began to occur to him concerning apparent contradictions in the Manichaean system. "For about nine years . . . I was a disciple of the Manichees, and for nearly all of this time I had been waiting with a kind of boundless longing for the coming of this man Faustus. For the other Manichees whom I met and who failed to produce any answers to the questions I was raising . . . were always putting forward his name and promising me that as soon as Faustus arrived and I was able to discuss matters with him, all these difficulties of mine . . . would be very easily dealt with and very lucidly explained" (5.6.10).

Faustus did arrive and Augustine found him to be a charming and eloquent man. "However, my thirst could not be relieved by expensive drinking vessels and a well-dressed waiter" (5.6.10). Although charming and well spoken, Faustus was unable to answer his questions. Augustine tells us: "I was upset when I found that, with all his disciples around him, I was not allowed to put a question to him and communicate to him the perplexities which troubled me by talking to him as man to man with each of us speaking in turn. In the end I did get a chance to do this" (5.6.11). Then it became clear that Faustus not only had no answer but was not even willing to pursue the questions. "He behaved with great modesty and would not venture to take up the burden" (5.7.12). "As a result of this I lost the enthusiasm which I had had for the writings of Manes . . . after I found that the famous Faustus had shown up so badly in many of the questions which perplexed me. . . . All the ambition I had had to go far in that sect simply collapsed once I had got to know the man" (5.7.13). Augustine looked back at this event from the perspective of his conversion to the gospel story and saw God at work in the events of his life, speaking to him through his emotions. It was the Logos of God that set him on fire for wisdom, filled him with a passion for the questions, spread discontent and depression over his life when the questioning was denied, and deflated his enthusiasm for the Manichees when Faustus retreated from the questions. Augustine concluded, concerning the loosening of his ties to the Manichees, "it was your doing, my God" (5.7.13).

42. Cited in Peter Brown, *Augustine of Hippo: A Biography* (Berkeley: Univ. of California Press, 1967), 45.

Augustine's surrender to the questions continued to function as the normative criteria of his quest, as he went on to Rome and flirted with the skeptical philosophy of the Academics only to move beyond them as he delved into the philosophy of the Platonists and finally came to embrace the stories of the gospel. The first test of each story remains its openness to questions and questioning. The second requirement is that the story must permit one to follow the questions wherever they lead, even if that takes one beyond the story one is in.

Hauerwas and Burrell's account of Augustine seems very much a post-Reformationist account that opposes faith and reason. Augustine's experience of faith, however, predates the later Scholastic separation and Reformation opposition of faith and reason. For him, these are not appropriate distinctions. Faith begins in a trust of the power of reason as manifest in the seductive lure of the questions, for that seductive power is nothing other than the Logos "herself."[43] The Logos that overtakes the self is not identified so much by a theory of rationality (although it eventually leads Augustine to embrace Neoplatonic theory) as by the existential experience of doubt and questioning, the experience of a transcendence that seductively carried Augustine beyond himself. For Augustine the restlessness and doubt that overtake the self are experiences of grace that manifest the trinitarian nature of the God who acts in time to seek out the self and seduce it into seeking its true origin and destiny.

Thus the opposition of faith and reason is alien to Augustine. Hauerwas and Burrell's account makes it seem as if faith is on a level where reasons are not appropriate. But reasons were appropriate—they were just not sufficient. Augustine tells us that his reading of the Platonists answered all his intellectual objections to the Christian faith and exposed the final and most difficult problem—the bondage of the will (7.20-21; 8.1). Augustine did come to hold that, very often, in order to learn profound truths, one has to humble oneself and believe in order to understand; that believing never meant putting an end to the questions, however, but only helped guide one into new horizons of more fruitful questions. Faith is always, for him, faith seeking understanding. As Peter Brown notes, "he did not believe that philosophy had proved sterile," but that the truth of the Catholic

43. At least twice in the *Confessions* Augustine refers to the Logos or Christ as the Wisdom of God in the feminine (8.8.174 and 11.9.264). Not all translations faithfully record the feminine gender present in the Latin, but Werner's does.

faith resided in its openness to the logos and its questions.[44] At the time he wrote the *Confessions*, Augustine could not imagine a faith opposed to reason or a submission of reason to "revealed wisdom" (in the gnostic sense) or an unquestioning submission to the authority of the church in opposition to reason. Later, that changed. Although Augustine was probably not aware of it, the seeds of his later authoritarianism were already contained in the narrative flaws of the *Confessions* itself (as I shall spell out later in this chapter and in the next). Nevertheless, faith at this time in his life was a surrender to reason—not to any theory of reason but to the radical, unsettling capacity for questions that underlies all theories and that leads us from horizon to horizon, theory to theory, story to story.

Augustine's surrender to the questioning of the logos was not alien to the gospel story he embraced but was the existential embodiment of his understanding that he lived within an unfinished story (in the period of the sixth day of creation, as he put it), in which truth is still an eschatological quest awaiting its final fulfillment. Perhaps that is why he embraced the gospel story as the fulfillment of his quest. It was the only story he found that was able to embody its incompleteness in its own story without surrendering to the nihilistic skepticism of the Academics and the intellectual dead end of the Manichees. The difference between Manichaean and Platonist Christianity was enormous. The Manichees offered esoteric knowledge that excluded "growth and intellectual therapy," whereas Christian Platonism offered the possibility of making "progress," the possibility of self-transcendence.[45] Conversion to the gospel narrative took him out of a story that made his life seem an "aimless wandering" and put him into an unfinished "journey" narrative. It was a narrative that allowed him to understand faith as setting out on a journey without knowing where he was going (Heb. 11:8) and to trust the questions to lead the way. This narrative was the most intellectually and emotionally true to his own experience of his quest for wisdom under the conditions of finitude.

This is the kind of master story that Speer should have had—a narrative that invites doubt and self-questioning, even of itself, a journey narrative affirming that the only way to retain our integrity is to surrender to the questions, which in turn forces us to face our self-deceptions. Hauerwas

44. Peter Brown, *Augustine*, 111–12.
45. Ibid., 112.

and Burrell's account of the role of the master story is problematic in that it places the criterion of truthfulness in the story. According to them, the truth of the gospel story that sets it apart from others is that it forces us to recognize that we are sinners. The story calls us into question. But because the story is the locus of the criterion of truth they seem not to see any way to pull free from the story and call it into question. Now this is a problem Hauerwas and Burrell themselves have highlighted with regard to the stories that held sway over Speer's life. "We can afford to let go of our current story . . . only to the extent that we are convinced that it does not hold the key to our individual identity."[46] This is true because each of us fears alienation—the experience of becoming a stranger to ourself. But if this is true with regard to the stories embodied in "the conventional roles we have assumed," why would not the same problem arise with regard to the master story? Indeed, the history of anti-Judaism intimately tied to Christian storytelling suggests that it does. A master story that does not permit itself to be called into question is ultimately demonic.

Hauerwas does offer a possible response by appealing to MacIntyre's notion of tradition as a "historically extended, socially embodied argument . . . precisely about the goods which constitute that tradition." A narrative tradition capable of producing truthful lives needs to recognize "that it is not final, that it needs to grow and change."[47] This is an important qualification but it is not sufficient. Nearly two thousand years of Christian history have shown that it is possible to engage in such arguments without ever seriously questioning (prior to the Shoah) the fundamental supersessionist presuppositions of the Christian story. There can be no substitute for the master story itself being put in question. Indeed, I would suggest that the way in which one distinguishes a master story from the stories that would identify us with our roles and our culture is that a master story demands that one call into question its own authority.

Hauerwas argues that the Christian self, character, and story are identical. "Our character is not a surface manifestation of some deeper reality called the 'self.' We are our character." My act is my own because "I am able to 'fit' it into my ongoing story" and accept it as an expression of my character. Both he and MacIntyre reject the existentialist notion of a

46. Ibid., 83.
47. MacIntyre, After Virtue, 207, quoted in Hauerwas, Peaceable Kingdom, 46; Hauerwas, Peaceable Kingdom, 45.

"transcendental self" (i.e., the self-transcending self that chooses itself), because they feel that it is too thin a notion of self, that it ignores the self's relational character as defined by its roles and responsibilities. Many feel, says Hauerwas, that there must be a such a deeper self, that "if we are to be genuinely free, a transcendental 'I' is required that ensures that we will never be completely contained by our character. The difficulty with this, however, is that such an 'I' must be impersonal, free from my history, which is exactly what makes us what we are."[48] Such a self appears to exist "in 'midair' above history."

I am sympathetic to Hauerwas's objections but not convinced by them. It is difficult to see how there can be anything like conversion without the self transcending itself. The precondition of all self-transcendence is the experience of becoming alienated from oneself. Hauerwas tends to treat alienation as a ethical disease, but Augustine's autobiography demonstrates that doubt and alienation are important ethical experiences that reveal the utopian capacity of the self to become what it is not, namely, a new self or new creature. Doubt reveals the infinite qualitative distance between the self and its story. Doubt is the *krisis* or separation that prepares one to embrace a new understanding of oneself through a new story.[49]

In rejecting a transcendental self, I think Hauerwas and MacIntyre are rightly reacting to a kind of gnostic alienation that disconnects one from the world and enables an arbitrary choice of self—what Tillich calls the option of autonomy (i.e., becoming a law to oneself).[50] Hauerwas specifically cites Timothy O'Connell's treatment of the transcendental self and the fundamental option. But O'Connell's abstract, disembodied approach is not the only way to account for self-transcendence. There is another alternative, the pilgrim self who is an alien (i.e., not at home in the world), because like Abraham, this self has set out on a journey without knowing where it is going (Heb. 11:8), trusting Transcendence to guide the way. This is the theonomous alternative of the self that is called beyond itself through surrender to the logos, that is, to the questions. When Hauerwas and Burrell describe the "shifting of horizon" that accompanied Augustine's abandonment of the Manichaean story, they come close to acknowledging

48. Hauerwas, *Peaceable Kingdom,* 39, 42, 39.
49. *Krisis* is the New Testament term for judgment; it is related to *krino,* which means "to separate."
50. Paul Tillich, *What Is Religion?* (New York: Harper & Row, 1969), 151ff.

this more historical kind of self-transcendence. In the act of faith as a surrender to the questions, one is both liberated from one's world and its stories and placed in a new relation of obligation to one's world (and its stories), especially to all aliens and strangers. Although one does, in the moment of doubt, experience a kind of "nakedness," to which O'Connell is alluding with his notion of a transcendental self, one is not trapped in an ahistorical self that disowns its character (i.e, its own history), as Hauerwas fears of the transcendental self, but rather one reclaims one's past in the mode of repentance in order to assume one's utopian destiny of becoming other than one's past, namely, a new creature.[51]

Hauerwas does, at least partially, call the master story into question, but he offers no account of what he is doing when he does it. As he suggests, when we cannot say what we are doing we are typically unaware of doing it. For the Augustine who read the *Hortensius*, truth is eschatological, hence truth resides in a surrender to the eschatological direction that the questioning logos opens up in one's life. On the basis of that normative experience of self-transcendence, he can recognize the gospel as a true story because it is a utopian story, that is, a promising yet incomplete and unfinished story.

There remains the question of truthful lives. Is Augustine's life a witness to truthfulness that legitimizes his story in the *Confessions*? To the degree that Augustine did grow more rigid and dogmatic in his role as an aging bishop besieged by "heresies," his life stands as a negative witness to the norm of self-transcendence he witnessed to in the *Confessions*. This failure on Augustine's part does not invalidate the normative stance of the *Confessions*. The *Confessions* do provide a successful norm for telling a true from a false story—so successful that Augustine himself can, at least in some of his actions, be condemned by it. Truthful lives do not always follow from truthful stories. But a truthful story has the utopian capacity to bring about judgment and the possibility of renewal so that we can begin again.

The tragedy of Augustine is that the man of spiritual adventure who tells his story in the *Confessions* later became the dogmatist who, during the Donatist and Pelagian controversies, advocated the use of state authority

---

51. See Timothy O'Connell, *Principles for a Catholic Morality* (New York: Seabury, 1978), 59; Hauerwas et al., *Truthfulness and Tragedy*, 32. See Hauerwas's discussion of the transcendental self in *Peaceable Kingdom*, chap. 3.

to suppress the questions of others.[52] As Augustine grew old, the man of faith became so taken with his own answers that he forgot the normativity of the questioning logos that guided his own narrative quest. His autobiographical narrative contains the seeds of contradiction that undermine its true genius. As we have already noted in our analysis of the theme of wrestling with God (in chap. 2), Augustine interpreted his conversion as a wrestling with God in which his self was defeated and all doubts were swept away. The paradox of this narrative account is that it destroys the very faith that brought about his conversion. This in turn gives rise to a further inconsistency, for, as Peter Brown's masterful biography indicates, Augustine did continue to doubt and to question, especially in the decade following his conversion, and leading up to his *Confessions*. But theologically the answers grew more and more important to him—more important than the questions. To the degree that we make the answers more important than the questions we make the finite more important than the infinite, and we end in idolatry—we make an idol of our answers. For our experiences of doubt and the questions such doubts raise, as Augustine well knew, are genuine and immediate experiences of the infinite, whereas our answers are always finite responses to the infinite. To substitute the answers for the questions is therefore to substitute the finite for the infinite, the sacred for the holy.

The Donatist and Pelagian controversies, in which Augustine (like his mentor, Ambrose) aligned the church with the state in order to suppress those who were different, reveals the final deformation of Augustine's once authentic conversion. Augustine's conversion to the logos was more authentic at age nineteen than at age thirty-three. Augustine was truer to the logos when he surrendered to the questions after reading the *Hortensius* than he was when he surrendered to the woman of Continence in the garden. Augustine's own story first offers us a narrative approaching the depth of the Jewish narrative tradition of chutzpah, a narrative capable of calling itself and its God into question, only in the end to take back what it offers. Augustine's life is finally a negative witness to transcendence and a tragic illustration of the truth that openness to the questions and to the stranger are two sides of the same coin. Our willingness to welcome strangers and

---

52. See Paul Johnson, *A History of Christianity* (New York: Atheneum, 1976), 112–22, for a discussion of Augustine's role in shaping the authoritarian state in Western civilization.

the doubts they bring with their alien stories is a decisive test of authentic faith.

A truthful story, as Hauerwas suggests, is one that, first, forces me to acknowledge my self-deception and recognize that I am a sinner, and second, prepares me to welcome strangers and their stories. The problem of sin is not so much the problem of failure as it is self-deception, which perpetuates the failure and transforms it into an expression of character. That perpetuated pattern over time reveals individuals and communities to be untruthful. By that criterion not only Augustine but virtually all the saints to whom Hauerwas appeals as models of "truthful lives"[53] present us with a serious problem. For it is almost impossible to find a single saint who did not subscribe to the myth of supersession that fed the history of Christian anti-Judaism, creating the massive, continuing, deadly self-deception that has shaped Christianity, not just since Constantine, but since the post-Pauline era of the New Testament. A Christian narrative ethic does stand or fall with its response to the Holocaust, as Hauerwas suggests, and unless it begins by acknowledging the untruthfulness of at least part of the gospel narrative (i.e., that part which teaches contempt for the Jews and the myth of supersession), it has nothing to say to a post-Shoah world. But if there is a parallel between the eschatological form of the gospel and our surrender to the questions, then the gospel itself can be redeemed, for it was only by denying the eschatological meaning of the title *Christos* or *Messiah* that Christians were able to apply the term to Jesus as if it were already an accomplished fact of his identity. Christianity achieved this identification by changing the meaning of the term, by replacing the eschatological emphasis with an emphasis on Christ/Messiah as the Logos incarnate.

If, however, the Logos itself is the reality that continually calls us into question and in so doing keeps us eschatologically open to living within an unfinished or utopian story, then to be a member of the body of Christ means that one has been grafted into the messianic-eschatological hope of those who await the coming of the Messiah and the transformation of all things. By denying the eschatological dimension of both "Messiah" and "Logos," Christians fell into the untruthfulness that allowed them to place

53. Hauerwas et al., *Truthfulness and Tragedy*, 80–98.

a premature closure on history and to substitute the ideology of the universality of Christendom for the particularity of the eschatological community of faith. The good news is not some ideology to be imposed on others but the eschatological event that occurs when we welcome the stranger. We do not bring Christ to the stranger—we meet Christ in the stranger (Matt. 25:35-40). Having been, themselves, reconciled to God while still enemies (Rom. 4:10), Christians are to be ambassadors of the good news (2 Cor. 5:19-21) that reconciliation between God and humanity is revealed when God, through the cross of Jesus, grafted Gentiles into the promises made to Abraham (Eph. 2:11-22). Strangers who are welcomed and affirmed in their differentness are the proof of that reconciliation. When we welcome strangers we welcome the Messiah (Christ), the kingdom of God draws near, and all things are possible—all things are made new.

After Auschwitz, the hermeneutical shift we have confronted in our encounter with Judaism requires that we recover questioning faith as normative in shaping Christian faith for the coming of the postmodern world of the next millennium.[54] When we wrestle with our doubts and questions we are wrestling with both God and the stranger, and when we welcome both, no one is defeated and human dignity is the victor. The Christology

---

54. This understanding of faith as a surrender to the questions, although often repressed, has played an important role in the history of Christianity, especially in the Scholastic movement of the late Middle Ages, when men such as Abelard in his *Yes and No* and Peter Lombard in his *Sentences* began the process of the secularization of thought by placing the apparently contradictory "truths" of Christian Scripture and tradition under topical headings in order to force dialogue and debate. It was a dramatic recovery of the Augustinian tradition of faith seeking understanding, of faith as a surrender to the questions. This early Scholastic methodology bears striking resemblances to the talmudic tradition (not in content but in attitude), and one cannot help but wonder if there was not also some influence from that direction on this volatile and creative period in the history of Christianity. Nevertheless, the fact that today we associate scholasticism with a tradition of rote answers bears witness to how difficult it is to keep such an understanding of faith alive in a tradition dominated by an emphasis on unquestioning belief and obedience. This same questioning faith appeared in the bold exegetical work of nineteenth-century Protestant scholars who used historical-critical methods. This tradition of questioning became fully secularized in the Enlightenment, which likewise began as a surrender to the questions and ended in its own dogmatic methods and answers so as to deny the link between faith and questioning. It remained for Kierkegaard and Nietzsche to call Enlightenment dogmatism into question. Both Nietzsche and Kierkegaard, however, overcompensated in the direction of faith as an irrational act embraced at the expense of reason: for Nietzsche, an irrational faith in one's own power of self-overcoming; for Kierkegaard, an irrational leap into divine transcendence. In our time, however, faith and reason, heart and mind, psyche and logos are finding a new unity in the synthesis of Bernard Lonergan's account (in *Method in Theology*) of the intentionality of questioning that underlies his theological method.

that could emerge out of this hermeneutical shift and the narrative reconstruction it requires would understand faith in Christ as surrender to the
Logos that questions all authority in the name of human dignity and seeks
the visage of the Messiah in the coming of the stranger. Such a Christology
would understand the attribution of the title *messiah* to Jesus as an eschatological act of faith and hope that one day the new age proclaimed by
Jesus will come, and suffering, injustice, and death will no longer threaten
human dignity. The life and death of Jesus would then be understood to
have been for the purpose of grafting Gentiles into the messianic hope of
the Jews. Like the Jews, Christians still await the coming of the Messiah.
Such an understanding might awaken a parallel audacity in Christians. It
might give them the audacity also to ask with impatience: How long, O
Lord?

This faith, that is a surrender to doubt, would result in a reordering of
the last words of Jesus. Christians have generally not been comfortable
with the dying words of Jesus in the earliest Gospels (Mark 15:34; Matt.
27:46)—"My God, My God, why have you forsaken me?" It is typical
of Christian piety (the Good Friday tradition of the "Seven Last Words"
for instance) to transform these words into the proximately last words,
saving for the very last the more comforting words of completion, "It is
finished" (John 19:30), and surrender, "Father, into your hands I commend
my spirit" (Luke 23:46). Ordering the words in this way emphasizes not
the audacity of Jesus to call God into question but Jesus' final surrender
and obedience. However, nothing in the Gospels requires us to read these
last words in this order. After Auschwitz we must invert this order. Christian
piety must begin with "It is finished," suggesting not (as John implies)
"it is accomplished" but "my life is over." This should be followed by
"Into your hands I commend my spirit" and finally by "My God, My
God, why have you forsaken me?" This order would suggest that the spirit
that Jesus surrenders is the same spirit that inspired the audacity (chutzpah)
of Abraham, Jacob, and Job—the audacity to call all authority, whether
human or divine, into question in the name of human dignity. This would
be more in keeping with the prophetic iconoclasm of Jesus as portrayed
in the Synoptic narratives, the spirit Jesus shared with the Pharisees, the
spirit that insisted that the Sabbath was made for human beings and not
vice versa.

In such a post-Shoah Christology, neither Jesus nor the God of Jesus
would be the answer to all questions but the questioning of all answers.

As with Job, this God would be "God with us" in our doubt and our questioning (even if it means a questioning of God) because God always takes the side of human dignity. In place of the idolatry of Jesus and of a god who demands unquestioning obedience, a post-Shoah Christian faith would free individuals from the demonic sacralization of finitude (which occurs whenever answers are given priority over questions) and once more open up the possibility of faith as a surrender to the infinite, a faith that welcomes the stranger so as to welcome the coming of the messiah.

If the Christian story is to prove itself capable of creating truthful lives, it will have to begin anew, after Auschwitz, by being truthful about its role in creating demonic lives in the past. Only on the basis of such honesty can Christian ethics be reconstructed to meet the high standard that Hauerwas proposes.

CHAPTER FOUR

DEMYTHOLOGIZING THE DEMONIC

THE MYTH OF DEMONIC INVINCIBILITY

The Shoah, Arthur Cohen suggests, is the occasion of a new revelation for all humankind. In *The Tremendum,* he deliberately adopts the language of the holy, forged by Rudolf Otto, to speak of this revelation. Otto spoke of the awesome and awful power of the divine as a fascinating and yet terrifying *mysterium tremendum.* The new revelation, however, is not divine but demonic.

It is possible to construct not only a history of holy events (such as the Exodus and Sinai) but also of demonic events, revelations of the dark side of history. These events Cohen describes as "caesuras," which reveal the "abyss of history" opened up by the *tremendum.* "In the time of the human *tremendum,* conventional time and intelligible causality is interrupted. In that time . . . the demonic tears the skein of events apart and man (and perhaps God no less) is compelled to look into the abyss." In Jewish history, Cohen identifies three such events: (1) the destruction of the First Temple, (2) the expulsion of the Jews from Spain, and (3) the Nazi deaths camps. Each threatened to destroy Jewish faith, hope, and a sense of meaning. In the first and second cases the Jews transcended this threat—in the first case by interpreting it as a chastisement for sin, and in the second case by turning to the secrets of mystical knowledge. Finally, with the Nazi death camps the abyss opened once more and "one-third of the Jewish people fell in."[1] This time neither guilt nor mystic hope was able to close the

---

1. Arthur Cohen, *The Tremendum* (New York: Crossroad, 1981), 20, 21.

abyss of the demonic. This caesura remains like an open wound. There can be no question of closing the abyss this time, Cohen argues. At best, one can hope to build a bridge over it, a bridge that will allow life to go on even as the wound remains exposed.

The manifestation of the demonic mimics the divine. Its sheer immensity produces a kind of awe, evoking both fascination and dread. The demonic is an inverted experience of the holy—one which replaces the *mysterium tremendum*, the power of life, with the *demonic tremendum*, the reign of death. The abyss of the demonic that has revealed itself in this century seems to Cohen absolutely inhuman and overwhelming in its immensity. The Shoah is a caesura in which the ground opens beneath our feet and threatens to swallow up all human meaning.

The *tremendum* of the Shoah is a "human *tremendum*, the enormity of an infinitized man" who seeks to conquer death by building a "mountain of corpses," that is, by the "magic of endless murder." This new caesura, says Cohen, reveals the demonic to be an all-too-human capacity. The *tremendum* is the inversion of life, "an orgiastic celebration of death." Unlike the divine *mysterium tremendum*, "it is the immensity of the event [i.e., the demonic *tremendum*] that is mysterious but its nature is not mystery." For it has its roots in "the triumph of technics by which procedures of dehumanization and distanciation were brought to their perfection. The evil is remarked less in its passion than in its coldness."[2]

Richard Rubenstein argues that this calculating, technical rationality made the death camps, as societies of total domination, possible. Genocide became a real possibility only after the pattern of *Kristallnacht* was rejected. Himmler opposed the crude methods of Goebbel's SA-instigated riots of *Kristallnacht*. Such tactics were socially disruptive, created bad publicity abroad, and were highly inefficient. He recognized that if the moral barrier to genocide was to be broken, the process would have to be "taken out of the hands of bullies and hoodlums and delegated to bureaucrats."[3] Bureaucratic structure separates ends from means. It separates the deciders from the actors. One learns to act upon orders from higher up without knowing or questioning the reason and thus not to feel responsible for the results.

2. Ibid., 19, 29, 41.
3. Richard Rubenstein, *The Cunning of History*, new ed. (New York: Harper & Row, 1978), 27.

"*It is an error to imagine that civilization and savage cruelty are antitheses.* . . . Mankind never emerged out of slavery into civilization . . . [but] moved from one type of civilization involving its distinctive modes of both sanctity and inhumanity to another." The only difference is that our modes of inhumanity are more efficient, "more effectively administered." The death camps represent the breaching of a "hitherto unbreachable moral and political barrier in the history of Western civilization . . . and . . . henceforth the systematic, bureaucratically administered extermination of millions of citizens or subject peoples will forever be one of the capacities and temptations of government."[4]

The genocidal program of the Nazis was a "thoroughly modern exercise in total domination" that required the efficient bureaucratic organization of an entire nation-state for the systematic purpose of totally exterminating an unwanted portion of its population. It started with the bureaucratic definition of who a Jew is, then proceeded to a bureaucratic process of systematically stripping those so identified of their citizenship and property rights, and finally subjected them to a systematic bureaucratic process of extermination in the gas chambers. "The destruction process required the cooperation of every sector of German society. The bureaucrats drew up the definitions and decrees; the churches gave evidence of Aryan descent; the postal authorities carried the messages of definition, expropriation, denaturalization, and deportation; business corporations dismissed their Jewish employees and took over 'Aryanized' properties; the railroads carried the victims to their place of execution. . . . The operation required and received the participation of every major social, political, and religious institution of the German Reich."[5]

The atrocities of the Holocaust are so overwhelming that they seem to demand a new mythology of evil. Eliezer Berkovits notes that the medieval rabbis sought to deal with the problem of God and evil in such a fashion as to circumvent the Gnostic-Manichaean view that the world is divided between two gods—one good and the other evil. They considered the alternative suggested by Isa. 45:6-7 that the one true God is the creator of both good and evil. But if the first (Gnostic) alternative absolved the good God of evil by making God only half a god, the second (Isaiah) seemed

4. Ibid., 92, 2.
5. Ibid., 4–5.

equally to diminish God by making the one God directly responsible for evil. In either case evil became an ontological reality beyond human control and human responsibility. Therefore, like their Christian theological counterparts, the rabbis compromised by drawing on Neoplatonic philosophy: Evil is not an active ontological reality or presence but rather an absence, a deprivation of the good. This option has the merit of explaining evil without attributing it directly either to the one God or to two. Evil is interpreted as a creaturely failure, a failure to will or enact the good. For the good brings harmony to creation and its absence produces a disharmony that causes chaos and suffering.

When measured against the atrocities of the Shoah, however, such an account of evil as absence or lack seems weak and inadequate. "Certainly after the holocaust," says Berkovits, "such naive and well-meaning ideas have become more untenable than ever. The evil that created the ghettos and the death camps and ruled them with an iron fist was no mere absence of the good. It was real, potent, absolute." Likewise, Arthur Cohen argues that in the light of the *tremendum*, "both God and man are in need of rethinking and redescription. . . . The sovereignty of evil has become more real and immediate and familiar than God. The question is not how can God abide evil in the world, but how can God be affirmed meaningfully in a world where evil enjoys such dominion."[6]

These are understandable responses to the overpowering atrocity of the Shoah. But the danger is that we may be allowing a new mythology of evil to emerge that is so overwhelming that it will be ethically immobilizing. The demonic can come to seem invincible. We are in danger of characterizing evil as a cosmic or ontological reality over which we have no control and hence for which we have no responsibility. Unless the demonic is demythologized, the power of evil that erupted during the Shoah will intimidate us into surrendering to a sense of hopelessness as we face our future in a nuclear age. The result will be total submission to the inevitability of the dominance of an evil, whose second coming may be nothing less than a global nuclear holocaust.

When one stands back and takes in the sum total of evil during the Shoah, it is overwhelming. When one looks at specific deeds of cold

---

6. Eliezer Berkovits, *Faith After the Holocaust* (New York: KTAV, 1973), 89; Cohen, *Tremendum*, 34.

atrocity, they are overwhelming. But when one examines the personal histories and day-to-day lives of persons who committed such deeds, one is struck with how ordinary most of these persons were. As Elie Wiesel points out, the Shoah demonstrated that "it is possible to be born into the upper or middle class, receive a first-rate education, respect parents and neighbors, visit museums and attend literary gatherings, play a role in public life, and begin one day to massacre men, women and children, without hesitation and without guilt. It is possible to fire your gun at living targets and nonetheless delight in the cadence of a poem, the composition of a painting. . . . One may torture the son before the father's eyes and still consider oneself a man of culture and religion."[7]

To understand how this was possible it is useful to turn to Robert Jay Lifton's study of the Nazi doctors. Lifton's interviews with physicians who served in the death camps offer us an intimate look into the lives and psyches of the professional physicians who played a major role in operating the camps. While these physicians were members of the SS and deeply committed to the Nazi ideology, and did in fact commit demonic acts, they were not quite what one might imagine. Lifton tells of commenting to a survivor of Auschwitz how he was struck by the "ordinariness of most Nazi doctors. . . . Neither brilliant nor stupid, neither inherently evil nor particularly ethically sensitive, they were by no means the demonic figures—sadistic, fanatic, lusting to kill—people have often thought them to be." To which the survivor replied: "But it is *demonic* that they were *not* demonic." The lesson of Auschwitz is that "ordinary people can commit demonic acts."[8]

DEMONIC DOUBLING AMONG THE NAZI DOCTORS

Lifton's brilliant study illuminates the power of *mythos* and *ethos* (i.e., story and its institutional embodiment) to seduce and transform ordinary human beings into beings capable of unspeakable evil. This transformation is perhaps nowhere more forcefully illustrated in Nazi Germany than in the corruption of the healing profession into a profession whose purpose

7. Elie Wiesel, *One Generation After,* trans. by Lily Edelman and Elie Wiesel (New York: Avon, 1965), 10.

8. Robert Jay Lifton, *The Nazi Doctors: Medical Killing and the Psychology of Genocide* (New York: Basic Books, 1986), 4–5.

was to authorize and legitimate systematic, bureaucratic mass murder or genocide. The Nazi myth of the pure Aryan race provided a "biomedical vision" that enabled physicians to consider it their duty to "kill in order to heal." Killing became a "therapeutic imperative." When Fritz Klein, a Nazi physician, was asked how he could reconcile his role in sending Jews to the gas chambers with his Hippocratic oath, he answered: "Of course I am a doctor and I want to preserve life. And out of respect for human life, I would remove a gangrenous appendix from a diseased body. The Jew is the gangrenous appendix in the body of mankind."[9]

The underlying narrative theme of Nazi mythology was cosmological. That is, it interpreted its social definitions as being built into the very structure of nature. "The nation would now be run according to what Johann S. [a Nazi physician] and his cohorts considered biological truth, 'the way human beings really are.' That is why he had a genuine 'eureka' experience—a sense of 'That's exactly it!'—when he heard Rudolf Hess declare National Socialism to be 'nothing but applied biology.' " The Aryan race was *by nature* the superior race. The Nazi vision was a "biocracy" in which the state was "no more than a means to achieve '*a mission of the German people on earth*': that of '*assembling and preserving the most valuable stocks of basic racial elements in this* [Aryan] *people . . .* [and] *raising them to a dominant position.*' " This biological-racist narrative legitimated surgical excision of the Jews by means of the death camps. The Jews were viewed as "agents of 'racial pollution' and 'racial tuber-culosis,' as well as parasites and bacteria causing sickness, deterioration, and death in the host peoples they infested. . . . The cure had to be radical: that is (as one scholar put it), by 'cutting out the "canker of decay." ' "[10]

If, as the tradition of narrative ethics argues, the rationality of our actions is determined by the narrative we understand ourselves to be in, then this story gave rationality and even a sense of moral duty to the Nazi physicians' task of having to "kill in order to heal." Once the narrative drama that these physicians understood themselves to be living within and the heroic roles that they were called upon to play were accepted as an accurate description of reality, then neither a Kantian deontology nor a utilitarian consequentialism could fault their actions. For the Jews were not human

---

9. Ibid., 15, 16.
10. Ibid., 129, 17, 16.

beings (always to be treated as ends and never only as means) but only subhuman agents of disease. In view of that subhuman status, the genocidal elimination of this alien minority was simply doing the greatest good for the greatest number.

The narrative interpretation of reality created by the Nazi movement proved itself capable of transforming demonic acts into moral obligations and of inverting even the sacred oath of physicians to heal. "In terms of actual professional requirements, there was absolutely no need for doctors to be the ones conducting selections: anyone could have sorted out weak and moribund prisoners. But if one views Auschwitz, as Nazi ideologues did, as a public health venture, doctors alone became eligible to select." The Nazi myth put them in charge of both nature and history and thus made them the authors of their own story. In this story, the physician played a key role as the representative embodiment of modern science and technology whose societal role as a healing professional gave ultimate legitimacy to the Nazi genocidal program against the Jews.

> In Auschwitz, Nazi doctors presided over the murder of most of the one million victims of that camp. Doctors performed selections—both on the ramp among arriving transports of prisoners and later in the camps and on the medical blocks. Doctors supervised the killing in the gas chambers and decided when the victims were dead. Doctors conducted a murderous epidemiology, sending to the gas chamber groups of people with contagious diseases. . . . Doctors ordered and supervised, and at times carried out, direct killing of debilitated patients on the medical blocks by means of phenol injections into the bloodstream or the heart. In connection with all of these killings, doctors kept up a pretense of medical legitimacy: for the deaths of Auschwitz prisoners . . . they signed false death certificates listing spurious illnesses. Doctors consulted actively on how best to keep selections running smoothly; on how many people to permit to remain alive to fill the slave labor requirements of the I. G. Farben enterprise at Auschwitz; and on how to burn the enormous numbers of bodies that strained the facilities of the crematoria. . . . The doctor standing at the ramp represented a kind of omega point, a mythical gatekeeper between the worlds of the dead and the living, a final common pathway of the Nazi vision of therapy via mass murder.[11]

How is it that ostensibly quite ordinary men and women, well-educated persons, medical professionals dedicated to healing and giving life, could

---

11. Ibid., 150, 18.

so totally and completely embrace this demonic genocidal process? The answer lies in a process that Lifton calls "doubling." Doubling is "the division of the self into two functioning wholes, so that a part-self acts as an entire self."[12] Doubling is not inherently demonic. It is rooted in our capacity for reflexive self-consciousness or alienation. It is the capacity to divide oneself into the observer and the observed, the capacity to disengage from one's own actions and to stand back and watch oneself as if one were somebody else. In this sense doubling is a fundamental characteristic of human self-consciousness and essential for ethical reflection.

The demonic potential of doubling emerges when the self that is observing (the self as subject) refuses to accept responsibility for the actions of the self that is being observed (the self as object). Demonic doubling originates through a fundamental process of self-deception that can occur when the self is placed in an environment radically discontinuous with its previous environment in its values and practices, such that one's previous self becomes dysfunctional. In the doubling process, the Auschwitz physician developed a second self "both autonomous and [yet] connected to the prior self that gave rise to it."[13] The physician needed the first self in order to continue to think of himself or herself as a good person and a good physician, and the physician needed the second self to perform his or her new responsibilities and duties in the new Auschwitz environment. The physician created a second, separate "killing self" as a means of psychological survival in order to keep the "true self" unstained by the guilt of his or her duties.

Doubling in this demonic sense, which is the focus of Lifton's study, is a response to being placed in an atrocity-producing institutional situation. The environment into which the Nazi doctor was introduced implicitly demanded that doubling occur, "to bring forth a self that could adapt to killing without one's feeling oneself a murderer." Lifton observes that when Nazi physicians came to Auschwitz they went through an initiatory process lasting about two weeks during which they developed their alternate or Auschwitz self. During this period a profound psychological conversion occurred: "In the beginning it was almost impossible. Afterward it became almost routine." The performance of "selections" was a kind of rite of

12. Ibid., 418.
13. Ibid., 419.

passage essential to this conversion. "The selections process had the ritual function of 'carefully staged death immersions culminating in honorable survival and earned rebirth' . . . via the formation of the Auschwitz self. . . . Selections . . . provide a ritual drama . . . [that] tended to absorb anxieties and doubts and fuse individual actions with prevailing (Nazi) concepts, as does ritual performance in general."[14]

The doctors were encouraged to understand themselves as a holy community, set apart from the world in order to save the world through the healing power of their "surgical" acts. This community was, of course, a demonic inversion of a holy community—a sacred society that had no place for the alien and the stranger. Indeed, the "SS was the élite 'community within the community.' . . . Faith in the *Gemeinschaft* became a source of murderous action and a crucial support for the Auschwitz self."[15] The doctors underwent a kind of mystical immersion and rebirth in the Nazi mythos as if "entering a religious order" where one must divest oneself of one's past self and be "reborn into a new European race." "One was asked to double in Auschwitz on behalf of revitalization that was *communal* . . . and *sacred*. . . . Hitler [spoke of] . . . 'the nothingness . . . of the individual human being and of his [or her] continued existence in the visible immortality of the nation.' "

Essential to the inducement of this conversion was being confronted with the social reality of Auschwitz as a massive, unchangeable fact. As one physician reported: "One couldn't . . . really be against it. . . . That is, mass killing was the unyielding *fact of life* to which everyone was expected to adapt." The ritual initiation of a doctor into the process of making the selections included a routine of heavy drinking and socializing during which the new doctors would be helped to accept what they were expected to do by those already adapted to the process. When a physician raised the question of how these things could be done, a process of reality therapy would begin, in which the newcomer would be brought to see that the fact that these camp inmates had been sent to Auschwitz meant that they were already dead. It was simply a matter of how and when. As one Nazi physician put it, "What is better for him [the prisoner]—whether he croaks . . . in shit or goes to heaven in [a cloud of] gas?" The massive,

14. Ibid., 425, 195, 432.
15. Ibid., 434, 435.

ever-present, all-encompassing bureaucratic process already had determined their fate unchangeably, and therefore the physician was encouraged not to feel personally responsible. Indeed, under the conditions of war, it was argued, physicians have a duty to "select." Why should the physicians' responsibilities be any less demanding than those at the battle front? One must not shirk one's duty, no matter how unpleasant. In fact, the more unpleasant, the more morally praiseworthy it was to have the "courage" to perform it. Thus the doctors became resigned to the killing structure. As one physician put it: "I'm here. I cannot get out. If prisoners come, that is a natural phenomenon. . . . And I have to do [make] the best of it." After approximately fourteen days of such personal struggling, the new physician no longer raised these questions, and "at that point one became an 'insider.' "[16] If there were any residual difficulties, the new physician would be assigned a mentor, someone he or she respected, to help work through the difficulties and adjust to the situation.

The doctor's professional identity also helped facilitate his or her acceptance of the paradox of having to kill in order to heal. For Lifton argues that becoming a medical student itself creates a form of doubling. "That doubling usually begins with the student's encounter with the corpse he or she must dissect, often enough on the first day of medical school. One feels it necessary to develop a 'medical self,' which enables one not only to be relatively inured to death but to function reasonably efficiently in relation to the many-sided demands of the work." Other professional roles also played into doubling. While anyone might undergo the process of doubling, "professionals of various kinds—physicians, psychologists, physicists, biologists, clergy, generals, statesmen, writers, artists—have a special capacity for doubling. In them a prior, humane self can be joined by a 'professional self' willing to ally itself with a destructive project, with harming or even killing others."[17] The temptation of the professional is to suppose that whatever he or she does as a professional is always healing.

Although the doubling occurs through an attempted repression of self-awareness, the prior self is conscious of this second self and must be held morally accountable for its actions, including the actual formation of the double. Lifton's findings are consistent with those of Hauerwas. It is the

16. Ibid., 196–97.
17. Ibid., 426–27, 464.

incipient consciousness of guilt and the refusal to face it that forces the self to double and fall into self-deception. The second self, therefore, is a product of a lack of courage to face one's life truthfully, an unwillingness to seek self-knowledge.

The double should not be confused with multiple personalities or psychosis. In schizophrenia the self is like a tree in which the self has splintered and shattered near its roots. In the case of multiple personalities the trunk is essentially sound and the split is higher up. In doubling the split "takes place still higher on a tree whose roots, trunk, and larger branches have previously experienced no impairment; of the two branches artificially separated, one grows fetid bark and leaves in a way that enables the other to maintain ordinary growth, and the two intertwine sufficiently to merge again should external conditions favor that merging." This impairment is temporary and "occurs as part of a larger institutional structure which encourages or even demands it."[18]

While both multiple personalities and doubling are responses to extreme environmental conditions, in the multiple personality these conditions occur in childhood as the personality is developing, and the personality splinters into selves that are totally unaware of each other. In doubling the splintering occurs in the adult personality, and the two selves are very much aware of each other. In doubling the one self knows what the other is doing but refuses to take responsibility for it; rather, it attributes responsibility for its actions to forces beyond itself.

"In doubling, one part of the self 'disavows' another part. What is repudiated is not reality itself—the individual Nazi doctor was aware of what he was doing via the Auschwitz self—but the meaning of that reality. The Nazi doctor knew that he selected, but did not interpret selections as murder. One level of disavowal, then, was the Auschwitz self's altering of the meaning of murder; and on another, the repudiation by the original self of *anything* done by the Auschwitz self. From the moment of its formation, the Auschwitz self so violated the Nazi doctor's previous self-concept as to require more or less permanent disavowal." The process of doubling restructured the Nazi doctor's conscience by transferring the functions of conscience to the new Auschwitz self, "which placed it within its own criteria for good (duty, loyalty to group, 'improving' Auschwitz conditions, etc.), thereby freeing the original self from responsibility for actions

18. Ibid., 423.

there."[19] Doubling is a shifting of narrative horizons—a migration into a new world, in which what would be immoral within the first world is perfectly moral and rational within the second. The new self exists within a new cosmos (a new institutionally embodied narrative), and that cosmos has built into it its own ethical norms to which the self must conform as long as it exists in that cosmos. Doubling is the coward's alternative to questioning the legitimacy of the new world one is being asked to inhabit— in this case the world of Auschwitz.

"Doubling is the psychological means by which one invokes the evil potential of the self. The evil is neither inherent in the self nor foreign to it. To live out the doubling and call forth the evil is a moral choice for which one is responsible, whatever the level of consciousness involved. By means of doubling, Nazi doctors made a Faustian choice for evil: in the process of doubling, in fact, lies an overall key to human evil."[20] The demonic double overtakes the personality not when that person wills to do evil. No, the will to evil is a secondary, parasitic act that depends upon a prior lack or absence of a will to truthfulness and self-knowledge. It is out of that absence or lack that the demonic double is born in self-deception. What makes self-deception possible is that the double emerges not through the commission of an act but through omission. The self does not have to do anything. The double emerges through not doing. Thus one can say to oneself: "How can I be responsible? I didn't do anything." In that moment of refusal to heed the inner demand for truthfulness and self-knowledge there is a failure of self-transcendence. In that moment the demonic assumes flesh, and evil becomes a real ontic presence. The demonic double is a substitute for genuine self-transcendence. Instead of surrendering itself to its own doubts and self-questioning, which would open the self to the infinite inner demand for truthfulness, the demonic double confines both itself and its victims to the hell of the closed totalitarian world created by its self-deception.

DEMONIC DOUBLING AND LUTHER'S TWO-KINGDOM ETHIC

The theme of the double, the *Doppelgänger*, is especially prominent in German history (Nietzsche, Hölderlin, Heine, Kleist, Goethe, Mann, etc.),

19. Ibid., 422, 421.
20. Ibid., 423–24.

but as Lifton points out, it is not unique to it, being found in authors of a variety of nationalities (Marlowe, Poe, Stevenson, Wilde, de Maupassant, Dostoyevski, etc.). Although Lifton does not explore the role that Luther's two-kingdom ethic may have played in the development of this doubling, I would argue that the influence of Luther's ethic on German culture contributed directly to the propensity of the Nazi doctors to develop a demonic double.[21]

We recall that Luther's ethic is based on the paradox that every Christian is always, at the same time, both a saint and a sinner. Luther's realism holds that in a world of sinners hangmen, even Christian hangmen, are necessary. Unlike the sectarians (e.g., the Anabaptists), therefore, Luther saw no problem in someone being both a hangman and a Christian at the same time.[22] These two roles reflect the dual modes of God's rule over the world through state and church—the left hand of God's justice and wrath and the right hand of God's grace and mercy, respectively. Luther's ethic demands that one develop a double self through which one's personal life is kept separate from one's public life. Luther's ethic suggests that every Christian must live with the paradox of being in two stories at the same time—the right-handed story of the sacred inner and personal kingdom ruled by God's gracious mercy, and the left-handed story of the secular outer and public kingdom ruled by God's just wrath.

The combination of Luther's insistence that one may be obligated in one's public role to carry out unpleasant duties (e.g., the hangman) and his emphasis on unquestioning obedience, even to an unjust ruler, forces the self to double when it performs its public duty. It is hard to imagine Luther's good Christian hangman performing his duty without doubling in the demonic sense. The very process of doing as a public duty what one would not do in one's personal life encourages a disavowal of personal responsibility for one's public actions and makes some higher authority (e.g., God or the state) responsible. Given the formative role of Luther's ethic in German culture, demonic forms of doubling may have been built

21. Lifton's reference to Luther in relation to the problem of doubling is limited to a perceptive footnote on the dialectical tradition in Germany in which he suggests, quite correctly as we shall see, that doubling may be related to Luther's concept of a God "who works by contraries" *(Nazi Doctors,* 428).

22. See Paul Althaus, *The Ethics of Martin Luther,* trans. Robert C. Schultz (Philadelphia: Fortress, 1972), 74.

into the culture. Thus Christian ethics played a preparatory role in promoting the eruption of the demonic type of doubling in Nazi Germany.

But it is not only the two-kingdom aspect of the Christian story, as Luther interpreted it, that contributed to the legitimation of the demonic double among the Nazi doctors. There is also a fundamental flaw in the narrative that accompanies and authorizes his two-kingdom ethic—the narrative that portrays the life of faith as a paradoxical wrestling with God. The way in which Luther appropriated the biblical story of Jacob wrestling with the stranger to express his understanding of faith departs from and inverts the meaning of the biblical story by authorizing unquestioning obedience to a God who is the archetypal model of the one who kills in order to heal. As we saw in chapter 2, standing in the tradition of Augustine, who wrestled with the God who slays in order to make alive, Luther spoke of God as a "hidden" God with whom he wrestled in an inner struggle. This God reveals himself through paradoxes that come dangerously close to breaking the unity of God into a Manichaean-Gnostic duality. The most dangerous of these paradoxes is that, as Luther put it, "When God brings to life, he does it by killing."[23]

In the light of the Shoah and Lifton's study of the ethic of the Nazi doctors, with their two-kingdom ethic of doubling and absolute obedience so as to be able to kill in order to heal, this strand of Augustinian (Catholic) and Lutheran (Protestant) narrative tradition and its understanding of two-kingdom ethics, which has largely dominated the Christian tradition, must be recognized for what it is: totally demonic, morally bankrupt, and permeated with the stench of death. Few have seen the pagan and demonic possibilities that lurk beneath the surface of the biblical narrative traditions with more clarity than Richard Rubenstein. When this dimension becomes dominant, the holiness of God becomes "more than a moral force. He who makes alive is also He who slays by His very presence. . . . I believe few men knew the truth about God in His holiness as did Martin Luther."[24]

---

23. See Gerhard Ebeling, *Luther: An Introduction to His Thought* (Philadelphia: Fortress, 1970), 236–37. (German edition, 1964.)

24. Richard Rubenstein, *After Auschwitz* (Indianapolis: Bobbs-Merrill, 1966), 125. Rubenstein also points out (p. 54) that Dean Gruber, a minister who saved many Jewish lives during the Holocaust himself believed that "for some reason it was part of God's plan that the Jews died, God demands our death daily." Despite their religious and political opposition, says Rubenstein, it is frightening to see that both Dean Gruber and Adolf Eichmann served their masters with "complete and utterly unquestioning fidelity."

The difference between the God of transcendence and the idol (even if the idol is a biblical one) is captured in these alternate narrative interpretations: the idol demands the total annihilation of our individuality, requiring our total obedience and conformity, whereas the living God invites our disputation and affirms each of us in our dignity as an other. This God demands only that we do the same for those others, those strangers, who are sent into our lives as an invitation to self-transcendence.

DEMYTHOLOGIZING THE DEMONIC

While dissatisfied with the account of evil as an absence, Arthur Cohen himself is aware of the danger of reinventing Manichaeism, in which "Evil" becomes an ontological reality, a demonically divine cause of all human atrocities such that, by its very existence, human beings are absolved of all responsibility for their actions. Sometimes Cohen seems to come dangerously close to this point himself. But what he is striving for is an explanation of evil that takes it more seriously than Neoplatonism and less seriously, metaphysically, than Manichaeism. He refuses to sever the tie between the demonic and the human, the tie without which no human being could be held responsible for his or her actions. It is possible that "evil can be a substantial presence, real, making claim (and hence affirming), exerting power (and hence an order of being). Evil may be accorded ontological station without our risking, as traditionally feared, that the universe would be delivered to its sovereignty and divine goodness denied. . . . All that is contended at this point is that evil is a real force, that its negativity and destructiveness are no less *an aspect of the human structure* than is that structure's potency for good, that the human labor to identify and subdue manifestations of evil remains as decisive as the human energy to augment and create. Evil has ontic reality no less than the good."[25]

Cohen chooses his words carefully: evil is not "ontological" but "ontic." It is not built into the essential structure of reality but emerges at the level of contingent relations. Once this concession is made, however, I think we are back at the very position Cohen sought to go beyond—namely, the understanding of evil as an absence or lack of the good. Robert Lifton's studies of doubling represent a descent into the abyss of the demonic that

25. Cohen, *Tremendum,* 33 (emphasis added).

demythologizes evil and returns the struggle with evil to the realm of moral responsibility. To acknowledge the demonic as a human capacity manifest through the phenomenon of doubling is to recognize evil as an ontic rather than ontological reality, in a way analogous to Neoplatonism. The Neoplatonic understanding of evil as an absence of the good is more adequate than it seemed at first glance. For the essence of this tradition is that evil is real but its reality is only ontic, not ontological. "Nothing but what is good can be evil," says Augustine, "seeing that every being is good, and that no evil can exist except in a being. Nothing, then, can be evil except something which is [in a] good." In other words, evil is (ontically) real but never final, never more definitive of reality than the good, because evil is always parasitic—it always depends upon some prior (larger or more fundamental) order of being that is good. It follows from this, according to Augustine, that "an evil will could not exist in an evil nature but only in a good one."[26] That is exactly what we see in the phenomenon of doubling. The second self, the Auschwitz self, depends on a prior self that does know something of truth, goodness, virtue, etc. But the second self manifests itself precisely as an alternate self that, on the one hand, lacks these characteristics and, on the other hand, accepts its own lack through an act of self-deception. By this act of self-deception, it draws parasitically upon the virtuous aspects of the first self for its own self-image while disavowing the second self as not being who one really is. Lifton helps us to see that the demonic depends upon the good for its existence while subverting and co-opting that good. What makes the Auschwitz self possible is the absence of a personal center (i.e., its decisions are made elsewhere, it need only obey without question), an absence for which it compensates through the art of self-deception, by claiming the virtue of the first self.

Among certain types of Christians a key test of orthodoxy is whether one believes in the personal reality of the devil. Such a test reveals an utter failure to understand the demonic. The demonic is the absence of the human or personal; it is the lack of a personal center that makes the demonic possible. But a lack or absence cannot exist in itself. It is not an ontological reality. Thus the demonic thrives only by feeding parasitically off the human—generating a second self, a double, which is inherently inhuman and which subverts and co-opts the humanity resident in the first self.

<hr>

26. Augustine *Enchiridion* 13.14; idem, *City of God* 12.6.

Nevertheless, that co-option is the ethical responsibility of the first self that chose the path of self-deception over that of truthfulness and self-knowledge and by that choice called this double into being. It is the surrender of control over one's life to this second inhuman self that makes an individual feel possessed by what Albert Speer called "alien forces." The palpable presence of evil requires no metaphysical source—it is the work of human hands. In making this claim, I do not wish to suggest a psychological reductionism any more than I would wish to invoke a mythical-metaphysical realism. Even the mythical story of the devil decribed him as a good angel corrupted—a good being in which evil became actualized.

When the self refuses to open itself to the infinite and to the doubt and self-questioning that the infinite implies, then the self (as subject) disowns its self (as object—the performer of a role) and attributes responsibility for its actions as an agent (i.e., performer of a role) to some higher authority (God or the bureaucracy, etc.). Into the vacuum created by the abdication of responsibility (the absence of a good will) then floods the powers (*stoicheia*) of this world, which are legion. These powers are the collective and impersonal forces embodied in every social order, powers that seek to replace the infinite with their own finite and sacred order. According to Walter Wink, institutions are more than just social arrangements. "Every organization is made up of human beings who make its decisions and are responsible for its success or failure, but these institutions tend to have a suprahuman quality. Although created and staffed by humans, decisions are not made so much by people as for them, out of the logic of institutional life itself."[27] These institutions have a spiritual ethos that "possesses us," integrates us, and moves us toward either good or evil. The demonic lies not just in the power of an institutional order to issue commands and have them obeyed out of fear, but in the ability of faceless bureaucracies to seduce us into embracing demonic acts as if they were morally and spiritually ennobling so that the demonic appears as the greatest good.

The real presence of evil, its palpability, comes from its co-option of human personal and social energy so that individuals attribute their actions not to themselves but to higher authorities. They sacrifice themselves in unquestioning obedience to these authorities, seduced by narratives that

27. Walter Wink, *Naming the Powers* (Philadelphia: Fortress, 1984), 110.

make doing evil seem good. The result is the unleashing of the extraordinary impersonal human energies that make demonic genocidal projects possible. An institutional order capable of producing an Auschwitz self is made by human hands, or perhaps we should say inhuman hands (provided we understand that inhuman is what human beings become when sacred bureaucratic powers replace God and take charge of reality). Nietzsche's madman wondered what games and rituals would have to be invented to be worthy of the death of God. The double, with his or her professional, scientific, technical, and bureaucratic expertise, discovered the appropriate ritual—the archetypal ritual of recreating the world, recreating it, of course, in his or her own image (e.g., the Aryan race), which means eliminating from the world all who are different or alien. Finite beings imagine being infinite to mean having absolute power over life and death. The Holocaust, Cohen argues, is the product of "an infinitized man" who seeks to conquer death by building a "mountain of corpses."[28]

Using this analysis of the Nazi doctors as our guide, we can say that the demonic emerges in society with the critical conjunction of three factors. First, there must be the creation of a mythological narrative that divides humanity into two camps: the children of light and the children of darkness, sacred and profane, good and evil, saved and damned—those who are the same and the those who are different (i.e., aliens or strangers). This myth demands and justifies that the forces of evil and chaos be removed in order to save the cosmos as the dwelling place for the true children of light. This division of humanity into opposing camps must not appear arbitrary. It must be given cosmological status so that these divisions appear not as the work of human invention, judgment, bias, or prejudice, but simply as reality, the way things are. In the case of the Shoah, this mythic narrative has a long history of development going back at least to the Christian myth of supersession. But the statement of this myth in cosmological terms occurs only with the Enlightenment, when being a Jew was redefined— from religious terms to secular, scientific, racial-biological terms.[29]

28. Cohen, *Tremendum*, 19.

29. Notice here that I give priority to myth and the power of ideation (the realm of Marx's superstructure) rather than to the social-institutional infrastructure. The tendency of the social sciences, Marxist and non-Marxist, has been to give priority to political and economic factors and to see mythic narratives and ideas as dependent variables. But the history of anti-Judaism or anti-Semitism is overwhelming evidence that the mythological or ideational can have the force of an independent variable with the power to alter the infrastructure of society. Although

Second, at some critical point an institutional revolution must occur to give massive social embodiment to this myth. In Nazi Germany this revolution began in the National Socialist Party as an unholy community that succeeded in transforming German society through the process of *Gleichschaltung* or "coordination." Without this second step, the Nazi myth of the Aryan race would have remained an impotent fringe phenomenon. Again, the institutional precedents for this can be found in the earlier institutional history of Christendom, religious and political, which stripped Jews of their citizenship and rights. (Hitler especially admired the bureaucratic authoritarianism of the Catholic church.)

The third and final factor necessary for the demonic is largely a response to the first two, namely, the process of doubling as an act of self-deception. Demonic doubling is undoubtedly present from the beginning, but once the myth has been embodied in the total institutional structure of society, doubling becomes a pervasive social phenomenon, not only in the death camps but also in society at large. The massive institutional embodiment of the demonic, legitimated by the mythic narrative, makes its bureaucratic structures appear impenetrable and unchangeable. The institutional order of society comes to be experienced as part of the natural order and thus simply a given that is not a matter for moral reflection any more than trees and mountains are. One is simply faced with "reality," and one must learn to accommodate by being "realistic." "Realism" is the language of the demonic whose purpose is to seduce us into thinking that we have no other choice. Again and again, the Nazi doctors justified what they "had to do" with the thought that nothing could be changed, that once the bureaucracy had selected the Jews for the camps they were already dead. Everything that followed was a mere formality realizing what had been predestined. Hence, the Nazi doctors did not see themselves as doing the selecting at all—that, in a sense, was already complete. Moreover, if they had any remaining doubts about the ugly things they had to do, the myth provided

---

economic and political factors do help to explain the waxing and waning of anti-Semitism, no infrastructural factors are persistent enough throughout this long history to explain the continued and pervasive influence of anti-Judaism and anti-Semitism. On the contrary, the myth alone can bring coherence to this dark history. Nothing is more symbolically expressive of the autonomy of myth than Hitler's insistence on diverting trains that could have carried troops to the front during the last months of the war in order to send as many Jews to the death camps as possible. There was absolutely no political, military, or economic advantage to such a policy. In fact, it was self-destructive. Yet it alone allowed Hitler to live out his own vision of his mythic destiny.

them with a language of moral obligation that required that they kill in order to heal. This was the sacrifice that they were called to make for the good of the whole *Volk*.

CONVERSION—RECLAIMING THE DOUBLE

Paul reflects on the ethical dimension of the capacity for doubling in his Letter to the Romans, where he tries to account for the paradox of his own behavior—the good that he intends, he does not do, and the evil that he does not intend, he does. Paul seems to suggest that it is as if he had two different minds or two different selves. He says that two laws are at work in him so that "with my mind I am a slave to the law of God but with my flesh I am a slave to the law of sin" (7:25). Thus, "Now if I do what I do not want, I agree that the law is good. But in fact it is no longer I that do it, but sin that dwells within me" (7:16-17). Paul is clearly speaking the language of doubling. Whether this is demonic doubling, however, depends on the story through which it is interpreted.

During his Manichaean phase, Augustine would have read this passage as vindication of the ontological duality of good and evil. Paul's true self, which loves the law, would be the result of an inner self or divine spark created by the high god, who is pure spirit and goodness. But this self is trapped in an evil body that generates its own self, which loves evil. This physical self is the product of the demiurge, who is the god of all evil. (Among gnostic Christians this took an anti-Jewish form of expression, for these two gods were identified with the god of the New Testament and the god of the Old Testament [i.e., the Tanakh] respectively.) Thus Augustine, recalling the follies of his youth, could explain to himself that the self that stole the pears was not the same self that was horrified by this act. In his true self he was good, he was not really responsible for what the evil self did. After his conversion to the Christian story, however, this explanation and application of Paul would not work, because in his new story there was only one God, who is wholly good; evil is a defection of the will from the good.

Thus, while for ten years of his life Augustine had experienced two selves at war within him, one loving wisdom and transcendence and the other the egoistic pleasures of the world, at the moment of his conversion we find Augustine confessing responsibility for both these selves. His conversion is a turning around or turning inward to memory. It is an act of reclaiming the double, of recalling the two selves manifest in his past, and accepting responsibility for the actions of both. Thus, says Augustine: "It was I who willed it [to surrender to God], and it was I who was unwilling. It was the same "I" throughout. But neither my will nor my unwillingness was whole and entire. So I fought with myself and was torn apart by myself. It was against my will that this tearing apart took place, but this was not an indication that I had another mind of a different nature; it was simply the punishment which I was suffering in my own mind. It was not I, therefore, who caused it, but *the sin which dwells in me,* and, being a son of Adam, I was suffering for his sin which was more freely committed."[30] Conversion conforms one to the image of the trinitarian God who is without image, a God whose selves are interdependent, three yet one. Conversion is for Augustine the resolution to the problem of doubling. The capacity to confess is for him the true test of authentic conversion, for it reveals the unifying act of self-transcendence whereby the self assumes responsibility for all doubling and hence for all its selves. What turns doubling into a demonic phenomenon is a Gnostic-Manichaean compartmentalization of the selves (i.e., social roles) so that one self need not assume responsibility for what the other self does. The demonic appears when the self splinters into many unrelated selves whose name is rightly "legion" (Mark 5:9).

But conversion resolves the problem only if the narrative through which one is converted upholds rather than annihilates the dignity of the self. The trinitarian God of the Augustinian Christian narrative tradition differs from Jewish narratives of the God of history in at least one important respect. As we have already noted, the God of Augustine and Luther wounds in order to heal and slays in order to make alive, while the God who comes as a stranger to wrestle with Jacob (Gen. 32:22-32ff.) wounds in order to heal but does not slay in order to make alive. This God inspires the audacity

---

30. Augustine *Confessions* 8.10. The "sin which dwells in me" is not the force of some alien power but the weakness of the human will, its inability to will one thing—a weakness Augustine mythologically attributes to the sin of Adam. Augustine goes on to point out that proof that we are dealing with one will that is weak (rather than two separate selves with opposing wills) can be found in our experiences of being divided by indecision not only between good and evil but also between two evils or two goods. If we were to follow the Manichees' logic we would then have to admit that we have either two evil selves or two good selves. Instead of multiplying selves, Augustine argues, it is more logical to account for this phenomenon by assuming a single self with a divided will.

or chutzpah to call all authority, even God, into question. The God of Jacob and Job wins not by defeating the human but by enabling the victory of the human. "Israel," we are told, means "one who wrestles with God and humans and wins." For such figures as Augustine and Martin Luther, the trinitarian God with whom they wrestled was the divine slayer who must defeat the person with whom God wrestles. In the Christian imagination, in contradiction to the biblical story of Jacob wrestling with the stranger, God must be the victor and human beings must be defeated. In this story there is a profound transformation of identity—a conversion. Jacob becomes Israel. In the Christian narrative imagination this conversion can occur only if there is a total death of the self and a total surrender of will in unquestioning obedience. But in the Jewish narrative imagination God seeks not the total annihilation of the self but rather the affirmation of its true dignity.[31] Jacob is wounded, but neither he nor the stranger is defeated. The stranger flees with the dawn and Jacob is blessed and enabled to walk away with only a limp. Judaism (especially through the book of Job) alone seems to have grasped the decisive criterion of transcendence, the in-alienable human dignity of the self created in the image of the God without image. No God worthy of the name would ask for the total sacrifice of that dignity, for it would be the same as asking for the giving up of one's being created in the image of the God. It would be to ask one to trade one's humanity for the demonic.

These two ways of interpreting the Jacob story represent two ways of dealing with guilt. The first exonerates the self of personal guilt through a total surrender to a higher will by means of an unquestioning obedience that absolves one of personal responsibility. One is simply doing what one is commanded to do—one's selfless duty. The second requires the self to take responsibility for its actions through a repentance that (through its doubts and self-questioning) wounds and heals, and in so doing allows both parties to walk away with their dignity. Jacob was wrestling with his guilt for the ways in which he had cheated his brother Esau in his youth. Now, after many years, they would soon be face-to-face. "The text says it clearly: Jacob is afraid. And Rashi, in his elegant manner, hastens to add that Jacob is afraid for two reasons: he is afraid of being killed and

31. For a provocative discussion of these different narrative perspectives see Mordechai Rotenberg, *Dialogue with Deviance: The Hasidic Ethic and the Theory of Social Contraction* (Philadelphia: Institute for the Study of Human Issues, 1983), esp. 81ff.

of having to kill. For he knows that one does not kill with impunity; whoever kills man, kills God in man. Fortunately, he is assaulted by an angel before he is assaulted by Esau. Who is the angel? Is it an angel at all? The text says 'Ish,' a man, but Jacob speaks of God. And though he emerges victorious from the struggle, his victory does not imply his adversary's defeat. Thus Israel's first victory teaches us that man's true victory is not contingent on an enemy's defeat. Man's true victory is always over himself."[32]

The ethical power of a narrative depends directly on how the narrative is interpreted. The Christian interpretation of the Jacob story requires a total death of the self, a total surrender of will in unquestioning obedience to the God who slays. Out of this surrender emerges a totally new self. Through the despair of the "dark night of the soul" or the "sickness unto death," the individual's own will is finally extinguished in a spiritual death experience. If there is a universal narrative theme in the history of religions—from the primal myths of eternal return in tribal and early urban societies on through the great myths of Christianity, Islam (whose very name means "to surrender"), Hinduism, and Buddhism—it is that of life through death, the return to chaos, the total annihilation (or surrender) of the self as the precondition for re-creation and new life. After Auschwitz we must be prepared to recognize that the spiritual death or surrender of the self encourages a dangerous surrender of moral autonomy to some higher authority that all too easily leads to a literal slaying of the other upon the command of this authority. This theme will be explored more fully in my next volume *The Ethical Challenge of Auschwitz and Hiroshima—Apocalypse or Utopia?* (SUNY Press) where I suggest that public policy in our nuclear age is largely guided by the narrative theme that erupted at Auschwitz, "killing in order to heal, slaying to make alive," a demonic theme whose consequences can only be apocalyptic. There is a fundamentally demonic fascination in virtually all religious traditions with the need for a total surrender of the self that is essentially pagan. Only the Jewish narrative tradition of audacity or chutzpah stands as a bulwark against this temptation. After Auschwitz, says Irving Greenberg, "Nothing dare evoke our absolute, unquestioning loyalty, not even our God, for this leads to possibilities of SS loyalties."[33]

---

32. Elie Wiesel, *A Jew Today,* trans. Marion Wiesel (New York: Vantage, 1979), 205.
33. Irving Greenberg, "Cloud of Smoke, Pillar of Fire: Judaism, Christianity, and Modernity after the Holocaust," in *Auschwitz: Beginning of a New Era?* ed. Eva Fleischner (New York: KTAV, 1977), 38.

CHAPTER FIVE
RECONSTRUCTING CHRISTIAN NARRATIVE ETHICS

ETHICAL PARADOX AFTER AUSCHWITZ

Despite the case I have made for the influence of Luther's two-kingdom ethic on the formation of the demonic double among the Nazi doctors, I would argue that the failure of Christian ethics during the Shoah can be thought of as a failure to maintain its two-kingdom ethic. Although Christianity began as a holy community, a separated community embodying an anthropological ethic of being in but not of the world, from the time of Constantine its ethic largely collapsed into a cosmological ethic of sacred cosmic order. Luther's Reformation theology, which significantly shaped the ethos of Germany, attempted to reinstitute a two-kingdom ethic. Opting for a paradoxical relation between the church and the world, he separated the realms of the sacred and the secular, which he believed had been dangerously fused together in the medieval hierarchical order of Christendom. The way in which he separated the two realms of church and state, however, permitted the paradoxical relation between them to collapse once again into a cosmological ethic and prepared the way for the eventual formation of the Deutsch Christian gospel of the Aryan Jesus.

The collapse of Luther's two-kingdom ethic is primarily the result of his privatization of religious experience. As the secularization of public order expanded during the Renaissance and Reformation, the public dimension of religious experience contracted. For Luther, the language of religion is the language of the inner person, and the language of the secular public order (of politics, science, etc.) belongs to the outer person. Because the kingdom of God is restricted to the inner and the kingdom of this world to the outer, the relation between the two ethical orders is rendered complementary rather than dialectical. The essential element of dialectical

153

tension between the two ethical orders is eliminated. As a result the two kingdoms fit together too comfortably. The ethical tension between the cosmological and anthropological orders collapses into a sacral ethic of unquestioning obedience. The result is a pseudo-two-kingdom ethic.

Luther's instincts were right in attempting to recover a two-kingdom ethic, but his own version failed to alter substantially the Constantinian model of church-state relations. After Auschwitz, Luther's paradoxical two-kingdom ethic must undergo a fundamental revision. What is at stake here is more than restructuring Protestant ethics. As I suggested in the introduction, a two-realm or two-kingdom ethic is an essential feature of every anthropological tradition (e.g., Jewish, Christian, Buddhist, Socratic) and essential to the critique of culture. Therefore, understanding what went wrong with two-kingdom ethics in the Christian tradition can point the way to a viable reconstruction that is of value to all holy communities.[1]

Jacques Ellul offers a reconstruction of two-kingdom ethics which directly addresses the weakness of Luther's ethic. Ellul, a sociologist as well as a theologian in the Barthian tradition, has written over forty books on the social and ethical aspects of our technological civilization. As a sociologist, Ellul took on the task of identifying, analyzing, and articulating the "cosmological ethic" of our technological civilization. But as a theologian, Ellul then responded to that ethic by developing his own desacralizing "anthropological ethic." Like Richard Rubenstein and Arthur Cohen, Ellul sees the cold and calculating technobureaucratic structure of modern civilization as demonic and dehumanizing. The technicist ideal of efficiency subverts all other values, for once a society has opted for the most efficient solution in every area of human activity (his definition of a technicist society), human beings must conform to technical requirements, no matter how dehumanizing, for less efficient solutions simply cannot compete. Ellul's sociological work seems to suggest that human existence is determined by and conformed to technical and social forces, but that remains true only within the horizon of a cosmological ethic. Within the horizon of an anthropological ethic of transcendence, individuals may yet find it possible to exercise the freedom to call society into question and initiate a social transformation—one that brings the Is under the judgment

---

1. This argument is more fully developed in my book *The Ethical Challenge of Auschwitz and Hiroshima—Apocalypse or Utopia?* (Albany: SUNY Press, 1993).

of the Ought. This possibility occurs, Ellul insists, not when a cosmological ethic is replaced by an anthropological ethic but, as Eric Voegelin would agree, when one embraces both in a paradoxical relationship.[2]

This paradox is expressed in Ellul's contrast of the sacred and the holy, which parallels Voegelin's distinction between cosmological and anthropological ethics (distinctions that I have adopted as foundational for my own work). Ellul departs from ordinary usage here by treating the terms *sacred* and *holy* as antonyms rather than as synonyms. The sacred performs the sociological function of integration and legitimation. Its positive function is to create a sense of order within which human life can be carried on. But its demonic propensity is to create an absolute or "closed" order (in which Is = Ought) that prevents the continuing transformation of self and society. Without such a self-transcending openness to the future, life ceases to be either human or free.

Thus for human life to be creative, Ellul argues, the claims of the social order to be sacred and unalterable must be relativized by that which is its opposite—the holy. The holy is that which is Wholly Other than society. Where the sacred demands integration and closure, the holy (as the Hebrew word *qadosh* indicates) demands separation and openness to transformation. A consciousness of the holy creates a feeling of tension and separateness between self and society. That tension prevents the social order from becoming absolute because it prevents the total integration of the self into society. This, in turn, forces the institutional structures of society to remain fluid and open to further development.

The paradox of freedom is that it is always an act of revolt against a limit. But the real limit, for Ellul, is a "combination of what is actually impassable and the inviolably sacred."[3] Our sense of sacral awe makes us accept the limits of a given social order as absolute and also makes us seek to conform to these limits. Only our consciousness of the holy can enable us to desacralize and rehabilitate the sacred so as to open a social order

2. Eric Voegelin, *The New Science of Politics* (Chicago: Univ. of Chicago Press, 1952), 61 ff.

3. Jacques Ellul. *The Ethics of Freedom,* trans. and ed. Geoffrey W. Bromiley (Grand Rapids: Eerdmans, 1976), 345. Usually freedom requires transcending a limit, but in some cases, Ellul contends, freedom requires the establishment of limits where there are none, for both the limit and revolt against it must be present for freedom to be actuated. As an illustration, Ellul uses the yachtsman who learns to tack against the wind and compensate for the tides. The only thing he dreads is the calm, the absence of limits or resistance, for then he can do nothing (ibid., 233).

to further development in the name of the infinite. The possibility of ethical freedom depends on the possibility of having a hope in something radically other than our technological civilization and its promises of fulfillment. For the hopes promoted by the mass media of our civilization serve only to integrate us into the collective social order as a sacred status quo. By contrast, a radically other hope would individuate persons, set them apart from the collectivizing influences of mass media, and give them the critical autonomy that belongs to an anthropological ethic.

Ellul's designation for this unique hope is "apocalyptic hope." When he speaks of apocalypse, however, he is not speaking of it in the literal and popular sense. On the contrary, "hope . . . can be situated only in an apocalyptic line of thought, not that there is hope because one has an apocalyptic concept of history, but rather, that there is apocalypse because one lives in hope."[4] Hope is apocalyptic not because it expresses a literal expectation of the end of the world but because the hope expressed in the book of Revelation breaks radically with the present order of things in order to inaugurate a new creation. An apocalyptic hope is a hope in the one who is both Wholly Other and the end (*telos*) of all things. Every person who is moved to embrace such a hope participates in the transcending freedom of God and inserts that freedom into society as a limit on its claims to absoluteness. Such a hope ruptures one's psychological dependence on "this (technological) world" and permits one to break free and engage in acts that violate the sacral status of efficient technique, the ideological or mythological hopes of consumerism, and the political illusions that dominate our technical civilization.

When Ellul speaks about this kind of hope, he takes Judaism to be the model and argues that Christians must also learn to live a diaspora style of existence as a holy community. "Israel is a people centered entirely on hope, living by that alone. . . . As the one hoping people of the world, it is Israel which provides us with the model for this age . . . an example of the incognito [i.e., its hidden presence as a holy community within the larger society]. In this age . . . I think that Christians . . . should take that as a model." Indeed, "if history is looked at closely, and without the usual Christian prejudice, it turns out to have been forged at least as much by

---

4. Jacques Ellul, *Hope in Time of Abandonment*, trans. C. Edward Hopkin (New York: Seabury, 1973), 208.

the Jewish incognito as by Christian activism." "There is only one political endeavor on which world history now depends; that is the union of the Church and Israel. . . . These two communities . . . must join forces so that, in effect, this Word of God might finally be written. . . . It would be written in counterpoint to the technological history of these times." Ellul is speaking not of an institutional merger but of a conversion of the church to share the same hope so as to support Israel "in its long march through the same night and toward the same Kingdom."[5] The Christian community is the wild olive branch that has been grafted onto the cultivated olive tree of Judaism precisely to share in this hope.

Ellul's importance for post-Shoah Christian theology and ethics is linked to the fact that he is one of those rare Christian theologians who takes the Jewish experience of faith seriously in its own right. The essence of apocalyptic hope is embodied, for Ellul, in the Jewish tradition of chutzpah or wrestling with God. In an age of God's silence and abandonment, hope assaults God and wrestles with God. Prayer, which Ellul calls "the ultimate act of hope," is the "demand that God not keep silence. . . . [It is] a striving with God, of whom one makes demands, whom one importunes, whom one attacks constantly, whose silence and absence one would penetrate at all costs. It is a combat to oblige God to respond, to reveal himself anew." It is motivated by a "commitment on behalf of man [that] is decisively bound to the commitment with God," from which "all further radicalism, of behavior, of style of life and of action" comes.[6]

For Ellul, a Christian ethic emerges out of this shared paradoxical hope against hope. The only force that is a match for the integrating power of the fascination and hope inspired by the sacred is an apocalyptic hope inspired by the holy. Herein lies the ethical power of the dualistic symbolism of anthropological ethics. Only one whose hope is not in this world would even dare to contravene the present sacred order. Every act of inefficiency in the name of human dignity, every act of intelligent compromise in a world of politically absolute positions, is an audacious act that serves to delegitimate the present order and introduce new possibilities of ethical freedom.

5. Ibid., 290–91, 297, 305 (Ellul alludes to Gabriel Vahanian's understanding of Scripture as the "living Word," given with our capacity for speech, which opens up the utopianism of the future rather than the written word, which ties us to the past), 304.

6. Jacques Ellul, *Prayer and Modern Man,* trans. C. Edward Hopkin (New York: Seabury, 1970), 167, 156, 164, 174.

Apocalyptic hope gives birth to an ethic of holiness, that is, of separation from the world. But unlike the sectarian, Ellul is not speaking of physical separation but of psychological and spiritual separation—that is, a change of hopes, from the claims for hope and meaning mediated by mass media to a hope in the Wholly Other. It is "separation . . . only for the sake of mission. The break has to come first, but it implies rediscovery of the world, society, and one's neighbor in a new type of relationship."[7]

Ellul's intellectual roots are in the work of the twentieth-century theologian Karl Barth and the nineteenth-century philosopher Søren Kierkegaard. But his fundamental stance on Christian ethics goes back even further, to the theologies of the Reformation and especially to Martin Luther's two-kingdom ethic. According to H. R. Niebuhr, Christians have historically responded to the problem of the two kingdoms in one of five different ways.[8] At one extreme, Christians have preached a "Christ against culture." This is the sectarian option that sees the world as totally evil and seeks to withdraw from the larger culture into its own separate world. At the other extreme, Christians have preached a "Christ of culture," which sees the world as Christendom—a culture that has so accommodated the ideals of the gospel to those of culture that it no longer sees the need for a clear distinction between them and so settles for a cosmological ethic. Between these extremes Niebuhr places three mediating options. For our purposes two are of immediate interest: the Augustinian-Calvinist model of "Christ transforming culture" and Luther's "paradoxical" model of the relationship between Christ and culture. (The third is the Thomist "Christ above culture" model.) Ellul's two-kingdom ethic is quite complex and does not fit into any of these. Instead, he plays these models off against each other in a complex dialectic. The surface structure of Ellul's ethic sets the sectarian "against culture" and "paradox" models in dialectical tension in order to generate a deep structure that is transformational.

This surface structure juxtaposes the Lutheran rhetoric of paradox and a sectarian apocalyptic rhetoric. Ellul draws on the apocalyptic sectarian traditions of Christianity with their ethical purism, harsh judgments of the world, anarchism and anti-institutionalism. Although he draws inspiration from these traditions, he is not a sectarian—far from it, for he substitutes

---

7. Ellul, *Ethics of Freedom*, 7.
8. See H. R. Niebuhr, *Christ and Culture* (New York: Harper & Row, 1951).

Luther's paradox of having to be in but not of the world for that of sectarian withdrawal from the world.

Beginning with the paradox that every Christian is always, at the same time, both a saint and a sinner, Luther developed a corresponding ethic of paradox. As we have noted, unlike the sectarian, he saw no problem in someone being both a hangman and a Christian at the same time.[9] These two roles reflect the dual modes of God's rule over the world through state and church—the left hand of God's justice and wrath and the right hand of God's grace and mercy, respectively. The secular and public role of the hangman reflects the need for an ethic of realism about the corruption of the world. In spite of that, the possibility remains for this same hangman, in his personal relationships, to transcend this cynical realism and to exercise compassion and forgiveness. In any society, one must be prepared to play both roles, in Luther's view, since even an entire society of saints would remain a society of sinners.

Luther's ethic is basically pessimistic. Its rhetoric is very similar to that of sectarian Christianity, whose pessimism is so great that it gives up all hope in this world and seeks to withdraw from it. Such sectarianism believes that it is really possible for an individual to leave the corrupt world behind, stop being a sinner, and become a saint instead. Luther found that incredible. Realistically, the best one can do, he thought, is accept the paradox that one will always be both a saint and a sinner. In Luther's view, there will always be a need for two distinct ethics, mediating the corresponding paradox of God's justice and mercy. In this context Luther came to understand "vocation" as a calling from God to live in the world paradoxically.

Ellul advocates a similar position in his two-kingdom ethic but with an important difference. Where Luther reconciled these two ethics by making one public and one private, Ellul insists that both be exercised in the public realm. In place of Luther's insistence that the public order is divinely decreed and cannot be changed, Ellul argues that God decrees both order and (eschatological or apocalyptic) openness to change and transformation.[10] Where Luther's paradoxical ethic establishes a complementarity

---

9. See Paul Althaus, *The Ethics of Martin Luther*, trans. Robert C. Schultz (Philadelphia: Fortress, 1972), esp. chap. 4. The example of the hangman is discussed on p. 74.

10. See my book, *The Thought of Jacques Ellul* (New York and Toronto: Edwin Mellen, 1981), especially the discussions of the sacred and the holy on pp. 115–21 and 162–76.

between two separate spheres (private/inner and public/outer), Ellul's para-doxical ethic establishes dialectical tension between two mutually limiting public modes of action (political/technical ordering and apocalyptic/es-chatological freedom), each of which requires the other. Christian ethics is invented out of the irreconcilable dialectical tension between the world and the gospel, between the sacred and the holy (i.e., between cosmological and anthropological ethics). In our world, that tension translates into a dialectical tension between the gospel and a technological ethic of effi-ciency. The point is not to resolve this tension but to maintain it. It is this very tension that prevents an ethic of efficiency from making an absolute claim on one's life and thus from realizing its totalitarian potentiality.

Ellul's ethic emerges out of the dialectical tension created when he fuses the Lutheran ethic of dual roles with the apocalyptic ethic of anti-insti-tutional anarchism. Ellul's placing of the Lutheran ethic of paradox in dialectical tension with the apocalyptic sectarian traditions seems to have eliminated the worst and drawn the best out of each stance. From Luther he has retained the importance of paradox without accepting Luther's in-stitutional fatalism. Ellul counters that fatalism with the anti-institutional anarchism of the apocalyptic tradition. However, he forces that tradition out of its sectarian withdrawal and unleashes its anti-institutional force right in the middle of our technological institutional order. In so doing, the apocalyptic element acts as a catalyst upon the paradoxical element in the surface structure of his ethic, and that potent mixture gives rise to an ethic of transformation at the level of deep structure.

Fundamentally, I think Ellul's position is this: In the short run the only way to make a dent in the dehumanizing forces of our technological civ-ilization and have any impact is to assume a sectarian attitude of rejecting the world. But one must do so without leaving the world—hence the paradoxical element in his ethic. In the long run, however, I think Ellul believes that such an ethic can have transforming impact upon even a technological society by fundamentally altering the relationship between human beings and technique, so as to transform techniques into instruments of human freedom. Hence the dialectic in the surface structure of his ethic generates a transformational ethic in the deep structure. The surface struc-ture determines the short-range effects of ethical action and in the process sets in motion the long-range effects of the deep structure. Ellul's emphasis on contradiction and paradox at the level of surface structure is strategic; it serves the logic of transformation at the level of deep structure.

The dialectical ethic of paradox has important implications in the area of professional ethics. Our professional roles belong largely to the realm of a cosmological ethic that establishes orderliness within society. One cannot really expect to exercise one's vocation to promote freedom and dignity (i.e., anthropological ethics) through one's professional role in isolation from the rest of one's life. Professional roles tend to be absorbed by the technical-bureaucratic system governed by the laws of efficiency. Therefore one must both carry out one's professional role but at the same time seek to be involved, through a voluntary role, in some aspect of social or public life touched by one's profession that will present a liberating counterbalance. For example, Ellul suggests that a professor, who is under professional obligation to deal with students, can express his vocation in a free relation with young people of a different kind and in a different context. Ellul himself has done so over the years by work as a volunteer with adolescent delinquents. He has not sought to make them obedient but audacious. He has not tried to adjust them to society but to transform their "negative non-adjustment into a positive non-adjustment," which will help them to discover their own freedom.[11]

In such a situation the professor sets aside his or her institutional role, sidesteps institutional rules and bureaucracy, and enters into a direct personal relationship that fosters freedom. Such involvement also serves to put one's professional role in perspective. The juxtaposition of roles helps to create the spiritual and psychological tension that prevents one from being totally integrated into (and identified with) one's professional identity as an expression of technical expertise. Such an identity would require one to act only according to the laws of efficiency. The juxtapositioning of roles, however, enables one to identify with the stranger, who is normally on the receiving end of one's actions. Such identification inspires the audacity (chutzpah) to call into question the limits of one's professional role, so that humanizing encounters can occur even within professional or institutional contexts. For Ellul, every human encounter that fosters individuality and autonomy removes one more individual from unquestioning obedience and total integration into the collective structures of social identity fostered by our mass-media, technical civilization. Every such individual represents one more audacious counterforce to the demonic totalitarianism of techno-bureaucratic rationality.

11. Ellul, *Ethics of Freedom*, 509, 508.

FROM ALIENATION TO ETHICAL AUDACITY

Majorities, Orthodoxy, and Order

As a liberation theologian, Juan Luis Segundo assumes an attitude toward the restoration of creation that has strong affinities with those Jewish messianic traditions emphasizing that human action must help make possible the coming of the messianic kingdom. Segundo thinks that Christians must cooperate with God in bringing the liberating and transforming presence of the kingdom into the world. Quoting Reinhold Niebuhr's critical judgment of Lutheran passivity under the Nazis, he argues that "the fatal flaw in the doctrine of two realms was that one realm was that of private and the other of official morality." The doctrine of justification by faith and its relation to Luther's two-kingdom ethic, Segundo argues, is ethically and politically enervating. By weakening the link between faith and works, "justification turns faith into the confident but essentially passive acceptance of God's fixed plan." This doctrine "eliminate[s] from theologico-political language any term that might suggest a causal relationship between historical activity and the construction of the eschatological kingdom."[12] The doctrine of justification undermines the motivation to engage in the active transformation of the world. For Segundo this is unacceptable. Yet he allows that Luther's ethic does address a legitimate paradox of the ethical life, for we are always both saints and sinners because as finite creatures we cannot address all the ethical problems we ought to. Even the best of us are forced to compromise some values in order to spend our energies safeguarding others. Nevertheless, neatly dividing the area of compromise between the public and private life made it too easy to have a good conscience.

The division of ethics into public and private tends to legitimate a psychological compartmentalization that encourages us to lead a double life in which the right hand pretends not to know what the left hand is doing. Ellul's insistence that both ethical realms or kingdoms must be public forces the right and left hand into a situation of explicit tension and conflict. This tension between the two ethical realms is essential to an anthropological ethic. Segundo also seeks to recast Luther's two-kingdom

12. Juan Luis Segundo, *The Liberation of Theology*, trans. John Drury (Maryknoll, N.Y.: Orbis, 1976), 143, 144. Segundo's quote on p. 143 is citing Niebuhr's article, "Germany," in *Worldview* 16 (June 1973): 14–15.

ethic along these lines, translating the psychological tension into a sociopolitical tension, in an attempt to correct its sociopolitical flaws. The paradox of ethical consciousness (i.e., the awareness of being at the same time both a saint and a sinner) has a sociological correlate: every member of a holy community is at the same time both a member of an oppressive majority and of a liberating minority. For Segundo, the transformation of society depends on a dynamic relationship between minorities and majorities in which the church as a minority holy community plays the revolutionary role of a "leaven."

In contemporary society, as Segundo sees it, both personal and societal transcendence are blocked by social structures frozen in place by ideological legitimations masquerading as common sense (i.e., "the way things are," the sense of reality that everybody, it is assumed, knows to be true). The infrastructure of functional social and economic institutional relationships is so arranged that it favors certain social classes at the expense of others. At the same time the fundamental interpretation of reality embodied in the symbolic narratives of the superstructure give a cosmological status to the social structure that legitimates the bias built into society in favor of the ruling elite by making it seem as if the social structure simply expresses the fundamental laws of reality. The goal of a liberation theology is to unmask this ideological bias and to inaugurate a social revolution that would seek to transform society in order to make its social structures more just and equitable. The problem is how to identify and promote transcendence within the structures of social process in a way that will open up a closed society.

In Segundo's view, Christianity ought to introduce transcendence into society. What transformed Christianity from an instrument of social change into an instrument for the ideological justification of the status quo was the fundamental theological decision of the early church to understand its mission as one of saving the whole world through a process of conversion.[13] Salvation became equivalent to transforming those who were different (all who were aliens or strangers to Christianity) into the sameness of Christian identity. Sociologically, the consequence of understanding salvation in this fashion transformed Christianity into a religion of the masses.

Following Max Weber's analysis, Segundo contends that as Christianity went from being a minority religion to a religion of the masses it abandoned

13. Ibid., 212.

its charismatic characteristics (i.e., its power to inspire social transformation) and underwent routinization.[14] To the degree that Christianity became a religion of the masses, it accommodated itself to the ideologies of the status quo. It became the religion of a sacred society—the Holy Roman Empire. The mistake of Christianity was to interpret its mission as one of transforming the world into a universal church. Segundo is convinced that the original message of the gospel was aimed not at the masses so much as "at minorities who were destined to play an essential role in the transformation and liberation of the masses."[15]

Minorities, Doubt, and Transcendence

For Segundo, it is a matter of sociological and historical consciousness to recognize that social transformation requires a break with dominant patterns of societal routine that can only be initiated only by a minority. Only a minority, which is not participating fully in the rewards of the dominant ideology, is in a position to be conscious of the dominant ideology and unmask its role in promoting injustice. "Theologies will be methodologically distinct and opposed depending on the way in which they tend to relate the Christian message to either mass or minority ideas and lines of conduct."[16] If Christianity is to serve as a force for human liberation, it must be prepared to embrace a minority status. This decision is methodologically crucial for theological ethics.

It follows from Segundo's social analysis that a liberating theology can only emerge out of the experience of being a minority, of being an alien or stranger. This is not a viable option for Christianity so long as it thinks of itself as a religion for the masses whose obligation is to transform the world into Christendom. Thus Segundo, like Hauerwas and Ellul, argues that Christianity must let go of its image of itself as the means of eternal salvation for the whole world and assume a diaspora status. Both Ellul and Segundo argue that Karl Barth provides the necessary theological insight to bring about this transformation. For, as Segundo explains: "in Barth's eyes, a universal victory of Christ over Adam implied that even faith ceases

---

14. For Weber's theories see *Max Weber: On Charisma and Institution Building*, selected papers edited by S. N. Eisenstadt (Chicago: Univ. of Chicago Press, 1968).
15. Ibid., 209.
16. Ibid., 228.

to be a precondition for justification and salvation. For him faith is not *a human disposition for winning divine salvation* but rather a *recognition of the fact* that redemption and salvation have been granted to all." In a manner paralleling our reading of Paul's Letter to Romans, Barth severs the relation between conversion/election and salvation. Salvation is universal, while conversion is understood as a response to election—election to a holy community as a saving remnant that provides a fermenting presence for the utopian transformation of society. The message of the gospel is that "God does not divide humanity thus to save the few and hurl the many into perdition. . . . Instead we could say that he uses the numerical few as a leverage point for raising up the many."[17]

Because Segundo retains Luther's emphasis on paradox, his view of the church as separate or holy community avoids being sectarian and elitist, for he argues that "there is no scientific value at all in dividing human beings into masses and minorities without specifying what fields or attitudes or activities we are talking about. All of us . . . are by definition, masses *and* minorities." Like Luther's saint who is also always a sinner, we all find ourselves belonging to both categories at the same time, because it is a condition of finitude that we must conserve energy. "In order to save energy for attitudes we value more highly in existence, we choose not to choose in most of the rest of our lines of conduct."[18]

Like Voegelin and Ellul, Segundo maintains that we need both order and transcendence for human life to be possible. Transcendence occurs in society precisely through the dialectical interaction of masses and minorities, in which the mass routines of society legitimate the necessary order that makes life possible, while minority communities embody the anthropological drive toward transcendence and transformation that keeps life open to the infinite and hence to the future and new creation. "All minority growth simultaneously conditions and is conditioned by the rise in the level of mass conduct. And that signifies a *cultural revolution.*"[19]

From Doubt and Alienation to Ethical Audacity

To speak of "cultural revolution," says Gustavo Gutiérrez, is to speak of the utopian revolution advocated by liberation theology. A revolution fueled

17. Ibid., 213, 228.
18. Ibid., 224–25.
19. Ibid., 226.

by "Christian hope . . . keeps us from . . . any absolutizing of revolution. In this way hope makes us radically free to commit ourselves to social praxis, motivated by a liberating utopia."[20] But Segundo would argue that it takes not only hope but also doubt. Segundo is especially valuable for his understanding of the role that doubt and its questions must play in a social ethic of liberation. For doubt and questioning form the foundation of his theological method. One cannot simply begin with the Bible, because our understanding and interpretation of the Bible tend to reflect the ideological bias of the commonsense world of the majority.

Theology does not begin with the Bible but with the experience of radical doubt and its questions. The foundational starting point that grounds Segundo's hermeneutical circle is not some absolute truth taken from the Bible but radical questions. All creative theology begins in questions that spring out of our present situation and "force us to change our customary conceptions of life, death, knowledge, society, politics and the world in general."[21] Transcendence emerges with our capacity to doubt, and the audacity to question, and to be suspicious.

Segundo describes his hermeneutical circle as a "methodology for ideological analysis" and the basis of human liberation. It is a methodology for calling the present situation into question in order to open it up to new and more humanizing possibilities. He breaks this hermeneutic down into four stages:

> *Firstly* there is our way of experiencing reality, which leads us to ideological suspicion. *Secondly* there is the application of our ideological suspicion to the whole ideological superstructure in general and to theology in particular. *Thirdly* there comes a new way of experiencing theological reality that leads us to exegetical suspicion, that is, to the suspicion that the prevailing interpretation of the Bible has not taken important pieces of data into account. *Fourthly* we have our new hermeneutic, that is, our new way of interpreting the fountainhead of our faith (i.e., Scripture) with the new elements at our disposal.[22]

The moment of transcendence begins in the moment of doubt that occurs within the alienated consciousness of those experiencing minority status,

20. Gustavo Gutiérrez, *A Theology of Liberation*, trans. and ed. Caridad Inda and John Eagleson (Maryknoll, N.Y.: Orbis, 1973), 137, 139.
21. Segundo, *Liberation*, 8.
22. Ibid., 19, 9.

that is, when one experiences oneself as an alien or stranger in the eyes of the majority. This doubt or suspicion separates us from the present horizon of interpreted reality; it creates the psychological distance that enables us to engage in a systematic critique of our society and its understanding of the Bible as filtered through this majority viewpoint. Finally, as the distortions of the prevailing ideology are identified and critiqued, new insight occurs into the meaning of the gospel as a message of hope and a call to repentance.

Segundo is prepared to admit that this new liberating praxis also expresses itself ideologically. As with hope for Ellul and Gutiérrez, for Segundo the role of faith as a surrender to doubt is to introduce an element of transcendence in relation to ideology. Ideologies represent our historical options, but faith as a surrender to doubt represents our capacity for transcendence through which we choose one option over another. Faith expresses "the spirit of freedom for history, . . . for the future, openness for the provisional and relative." If ideology represents "the answers," that is, the accepted wisdom, learning, or knowledge that defines the horizon of one's culture, then faith as a surrender to doubt represents for Segundo a deutero-learning, a learning to learn that calls into question and transcends every given horizon.[23] The biblical record itself represents such deutero-learning, which has expressed itself in the different ideologies of its historical layers without being reduced to any of these ideologies.

The problem is what ideology to choose and by what criteria. The answer lies in the capacity of faith to guide critical rationality and to evaluate appropriately the ideological options. For faith "throws new light on everything, manifests God's design for man's total vocation, and thus directs the mind to solutions which are fully human." Faith as deutero-learning gives rise to a renewal of intelligence and imagination, whose fruit is a "secular inventiveness and creativity." Faith "consists in entrusting the meaning of our life to a process of illumination and knowledge directed by God himself."[24] Such a critical theonomous rationality finds its guiding norm in the chutzpah that defends human dignity, taking the side of the poor and the oppressed, those who are the least in our society and hence its true aliens and strangers.

23. Ibid., 110, 108.
24. Ibid., 167, 110 (quoting Vatican II, *Gaudiem et spes,* no. 11), 118, 179.

For Segundo, as for Augustine, faith can renew intelligence because faith is first of all a surrender to doubt. What we have learned from our interpretation of Augustine's *Confessions*, which places the key to his conversion in a surrender to doubt, amplifies Segundo's account by making it clear that not only social location (i.e., marginality or minority status) but also the inward experience of the Logos itself generates our experience of doubt. This experience is an alienating and hence liberating experience of grace that makes us strangers to ourselves even as it opens us to the infinite and makes us audacious on behalf of the stranger with whom we now identify.

ETHICS AND THE SOCIAL
ECOLOGY OF CONSCIENCE

The power of an authentic master story to subvert demonic doubling and to transform our capacity for doubling into compassion and responsibility for the other depends on its ability to inspire both faith as a surrender to doubt and openness to the stranger. In Stanley Hauerwas's view, an authentic master story would short-circuit the propensity for the self-deception that makes demonic doubling possible. It would "spell out in advance the limits of the various roles we will undertake in our lives." When we lack such a story we lack the skills necessary to question and "challenge the demonic," and thus we fall prey to alien powers. In his view, professional and bureaucratic roles lend themselves to self-deception, because they offer a ready-made self that one can, so to speak, step into and totally identify with. Therefore, ethical responsibility is possible only if one can prevent total identification with one's roles.

It should be clear by now, however, that the master narrative itself can be the crucial problem. If the master story is the measure of good and evil, what is the measure of the master story? My reservation concerning Hauerwas's position is that he does not allow for an adequate distancing of the self from its own master story. He rejects the notion of an existential or transcendent self, standing apart from all stories which is capable of choosing its story, since choosing only makes sense (i.e., avoids being arbitrary) within some narrative or other. I have suggested, however, that there is another possibility besides either the disembodied transcendent self or the self that is totally identified with its master narrative. That is, a story can be a genuine master story only if it puts itself in question by encouraging a surrender to doubt and self-questioning—questioning all authority, both secular and sacred (including divine authority), as in the Judaic tradition of the dialectic of trust and audacity (chutzpah). The merit of such a dialectic is that it never permits a total identification of the self with the master story except in the mode of alienation whereby it is encouraged to question all stories, including its own master story, and yet does not need to abandon this master story precisely because the story itself encourages (unlike Manichaean stories) such questioning of itself. Such a story has the paradoxical character of being both dependent on and independent of narrative.

The story that Speer and the Nazi physicians at Auschwitz lacked was a story that would have demanded that they question all authority, whether sacred or secular, precisely in the name of the human dignity of the alien and the stranger. The application of such a story as normative in one's life would require precisely the kind of reconstruction of Luther's two-kingdom ethic in which we have been engaged. The alternative to a two-kingdom ethic cannot be a one-kingdom ethic, for that is exactly what the Nazis tried to construct—a cosmological ethic expressed in the biocratic myth or story of the pure Aryan race. A two-kingdom ethic is absolutely essential, for the second kingdom, the second ethical realm that counterbalances the cosmological so as to protect human dignity, is precisely the anthropological ethic of individual conscience. In this sense every two-kingdom ethic creates a type of doubling. But in an ethic of the holy, as opposed to an ethic of the sacred, the realm of individual conscience is not to be sealed off from the public realm, as Luther's ethic tends to do. That bureaucratic-Manichaean compartmentalization of selves is what makes doubling a demonic phenomenon. As Jacques Ellul's work suggests, rather than eliminate a sacral ethic to replace it with an ethic of the holy, both the ethic of the sacred (cosmological) and the ethic of the holy (anthropological) must operate in the public realm to create precisely the irreconcilable tension needed to prevent the self from identifying absolutely with any one of its roles or stories.

Far from being storyless, as the Enlightenment myth of the third age suggests, the modern person's actions are still governed by narratives, or at least by fragments of narratives. The moral complexity of our modern lives has to do precisely with the fact that every one of the social roles we embrace in constructing our social identities has a story or complex of stories attached to it, which we consciously or unconsciously absorb. Our spouse and our children implicitly convey stories to us about what it means to be a good marriage partner and parent. Our coworkers and professional colleagues communicate to us stories that imply still further expectations and obligations. Our employer conveys to us a story about what it means to be an efficient and effective member of the organizational team. Our friends obligate us through yet other stories. And so it goes: with every social role that we embrace we add a new narrative or collection of narratives, and therefore another narrative self, to our repertoire. The problem is that the narratives that structure our role in each institutional context seem to demand all of our time, talents, and our very being. The narratives that structure the workplace seem to make being a good worker the ultimate value. The narratives that structure our marriages and family life seem to make another set of obligations absolute and primary; and likewise with our friends, etc. Nobody wants just a piece of us, everybody wants our whole being.

The lesson to be learned from our encounter with Speer and with the Nazi doctors is that an adequate ethical response to the eruption of the demonic will require the fostering of a consciousness of the complex socioecology of the modern self, an awareness that a pluralistic institutional environment makes us plural selves. If the modern self is a self that chooses its own identity, the very ambiguity of its identity creates a hunger for the unambiguous identity that the prestige of professional identity especially offers. There is a dangerous need in this self to find its fulfillment in its bureaucratic and professional roles.

In the anthropological traditions of holy communities, the unique function of religious stories is to ask us to put our whole life into perspective and to weigh and balance the obligations placed upon us by the diverse narrative contexts of our lives. Unlike the sacred society and its integrated institutions, the holy community, as an alternate or separated community, is the only institutional context in which the narratives ask us not to give our ultimate loyalties to it as one more institution but to put all our loyalties into an ultimate perspective, to weigh them against each other, and judge them by the measure of human dignity (i.e., the unseen measure of the God without image in whose image we are created), especially the dignity of the stranger.

The challenge of the ethical life in our time has to do with the complexity of the narrative expectations that are placed upon us in each of the institutional contexts of our lives. The role expectations that we encounter as we enter a particular institutional context represent an implicit morality that defines the good for that institutional context. In this sense every context generates a "persona" or self and a corresponding morality. The ethical dilemmas of modern consciousness have to do with mediating the conflicting demands of the diverse selves we find dwelling within us. This is a uniquely modern ethical problem, for in a premodern sacred society one would be born into a story that would define identity in a more or less permanent set of role expectations for the whole of one's life. By contrast, the modern self identifies itself not with its roles but as the chooser of its roles.[25] The modern self, says Lifton, is a protean self, constantly shifting and changing in its identity, as it experiments with possible and actual identities without feeling irrevocably tied to any of them.[26]

Modern consciousness is rooted in a sociohistorical awareness that cultures are humanly made and not part of the cosmic order of nature; hence human identity, rather than being the product of a rigidly fixed human nature, is also humanly constructed through our choices. The precariousness of human identity in a modern society can easily lead to a nostalgia for more secure times when people knew who they were and which way was up or down. This nostalgia explains the attraction of both totalitarian and fundamentalist movements. Lifton posits that the Nazi movement was an attempt to return artificially to a premodern sense of unity among cosmos, self, and society.[27] But modern historical consciousness, with its awareness of cultures as humanly created, is like a second "fall." It is a loss of innocence that can never be recovered. Any attempt to return to a primal order of nature will have to be artificially enforced and therefore totalitarian, and literally apocalyptic.

The Nazi vision of the Third Reich represents a nostalgic attempt to ward off modernity by denying the importance of individual dignity and its ecological context, institutional pluralism. The essence of that attack

25. Not that all our roles are chosen: we are still born into our families without being consulted, although even here persons make choices as to whether to accept the roles as given.
26. See Lifton's "Protean Man" in *The Psychoanalytic Interpretation of History*, ed. Benjamin B. Wolman (New York: Basic Books, 1971), 33–49.
27. See chap. 21 of *Nazi Doctors* for an extended discussion of this "nostalgia."

was Hitler's systematic bureaucratic program of *Gleichschaltung*, by which the institutions that protected human dignity (by placing limits on the power of the state) were systematically de-legitimated as autonomous institutions and re-integrated as components of the Nazi bureaucratic state. *Gleichschaltung* "means 'coordination' or 'synchronization' and also connotes the mechanical idea of shifting gears." It is a technological metaphor for a bureaucratic totalitarianism in which "all political, social, and cultural institutions were to be totally ideologized and controlled by trusted Nazis. . . . It also expressed the vision of absolute unity, of the totalized community (*Gemeinschaft*), of making all things and people one."[28]

Hitler had been chancellor of Germany for two months when, through the Enabling Act, as a kind of emergency powers act, he persuaded the Reichstag to disband for a period of four years and give him absolute authority to deal with the various internal enemies, those aliens and strangers who were trying to destroy Germany. By the time these emergency powers expired, Hitler totally controlled the government and could ignore the expiration. In the summer of 1933, then, Hitler began his systematic policy of *Gleichschaltung*. Its purpose was to remake the German government bureaucracy into an extension of the Nazi party and policy and to bring all organizations in German society under the control of the party. "The first step in *Gleichschaltung* occurred in March 1933 with the abolition of state governments. Each state was now to be governed by a Reich governor appointed by the party. . . . The next major change came at the beginning of April, with the reform of the civil service. This reform called for all 'non-Aryans,' . . . to be retired. . . . [All of] which had the effect of Nazifying the entire police, judicial and bureaucratic apparatus of the state." In May the labor unions were abolished and in June all political parties were banned. "There was no longer any effective center of opposition to the Nazis. . . . Within the first three months that Hitler was chancellor, all effective means of legal redress were rendered impotent."[29] The result of *Gleichschaltung* was the total destruction of the social and ethical ecology of the modern individuated self and the beginning of a totalitarian bureaucratic process whose purpose was to destroy all aliens and suppress all German individuality in the mythical and mystical collective reality of the Aryan *Volk*.

28. Lifton, *Nazi Doctors*, 33, 34.
29. Peter J. Haas, *Morality After Auschwitz* (Philadelphia: Fortress, 1988), 121–22.

Modern secular societies are institutionally pluralistic.[30] If the institutions of premodern cosmological societies were tied or bound together by the sacred (as the Latin root for "religion," *religare*, "to bind," suggests), secularization is precisely the untying of these bonds. Secular societies tend to differentiate into semiautonomous institutional systems (economic, political, cultural, etc.) with no single center of control. This differentiated institutional complexity without a controlling center forms the pluralistic social and moral ecology of the modern self. The modern self's freedom to choose itself resides in its political, cultural, and religious freedom to construct its own network of institutional roles and relationships and to alter that network as the vicissitudes of one's personal odyssey require. The freedom of the existential self would be little more than a fiction apart from its modern sociohistorical context. The institutional complexity of the modern, decentralized secular city provides the natural moral ecology for the utopian self—the self that is open to its infinite possibilities. Even as we imagine it in nature, so within the utopian horizon of the technological city, social complexity—the Babel of diverse communities and their narrative traditions—provides a potentially hospitable environment for life. The destruction of that complexity threatens human existence. The ethical task of the church and the synagogue as holy communities is to promote the life-enhancing potential of our complex moral ecology. The holy community, with its anthropological ethic, should guide each individual to find that mean between the extremes, whereby the self (as decision maker) assumes responsibility for all its selves (i.e., social roles) and distributes its time, energy, and loyalties among its various institutional roles in a way that sustains the ecological complexity of both one's self-identity and one's society.

The diversity of identities we take on in our various social contexts is a potential moral resource. Our capacity to move consciously and comfortably between diverse roles or identities represents a sociological differentiation of consciousness.[31] Differentiated social consciousness enables

30. One might think that certain communistic countries, which are officially atheistic, might contradict this observation, but I think not. More than one scholar has argued that such societies bear an uncanny resemblance to premodern sacred societies. The confusion is usually due to identifying "religious" and "sacred" with "theistic." But theism only expresses one type of experience of the religious or sacred. On this model, only a democratic society can be "secular" and "modern."

31. This sociological differentiation parallels the intellectual differentiation of consciousness articulated by Bernard Lonergan. Intellectual differentiation allows us to move comfortably among the linguistic realms of (pragmatic) common sense, (relational) theory, and (symbolic) transcendence without confusion. See *Method in Theology*, 81ff.

each of us to relate all our various selves (social roles) to each other and to assume responsibility for all of them. The failure of such a differentiation leads to a Manichaean compartmentalization of selves, such that the right hand pretends not to know what the left hand is doing. The very diversity of social roles, when consciously embraced, is mutually limiting and thus prevents any one of them from making absolute claims on our life. At the same time our ability to assume diverse roles facilitates our ability to identify with the other who will be affected by our actions. In the Jewish and Christian narratives that advocate welcoming the stranger, we are encouraged to welcome strangers by first remembering that we too were once strangers. The role of the master story is to encourage one to embrace a diversity of roles in order to identify with one's neighbor, the stranger, and even one's enemy, and in the process to prevent the demonic total identification with a single community, institution, or role.

In a sense, the secular city demands that we consciously assume multiple personalities. It was Plato who once suggested that the inner self or soul is like an inward city that mirrors the outer city. For justice to reign in the outer city, it must first reign in the inner city. The diverse desires within the soul are like citizens of a city all clamoring for what is due them, and they must be rightly ordered by *dike* (justice). If one fails to rightly order them, these citizens within will remain in disharmony and that inner disharmony will be mirrored in an outer disharmony, manifest in diverse forms of injustice in the outer city.[32] By analogy we can understand the diverse roles or selves we internalize in the plurality of institutions of modern society as constellating an inner city. Both this inner city and the outer city are rightly ordered only when we surrender to the inner demand of the Logos and its questions. When we do not consciously do so, the voices of our inner community, through our dreams, force themselves upon our consciousness and demand a hearing for the alien and the stranger, for the poor and oppressed, within and without. In this situation justice is a constantly renegotiated ecological balance, within and without, whose purpose is to protect the ecology of institutional pluralism necessary to sustain human dignity and interdependence.

32. See Eric Voegelin's discussion of Plato's *Republic* in vol. 3 of *Order and History, Plato and Aristotle* (Baton Rouge: Louisiana State Univ. Press, 1957), 46–134. "The psyche is a society of forces, and society is the differentiated manifold of psychic elements" (p. 125). For a discussion of dreams and the right order of the soul see 126ff.

If conversion is fully to reorient the self to the infinite through surrender to the questions and openness to the stranger (i.e., to the Wholly Other and the holy other), Robert Doran contends that this conversion must transform the deepest levels of our personality. Influenced by C. G. Jung's theory that dreams and other images cast up by the psyche have a teleological function, Doran suggests that such images try to bring to consciousness a compensating function.[33] They compensate for the narrow focus of our ego-centered consciousness, which neglects both the needs of the world beyond our egos and our own inner need for self-transcendence and transformation. The image brought up by the dream functions to make our ego consciousness aware of its neglect and thus to reorient our deficient or dysfunctional modes of consciousness toward self-transcendence. Such images therefore function to promote transcendence of the limitations of our biased consciousness.

The existential drama of our lives has a social and historical context. We shape our lives "in the presence of others, who also are actors in life's drama." The shaping of our identity occurs within the context of a community in the process of historical becoming. "What images we admit into consciousness will be a function of our antecedent willingness or unwillingness to accept the insights that are needed if we are authentically to constitute the human world and ourselves within the parameters set by the historical process."[34] Thus when the social context of the drama of life is governed by the ideological bias of one's family, class, race, nation, etc., the needed images will not be available.

Just as the existential formation of our identity, when dominated by ideology, blocks access to the imagery of the psyche, so the existential reorientation of the self brought about by conversion reaches down into the unconscious to release those images. "One must locate a domain of imaginal production where images are released unhindered by the guardianship of waking consciousness under the dominance of the biases" of

33. See Robert Doran, *Subject and Psyche* (Lanham, Md.: University Press of America, 1980). See esp. chap. 5, "Psyche and Intentionality." Both Jung and Doran talk about the wholeness of the self, but I am inclined to think of the self rather as an unfathomable openness to the infinite. The term *wholeness* seems to suggest closure, but the self can never be enclosed. The human self shares in the transcendence of a God who can never be named or imaged.

34. Doran, *Psychic Conversion and the Theological Foundations: Toward a Reorientation of the Human Sciences* (Chico, Calif.: Scholars Press, 1981), 176–77.

current ideologies. This domain is the dream, which is "the key to psychic conversion."[35] "Psychic conversion" is the name Doran applies to the conscious attempt to question our dreams so as to elicit ethical insight into our lives and bring about the necessary emotional or empathic transformation of our selves that will release us from all inhibitions to ethical action.

The dream is a barometer for measuring the degree of one's self-transcendence. It "displays the current linkage of image and affect. If one's subterranean life has been made the unwilling victim of one's own repression of conscious insight, the dream will display the plight, the crippled condition, the anger, the violence, the perversion, the helplessness of the oppressed." The dream accuses one for one's refusal to heed the call for self-transcendence and seeks to awaken one's compassion for the stranger. The crippled and disfigured images in one's dreams are the inner victims of one's own self-deception (i.e., the violence one is doing to oneself), which permits one to neglect the inner demands for truth, justice, and compassion and which therefore allows one to act toward others in the world without truth, justice, or compassion. Thus the dream suggests the degree to which the subject is resisting or cooperating in the promotion of his or her own self-transcendence. The bizarre and crippled images of one's psyche are meant as a compensating corrective to one's conscious orientation. The dream warns of the distance between one's conscious attitude and the demand for self-transcendence or selfless compassion. Since the drama of one's own life is embedded in the sociohistorical drama of one's time, the dream is also of "historical and political significance. . . . The dreams of an existentially capable adult are a cipher precisely of one's existential participation in the promotion, obstruction, or decline of the human good."[36]

Robert Lifton's study of the Nazi doctors gives a dramatic example. A Nazi physician, Ernst B., who was assigned to the death camps, thought he recognized a Jewish friend from his youth among the camp inmates. But when he later sought to find him he had no success. Then he began to have recurrent dreams about this friend, Simon Cohen. "He was always a very attractive young man. And now [in the dream] he had really

35. Ibid., 178.
36. Ibid., 180, 181.

deteriorated. . . . And he looked at me with a reproachful, beseeching expression . . . sort of [saying], 'It can't be possible that you stand there and I am . . . [like this] . . .' or more like a disappointed expression: 'How can you belong to those people? That can't be you.' " Lifton comments on these experiences: "We can say that the illusion [of seeing his friend in the camp] (as it probably was) and the dream were insistent assertions of Ernst B.'s humanity, and of his discomfort and guilt at being part of the Auschwitz machinery. *In their questioning* of his personal camp reality . . . they expressed his resistance to succumbing, or at least succumbing completely, to the very 'Auschwitz mentality' he was in the process of discovering."[37] It is significant too that this physician who had never fully confronted his moral culpability in the perpetration of Auschwitz continued to have this dream in the decades after the war, right up to the time of the interview in the 1980s.

There is a correlation between the strangers and aliens, the poor and the oppressed of one's psyche, and those of one's society. The latter are the product of the former and both demand the preferential option of one's attention. The poor and the oppressed are the victims of "social and economic systems [which] are nothing other than the intersubjective neglect of the movement of [psychic] life writ large and, as it were, 'projected' into the dialectic of history."[38]

Initiated by religious conversion, psychic conversion sensitizes the self to its own inner demands for self-transcendence and promotes the surrender of the self to its questions (i.e., to the infinite) and as a result to its social analogue—the stranger. Psychic conversion "reaches into and transforms the unconscious itself," opening it to the infinite and to the stranger. For "spontaneous psychic images function in human consciousness in a manner analogous to the role that questions play in intelligence, reflection, and deliberation."[39] This convergence of image and question renews both imagination and intellect and thus unites emotion and intelligence so as to release the ethical impulse in self-transcending actions on behalf of the stranger.

The lesson one should draw from this understanding of conversion is that it is a twofold process whose authenticity is measured by our ability (1) to surrender to doubt and its questions and (2) to welcome the stranger,

37. Robert Lifton, *Nazi Doctors,* 306, 307 (emphasis added).
38. Doran, *Psychic Conversion,* 150.
39. Ibid., 192, 200.

in which each enables and reinforces the other. For it is the presence of the stranger in our midst, perhaps more than anything else, that calls forth into consciousness troubling dreams and troubling questions. The stranger prevents us from being totally enclosed in a world of sameness. By his or her otherness, the stranger keeps our world open to the infinite and invites a utopian self-transcendence that can make all things new. The strangers who are sent into our lives and our dreams come bearing the invitation to self-transcendence.

The inner individuality and autonomy necessary to the ethical life are not the antithesis of community and human interdependence but rather the natural outgrowth of it in which the inner strangers of our psychic life are intimately related to the outer strangers of our social life. We become selves only in communities of interdependent selves. As bodily creatures our individuality is sustained by an ecological interdependence that is nothing less than a cosmic unity in diversity. As linguistic creatures, our most private thoughts are made possible only through a public language passed down to us through our communities over generations and steeped in symbolic narrative dimensions of meaning of which we are barely conscious. The Cartesian isolation of the ego is a naive myth, for our very self-consciousness is dependent on this public language. Our self is far more public than it is private, and our unique individuality and autonomy as ethical creatures only gradually emerge (from childhood into adulthood) through the sustaining nurturance of this sociohistorical ecology.[40]

PERSONAL AND PROFESSIONAL RESPONSIBILITY AFTER AUSCHWITZ

In this context, the concern of Hauerwas to find a master story that prevents a dangerous one-sided identification with any one institutional role, especially our professional identities, and Jacques Ellul's reconstruction of Luther's two-kingdom ethic reinforce each other. Ellul argues that our professional roles tend to be absorbed into the cosmological order of society,

40. Contrary to the usual interpretation of Jung, I would argue that the notion of Jung's collective unconscious finds its intelligibility and plausibility far less in biology than in the fact that our consciousness and unconscious are impossible apart from the mediation of language that is inherently communal. The "archetypal images" are in the linguistic structures that shape consciousness.

which is governed by the laws of technical efficiency. Therefore, one should not expect to promote the concerns of an anthropological ethic for freedom and human dignity directly through one's professional role. Like Luther, Ellul advocates a kind of doubling—that is, the development of an *other* self. But unlike Luther, for Ellul this other self must be engaged in relating to the same people in the same public realm in which one performs one's professional role. But this self must be involved on a purely voluntary basis and use one's talents and skills outside the usual institutional constraints in order to assist others in developing their own autonomy and sense of dignity. Thus, unlike the double of the Nazi physician, this other self is an advocate for the very people that are affected by one's professional role. By entering into direct personal rather than institutionally and professionally mediated relationships, one comes to identify with the alien and the stranger who is the recipient of the effects of one's professional role. The juxtapositioning of roles prevents the self from being totally integrated into its professional identity.

All of this will have a spillover effect on the professional role that the self assumes. That is, the self's professional ambition and identity, which integrate him or her into our technological, mass-media society, would be held in check by the psychic tension of one's nonprofessional, personal sense of identity developed in nonprofessional contexts with other persons. Professional ethics can begin only when we discover the limits of what it means to be a professional, limits that become clear only by stepping outside our professional identities.

For instance, it is far more likely that a corporate pharmaceutical executive will think twice about marketing a drug that has not been adequately tested if she remembers that she too is a consumer with a husband and children who are potential users of this drug. On the other hand, if this executive has gone the path of Albert Speer and totally identified with her professional role, even to the point of sacrificing her family relationships, then she is far more likely not to experience such qualms of conscience. In such a context, it becomes clear that the family can be privatized no more than any other institution in society. The family belongs to the same public realm in which this executive will market her product.

Professional ethics begins with the experience of alienation from our professional role. This alienation occurs when we have "passed over" into the life and the experience of the other. Becoming a stranger to ourself, seeing ourself through the eyes of the other, enables us, as professionals, to come back with new insight into the responsibilities (and limits) of the professional role. Apart from that consciousness, no professional associations and no set of professional ethical rules will be of any use. Once we have experienced our own world through the eyes of the stranger, that experience will infiltrate our professional roles. Physicians, lawyers, corporate managers, etc., need to be involved in the institutional diversity of the urban world and its various voluntary associations. The persons we meet in these diverse, nonprofessional, institutional contexts are the bearers of our conscience. Nazi death-camp physicians lived in an isolated and simplified socioecology in which such diverse contacts were discouraged and made virtually impossible. However, contacts as simple and basic as a visit with their wives and children typically created an uneasy conscience and an accusing dream life, for their families reminded them of their prior self and its values. Although officially forbidden, the formation of friendships between the Nazi doctors and the prisoner physicians who worked under them did occur, with similar results.[41]

Our willingness to respond to the call of conscience placed on us by our relationships with family and friends is perhaps our strongest capacity. But as we go from family to friends to acquaintances to strangers the call to conscience grows progressively weaker. A cosmological social order reinforces this hierarchy of remoteness by keeping everyone in their place. In contrast, the unique moral task of a holy community is to place the self in intimate contact precisely with those at the weak end of this hierarchy—acquaintances and strangers—both by welcoming strangers into its community and by demanding through story and parable that its members go beyond the community to seek out the alien and the stranger. Provided it has not conformed to the world, the church or synagogue is that unique social space (quite unlike our professional associations and even our spontaneous friendships) in which we are forced to relate to people who are not a mirror image of our own tastes and values. The holy community

41. See Lifton, *Nazi Doctors,* 303ff. One physician went to his superior in Berlin and indicated he could not do the selections. To which his superior replied, "I myself could not do it either. I also have children" (pp. 308–9). For another such case see 400. But the family also provided some physicians with a rationale for what they "had to do" (see 395ff.). Generally, the physicians were discouraged from having their families with them in the camps, since answering the inevitable questions of a wife or child only made what they had to do more difficult.

thrives when it is a community of strangers, a community that remains perpetually open to welcoming other strangers. A holy community dies when that milieu of differentness is sacrificed on the altar of sameness, which results in the collapse of the separateness of the holy community and its integration into the collective order of a sacred society.

Professional identity stands caught in conflicting crosswinds at the intersection between the cosmological and the anthropological orders of society. Cosmological values of sacred order serve to provide society with its needed stability, so that life can go on. Anthropological values remind us of the priority of human dignity over sacred order—that society is made for human beings and not human beings for society. On the one hand, professional roles serve to promote the sacred order of society; on the other hand, the notion of "profession" is rooted in the anthropological and utopian tradition of transcendence. In a technological society the tension between the cosmological and the anthropological ethical dimensions, a tension that has always been present, is heightened. For professionals, whose primary community is an alternate community with its own standards of excellence measured directly by the good they do for those they serve, are working increasingly within large corporate or government bureaucracies, whose criterion for measuring the professional is his or her contribution to efficiency and profits and his or her political loyalty (i.e., unquestioning obedience).

According to Alasdair MacIntyre, every society has its cast of *"characters* [which] are the masks worn by moral philosophies." They are the leading characters in a society's story—professional and public identities taken by society as orienting models. Each character "morally legitimates a mode of social existence."[42] In the modern world, three characters legitimate the implicit moral philosophy of our technical society—the manager, the therapist, and the aesthete. All three embody an emotivist ethic that has its roots in Nietzsche's will to power. This emotivist ethic, which assumes that values are arbitrary and preferential, has its social correlate in Max Weber's theory of the technical or bureaucratic society.

In this bureaucratic order we are asked to lead a double life: with a public self that is technicist (e.g., the manager or therapist) and a private

42. Alasdair MacIntyre, *After Virtue* (Notre Dame: Univ. of Notre Dame Press, 1981), 27, 28.

self that is hedonist (the aesthete). "The bifurcation of the contemporary social world into a realm of *the organisational* in which ends are taken to be given and are not available for ethical scrutiny and a realm of *the personal* in which judgment and debate about values are central factors, but in which no rational social resolution of issues is available, finds its internalisation, in its inner representation, in the relation of the individual self to the roles and *characters* of social life." These characters are the modern embodiments of a secular two-kingdom ethic in which the anthropological dimension is reduced to the ineffectiveness of the socially disembodied emotion of the aesthete. Neither the managers nor the therapists see it as part of their professional role to debate the ends to which their expertise is put. They "restrict themselves to the realms in which rational agreement is possible—that is, of course from their point of view the realm of fact, the realm of means, the realm of measurable effectiveness."[43] These characters bring to mind Jacques Ellul's analysis of the technical society. Ellul's analysis suggests that one more character needs to be added—the professional communicator. The manager brings efficient order to the public realm. The therapist helps the individual adapt to the requirements of efficiency. But the capstone of the cosmological order of a technical civilization is "the communicator" (the TV newscaster, the advertiser, and the dramatic entertainer), who dominates the mass media and provides society with its cast of narrative models. The media sustain the mythos of the well-adjusted manager who will be rewarded for conformity to the bureaucratic demands for efficient order with the promise that he or she will be able to live his or her private life on the model of the rich aesthete who indulges every whim and fancy in a life of consumerist hedonism. The conjunction of the scientific and technical expertise of the professional role and the aesthete's promise of hedontistic reward serve to legitimate the technical order as an order of unquestionable efficiency and effectiveness. To the degree that professional roles become patterned on these types they are conformed to the cosmological order of a technological society.

As Robert Lifton notes, however, the professions have deeper roots in an anthropological tradition of transcendence that sought to tie technical skill to a higher advocacy. The original context for the notion of profession

43. Ibid., 33 (emphasis added to "the organisational" and "the personal"), 29.

was religious. If one joined a monastic order, one made a profession of one's faith in answer to one's vocation or call to the religious life of the holy community. During the late Middle Ages the guilds (*universitae*) emerged. They were distinctive communities made up of those who shared the same technical skills. During the Protestant Reformation the religious notion of vocation and profession expanded to include not only a religious calling to the clerical life but also the skilled callings of guild members to serve the good, not only of the city of God but also the human city. As these professions underwent further secularization during the Enlightenment, "the image of the profession shifted from the proclamation of personal dedication to transcendent principles to membership in and mastery of a specialized form of socially applicable knowledge and skill. . . . Overall the change was from advocacy [i.e., of certain values that the community must remain cognizant of in order to be human] based on faith to technique devoid of advocacy."[44]

Thus professions as self-organized bodies of skilled technicians have their historical roots in the guilds (*universitae*) of the late Middle Ages. The first universities emerged out of the guild system as centers of professional training with a focus on medicine, or law, or theology. These guilds were incorporated, self-governing communities, which set standards for meeting the needs of society, especially in the newly incorporated free cities, first of Italy and then of northern Europe. As such, the professional societies resembled holy communities in being communities set apart from society, with their own internal stories and traditions into which one had to be initiated in order to practice one's calling for the good of society.

Medicine, law, and theology as professional disciplines draw upon our knowledge of nature, society, and God (i.e., transcendence) in order to promote the good of the human city. In the modern university that knowledge is mediated by the natural sciences, social sciences, and the humanities and informs the wide variety of professions that have proliferated in the intervening centuries. A society that protects the dignity of the stranger requires that these realms of knowledge and their uses by the professions be structured by a scale of values open to transcendence. While the stability of the social order will be legitimated by the values of the majority, it is

44. Robert Lifton, *The Life of the Self: Toward a New Psychology* (New York: Basic Books, 1979), 168.

the task of minority holy communities to insist that values which protect human dignity be respected in the actual distribution of the goods of society—holding up hospitality to the stranger as the definitive measure of a just society. Without audacity on behalf of strangers, justice becomes biased, social order begins to disintegrate, and the well-being of large sectors of a society will be ignored.

It is the task of the professions to ensure that the values of self-transcendence that protect human dignity are operative at every level in the distribution of a society's resources. This cannot occur when professional concerns are restricted to serving the self-interests of professionals and the elite social classes they may identify with (i.e., those who are "the same"). It can occur only when self-transcendence is operative in every profession—a self-transcendence that expresses itself through a surrender to doubt and an openness to the stranger. There is no justice in medicine without such self-transcendence, as the Nazi racist practice of medicine that used Jews and others as "guinea pigs" demonstrates. Law without self-transcendence sacrifices justice to a law and order that merely protects the special interest groups of the status quo as it did in Nazi Germany. And theology without justice ends in a self-serving exclusiveness well illustrated by the Deutsch Christians. A just society requires an audacity on behalf of human dignity on the part of professionals. This can occur only to the degree that the professional communities of medicine, law, and religion operate as holy communities in dialectical tension with the larger society. Thus the two ethical realms of cosmological order and the anthropological self-transcendence intersect in those professional communities which separate themselves from the larger society in order to transform that society. And the two realms intersect in the lives of professional persons as the dialectical tension between their professional identity and their other roles and identities in society.

The alternative to the "disembodied self" (i.e., the demonic double) of the Nazi doctors that has severed its ties to the socioecological complexity that sustains it, Robert Lifton suggests, is the "embodied self" which consciously maintains its rich and complex ties of interdependence within its socioecology. The embodied self affirms not only its interdependence with its neighbor who is the same but also with the stranger who is different and whose presence keeps it open to self-transcendence and self-transformation. "Our understanding of the embodied self," says Lifton, "includes a continuous symbolic or formative process with constant creation and re-creation of images and forms; an awareness of larger social and historical projects around one; and a capacity to confront the idea of one's own death as related to broader principles of life continuity or larger human con-nectedness."[45] This symbolic process that mediates our links to the larger social and historical projects in which we live, move, and have our being can occur only through an ongoing dialogue between one's own narrative tradition and the narrative traditions of the stranger.

When professionals find their destiny through stories that encourage doubt and also hospitality to the stranger, they become midwives of the utopian destiny of the city. For by living within such stories and having surrendered to the questions, they no longer seek to control this destiny but rather nurture its theonomous dynamic of self-transcendence through which all things can be made new. But when professionals fail to find their destiny in such stories, they end up reducing their professional calling to a self-serving elitist morality, guided by a will to power, which would impose a demonic and dehumanizing totalitarian morality on all others— a truth well illustrated by the Nazi doctors. As we face the future, we have two choices. We can live in an apocalyptic world that has succumbed to the mythic narrative of professional-technological control of our destiny or we can call this professional-technological mythos into question in the name of utopianism, which prefers to leave our world unfinished and open to its infinite possibilities. For when we welcome the stranger, the reign of God draws near and all things become possible.

45. Lifton, *Nazi Doctors*, 500.

EPILOGUE
ON WRESTLING AND RECONCILIATION

In the course of this book I have sought to defend a central thesis of contemporary narrative ethics theory: namely, that the story we understand ourselves to be in defines the meaning of good and evil for us and shapes our ethical behavior. I have tried to show that one can account for a major difference between Jewish and Christian ethics, the difference between audacity (chutzpah) and unquestioning obedience, in terms of alternate interpretations of the story of Jacob wrestling with the stranger as a normative model of faith. The Jewish tradition has retained the biblical emphasis that authorizes an audacious faith relationship with the God of the covenant, a relationship of wrestling and debate. By contrast, the Augustinian-Lutheran traditions of Christianity have reinterpreted the story of Jacob wrestling with the stranger so as to make God, rather than the human partner, the victor. As a consequence, faith is redefined as a total death of the self through a total surrender to God—a surrender that results in unquestioning obedience. We saw, then, how this ethic of unquestioning obedience to the God who *wounds in order to heal and slays in order to make alive* prepared the way for Christian cooperation with the imperative of the Nazi narrative that made it a moral obligation *to kill in order to heal*. We concluded that the way we tell our stories is critical, for the interpretation determines the ethical consequences that follow from the story. On the basis of this analysis I have argued that, after Auschwitz, Christians must abandon their traditional ethic of unquestioning obedience and recover the audacity of a faith that calls into question all authority, whether divine or human.

Christians have found it hard to imagine the divine-human relationship in this way. It seems sacrilegious and sinful to call God into question. That is a misperception, however, for the audacity to call God into question is not rooted in some kind of sinful ego-centered rebellion against God's will but in faithfulness to God's word and in defense of God's creation— reminding God of past deeds and promises. Audacity (chutzpah) is motivated by compassion for God's creation and especially for the stranger. Such compassion is stirred by the experience of the holy as the infinite or Wholly Other. When we allow the experience of the sacred rather than that of the holy to shape our ethical imagination, however, the result is an obedient faith, which can easily lead to the violation of the sanctity of human life, especially that of the stranger, as the evidence of the Shoah indicates. When the dignity of the stranger is violated, the image of God is violated and the very transcendence of God is attacked. Genocide is a disguised attempt at deicide.

To wrestle with God so as to win, as the Genesis story makes clear, is not an attempt to defeat God. For our normative model of the wrestling match between God and Jacob is one in which Jacob wins but the stranger (God) does not lose—that is, Jacob is wounded yet blessed, and both he and the stranger walk away with their integrity. The wrestling match between Jacob and the stranger brings to mind an earlier story from the Mediterranean world with a similar lesson—the Epic of Gilgamesh. Gilgamesh, the young prince of Uruk, lorded his power over others with unbridled arrogance. When the citizens of Uruk complained to the gods, the gods sought to remedy the problem by creating a twin for Gilgamesh named Enkidu. Enkidu is Gilgamesh's double; he is said to be like Gilgamesh "to a hair" (except that he is slightly shorter). Enkidu comes to Uruk as a stranger, sent by the gods as an equal to Gilgamesh, in order to teach him a lesson in humility. When they first meet they wrestle until exhausted without either one clearly conquering the other. As a result the two gain a mutual respect and become inseparable friends. Indeed, one might say they were closer than brothers.

The story of Jacob wrestling with a stranger is part of a larger tale that is similarly about unbridled arrogance in the rivalry between two brothers, Jacob and Esau (Gen. 25:19—33:20). Even in the womb, we are told, these two struggled to see who would be born first. While Esau, the firstborn, impetuously sold his birthright, Jacob was no less guilty for tricking his father, Isaac, into granting him the blessing by pretending to be Esau. Jacob sought to lord it over his brother Esau and was forced to flee for fear of Esau's anger. But the day came when Jacob repented of his actions and wished to be reconciled with his brother. Sending a large gift of livestock before him in preparation for his return home, he hoped his brother would forgive him even as he feared that Esau might seek revenge. On the night before he was to meet his brother he camped alone by the river Jabbok. On that night he was accosted by the stranger and wrestled until dawn. During that night his hip was wounded by the stranger who refused to give his name even as he blessed Jacob and changed his name to Israel, meaning "he who wrestles with God and man and prevails." In that wrestling match, although Jacob won, the stranger did not lose. Both walked away with their dignity intact. On that day Jacob was reconciled with Esau. They embraced each other and wept. Then Jacob insisted that Esau accept the gifts he had sent even as Esau attempted to decline. Jacob, however, filled with gratitude, would not hear of it, and told Esau, " 'I came into your presence as into the presence of God, but you have received me kindly, so accept the gift I have brought for you; since God has been generous to me, I have all I need.' And he urged him, and Esau accepted" (Gen. 33:10-11).

From chapter 2 onward, I have made much of the ethical importance of Jacob not being defeated in the wrestling match with God. It is fitting to conclude by returning to the theological themes of our discussion in the first chapter, for this same story is also pivotal for a theological understanding of the relationship between Jews and Christians. Here, as with its ethical dimensions, how we interpret the story makes all the difference. It determines whether we end up in the post-Pauline myth of supersession or affirm Paul's own understanding of Gentiles as being grafted onto the holy root of Israel. For in Paul's Letter to the Romans, he uses the story of the wrestling match between Jacob and Esau as a metaphor for the relation between Jews and Gentiles (i.e., Christians).

As retold by Paul, this story has been typically interpreted as an authorization for the myth of supersession. It is not hard to see why. After all, Paul seems to be speaking plainly:

For not all Israelites truly belong to Israel, and not all of Abraham's children are his true descendants; but "It is through Issac that descendants shall be

named for you." This means that it is not the children of the flesh who are
the children of God, but the children of the promise are counted as descendants. For this is what the promise said, "About this time I will return and
Sarah shall have a son." Nor is that all; something similar happened to
Rebecca when she had conceived children by one husband, our ancestor
Isaac. Even before they had been born or had done anything good or bad
(so that God's purpose of election might continue, not by works but by his
call) she was told, "The elder shall serve the younger." As it is written, "I
have loved Jacob, but I have hated Esau." What then are we to say? Is there
injustice on God's part? By no means! For he says to Moses, "I will have
mercy on whom I have mercy, and I will have compassion on whom I have
compassion." So it depends not on human will or exertion, but on God who
shows mercy.

(Romans 9:6-16)

God's decision would be unjust only if God were truly arbitrary. But, as
Paul argues, God imprisons both Jew and Gentile in their disobedience
only to have mercy upon all (11:32). The real point is the inclusiveness
of God's mercy rather than what human beings do—or do not do.

By the time Paul's letters were gathered together to be passed around
in the churches some thirty years after his death, the Second Temple had
long since fallen to the Romans and the Christian myth of supersession
was firmly in place. Passages like this seemed self-evidently to fit perfectly
within the frame of the new interpretation. According to the supersessionist
mind-set, it seems perfectly obvious that Paul is saying that the Jews are
not the true Israel. Rather, the younger child, Christianity, is the true Israel.
From this time forward "the elder shall serve the younger."

The problem with the supersessionist view is that it forces an interpretation on Romans that is alien to Paul, who wrote before the fall of the
Second Temple and the emergence of the supersessionist narrative. As we
saw in the first chapter, this supersessionist interpretation contradicts important themes in Romans that emphasize God's reconciling mercy toward
Jew and Gentile alike. The supersessionist interpretation works only by
systematically ignoring the dialectical balance of Paul's argument whereby
he shows that neither Jew (chap. 3) nor Gentile (chap. 11) has any advantage
or cause for boasting; that is, neither has any cause for lording it over the
other. It ignores, as well, Paul's insistence that while "not all Israelites
are true Israelites," the true children of the promise are the descendants
of Isaac, who are, of course, both the children of Jacob and the children

of Esau (9:7-8). Finally, it ignores Paul's description of the tortuous relationship between Jews and Gentiles as a jealous wrestling match modeled on the story of Jacob and Esau. That is, it ignores the fact that Romans, like the Genesis story, ends in the reconciliation of Jacob and Esau.

Paul's account of the rivalry between Jews and Gentiles in Romans deliberately mirrors the story of the rivalry of Jacob and Esau in which Jacob claims to be who he is not (namely, Esau) but finally repents of his arrogance and seeks reconciliation. It is no accident, then, that we find the Gentiles in the role of Jacob, the brother who sought to usurp the inheritance of his elder brother. It is Jacob (gentile Christians) who needs to return to Esau (the Jews) in repentance as if returning to the presence of God. Here, our post-Shoah reading of the dramatic reversal of Job and his comforters (Job 42:7-9) from chapter 1 is reinforced by the story of Jacob and Esau. It is Jacob who needs to repent of his arrogance, his lording it over his brother, his thinking himself better than his brother. It is the tragic irony of Christianity that it turned a story of reconciliation into a story of supersession. Faced with the opportunity to acknowledge, (as Jacob had), their guilt in usurping the identity of the elder brother, Christians refused the possibility of reconciliation and instead rewrote the story so as to make themselves the victor and the Jews the defeated. Having identified the Jews as the defeated and rejected, they felt no moral responsibility for their oppression of the Jews since they were acting in obedience to a higher authority. Here the ethical and theological reinterpretations of the story of Jacob wrestling with God/Esau converge to produce an unquestioning obedience to the god who slays in order to make alive. The consequences of interpreting Jacob to be the victor in the wrestling match with Esau are as grave, erroneous, and demonic as the consequences of interpreting God/the stranger to be the victor in the wrestling match with Jacob.

Romans 9–11 is a Pauline recapitulation of the Genesis story of Jacob and Esau. The theme that Gentiles need to repent of their arrogance toward Jews dominates Romans 11. Paul warns Gentiles that if they think themselves better than the Jews they will be cut off from the covenant into which they have just been grafted (11:22). He explicitly dismisses the idea that the Jews have been rejected (v. 1) for God never revokes his promises (v. 29). He insists that gentile Christians do not replace the Jews but have, through Christ, been grafted onto the holy root of Israel to share in the promises made to Abraham (v. 17). Thus Gentiles should not boast, for "it is not you that support the root, but the root that supports you" (v. 18). Paul wants Gentiles to know this so that they will not "be conceited" and think themselves better than the Jews. He goes on to insist that Jews have been "enemies" of God (that is, have wrestled with God and with the Gentiles) for the sake of the Gentiles. But their own election has never been in question (vv. 28-29). As I argued in chapter 1, Paul sees God as hardening the heart of both Gentiles (the Egyptians—9:15-17) and Jews (11:11) at particular times in history so as to create from each a saving remnant through a jealous rivalry with the other. Because of (and through) this saving remnant (the hidden righteous, we might say) God comes to shower his mercy (as he would have at Sodom and Gomorrah) on all, the just and the unjust alike (9:29). Justification is, as Lloyd Gaston has argued, through *faithfulness*—through the faithfulness of a God who never revokes his promises and through the faithful witness of a saving remnant from among both Jews and Christians.

A primary theme of this book has been that ethics is about how we treat the stranger. When we wrestle with the stranger we wrestle with God. When we welcome the stranger we welcome God and God's messiah. For those of us who are Christians, the strangers whom we must learn to welcome, above all others, are the Jews. In this book I have been engaged in a critique of my own tradition through a process of passing over into the stories of Judaism and the Jewish people from a post-Shoah perspective. Some who read this book will feel that I have been too hard on Christianity and too easy on Judaism. There may be some truth in this accusation. The inherent bias of alienated theology as an inversion of apologetic theology is to critique the realities of one's own tradition from the perspective of the virtues and ideals of the other's tradition. As such, it is an attempt to redress an imbalance in the history of the Christian tradition.

Perhaps, in the sweep of history, Jews have not always welcomed the stranger as they ought to have. To the degree that the biblical and talmudic injunctions to do so were restricted to "resident aliens" in the land of Israel—interpreted as those who were candidates for conversion—then Jews, too, need to radicalize this ethic after Auschwitz. Jacob Neusner has suggested that Judaism has not fared any better at making a place for the "other" than other religions have. It seems to me that Judaism has not felt compelled to turn the entire world into an image of itself the way Christianity has.[1] If Jews have not always created a positive place for the "other" (the stranger) within Judaism, at least they have not held the view that the whole world needs to be Jewish. They have been willing to allow that there are others outside Judaism, others worthy of God's saving love and compassion. Christians have on the whole found it difficult, if not impossible, to make such an affirmation.

My purpose in this book has been to critique Christianity, not Judaism. As Irving Greenberg's critique of Jewish orthodoxy after the Shoah makes clear, however, Judaism is not above criticism, a critique radicalized by the experience of Auschwitz. Moreover, it may be that in our time and place the Palestinians are the strangers who represent the greatest ethical challenge for Jews. But if that is the case, it is tragically complicated by the fact that while the Palestinians may be the significant minority in the state of Israel, they are also Arabs, and as Arabs (whether Muslim or Christian) they are part of an overwhelming majority that both surrounds Israel and at the same time represents an internal threat. For that Arab majority, it is the Jews (especially Israeli Jews) who are the strangers who need to be welcomed. The policies of Israel toward the Palestinians can and should be questioned. But we cannot adequately assess the situation if we ignore the fact that the existence of the state of Israel and its Jewish citizens remains precarious precisely because of historical conditions shaped largely by the Muslim and Christian traditions, both of which have subscribed to the myth of supersession, which sees the very existence of Jews as a "problem." Peace in the Middle East is not exclusively a "Jewish problem." It depends far more upon Christians and Muslims than it does upon Jews.

The time has come when all religious (and secular) communities must find a way to make the existence of the stranger more than just allowable, more than just tolerable. We live not only after Auschwitz but also after Hiroshima. We can no longer afford the luxury of rejecting the stranger. We can no longer afford to turn stories of wrestling and reconciliation into stories of killing in order to heal. For in a nuclear age the power of our weapons exceeds our focus on those we would choose to hate and transforms

1. See Neusner's article, "Thinking About 'The Other' in Religion: It Is Necessary, But Is It Possible?" and my response, "Ethics After Auschwitz and Hiroshima: The Challenge of the 'Other' for Jews, Christians, Buddhists and Other Strangers in a Technological Civilization," in the *Journal of the American Association of Rabbis* 6, no. 2 (June 1990).

the weapons of genocide into weapons of omnicide—weapons that promise to bring all of life (human and nonhuman) to an end, to engulf us all in a holocaust to end all holocausts. In this sense, ethics after Auschwitz leads us inevitably to expand our ethical reflection to consider human dignity, human rights, and human liberation on a global scale. That is the task I have embraced in *The Ethical Challenge of Auschwitz and Hiroshima— Apocalypse or Utopia?*

INDEXES

NAMES

Abraham, 52
Adam, 36
Allen, W., 61
Ambrose, 18, 111
Antony, 111
Aquinas, T., 63
Arendt, H., 68, 104
Augustine, 1, 15, 19, 63, 75, 97, 109–23, 142, 168

Barth, K., 60, 79, 158, 164–65
Berger, P., 41
Berkovitz, E., 55, 106, 108, 131–32
Burrell, D., 97–98, 104–5, 109–10, 113–14, 118, 120

Cain, 19
Calvin, J., 1, 63
Cicero, 115
Chrysostom, J., 19–20
Cohen, A., 22, 129–31, 143, 146, 154
Comte, A., 41
Constantine, 18, 62, 85, 107

Doran, R., 175–78, 183–84
Dunne, J., 3

Eckhardt, A., 26
Ellul, J., 12, 30, 154–62, 164, 167, 169, 178, 182
Esau, 150–51
Eusebius, 62–63
Eve, 36

Fackenheim, E., 15, 23, 26, 55, 58
Faustus, 117
Fein, H., 60, 66
Flannery, E., 19

Gallin, A., 69
Gandhi, M., 3
Gaston, L., 15, 30–37
Gilgamesh and Enkidu, 188
Goethe, W., 69
Gogarten, F., 80
Gordon, S., 61
Greenberg, I., 15, 41–45, 55, 57
Gutiérrez, G., 165–67

Hauerwas, S., 15, 90, 93, 96–97, 104, 105, 106, 108, 109–10, 113–14, 118, 119–21, 138, 164, 168, 178
Hegel, G., 41
Hirsch, E., 79–81, 86
Hitler, A., 17, 19, 25, 49, 60, 71, 72, 80, 86, 100–1, 103, 108, 137

Jacob/Israel, 1, 2, 150–51, 187
and Esau, 16, 188–94
Jeremiah, 55
Job, 55, 150
Jung, C., 175
Justin Martyr, 18

Kant, I., 68, including n.26

Kierkegaard, S., 41, 73, 75, 79, 158
King, M. L., Jr., 3
Klein, F., 134

Lane, B., 51
Laytner, A., 50
Lifton, R., 16, 70, 133–40, 143–51, 171, 176–77, 182, 184–85
Littell, F., 19, 59–60, 70, 72, 104
Lonergan, B., 92
Luther, M., 15–16, 20, 27–28, 73, 75, 81, 140–43, 153–62, 178

MacIntyre, A., 91, 93, 120–21, 181
Marcion, 28–29, 74, 86
Müller, L., 79
Müntzer, T., 73

Neusner, J., 53, 192
Niebuhr, H. R., 158
Niebuhr, R., 162
Nietzsche, F., 24, 146, 181

O'Connell, T., 121
Origen, 18
Otto, R., 129

Paul, 24, 27–37, 45–47, 64, 74, 105, 111, 113, 124, 148, 165, 189–92
Paul VI, Pope, 59

195

Pawlikowski, J., 25
Plato, 75, 174
Ponticianus, 111

Rabbi Eliezer be Hyrcanos, 53
Rabbi Levi Yitzhaq of
  Berditchev, 54, 55
Rabbi Yirma, 53
Rabbi Yoshua, 53
Rilke, R. M., 69
Rubenstein, R., 22–23, 26,
  40–41, 57, 130, 142, 154
Ruether, R., 21, 108

Sanders, E. P., 15, 30–37
Sartre, J., 59
Segundo, J., 162–68
Simplicianus, 111
Speer, A., 16, 97, 99–105,
  108, 119, 179
Steiner, G., 69
Stendahl, K., 15, 29–37, 74

Theodosius, 18, 62, 85
Thoma, C., 26
Tillich, P., 4, 8, 9, 11–12,
  121

van Buren, P., 26
Victorinus, 111
Voegelin, E., 9, 10, 155

Weber, M., 41, 163, 181
Wiesel, E., 23, 42–43, 55–
  56, 58, 133
Wink, W., 145
Wittgenstein, L., 96

Yoder, J., 73

Zinzendorf, 73

SCRIPTURES

Genesis
  11:1-9—4
  18:16-33—35, 52
  18:25—38
  22—52
  25:19—33:20—188
  32:22-32—1, 42, 53, 77,
    80, 116, 149
  33:10-11—189

Exodus
  23:9—83

Deuteronomy
  10:19—83
  30:19—71

Job
  1:1—2:10—37
  4:8—38
  8:3—38
  9:17—38
  9:2, 16–17—37
  10:2—37
  11:4-6—38
  27:5-6—37
  31:35—37
  38:4—39
  40:8-9—39
  42:6—39
  42:7-8—39
  42:7-9—191
  42:10-17—37

Psalms
  117—77

Isaiah
  45:6-7—13

Matthew
  5:43-48—85
  12:33—27
  16:25—73
  25:31-46—85, 125
  25:35—85
  27:46—73, 126

Mark
  5:9—149
  8:27-33—44
  15:34—73, 126

Luke
  10:25-37—85
  11:1-13—73
  18:1-8—73
  19:42-44—28
  20:9, 16, 19—28
  22:42—62
  23:46—126

John
  8:41-43—20, 29
  19:30—126

Romans—32-37
  3—190
  3:9—32
  3:29—32
  3:3-4—33
  4:10—125
  4:16—32
  4:24—35
  5:10—34
  7:16-17—148
  7:25—148

9:6-15—190-91
9:15-17—33, 192
9:16—32, 34
9:29—35, 192
11:1—191
11:5-7—34
11:11—34, 192
11:14—34
11:17-18—192
11:18—35
11:19-20—36
11:22-36—191
11:25—32, 33, 36
11:25-26—33
11:29—33, 191
11:28-29—34, 46, 192
11:32—34, 35, 190
11:33—34
11:36—34
13:1-7—63-64

2 Corinthians
  5:19-21—125

Ephesians
  2:12-13, 19—45
  2:11-22—47, 125

Philippians
  2:1-8—62

Hebrews
  8—21
  11:1—76
  11:8—116, 119, 121

Revelation
  3:12—46

SUBJECTS

Absolutism, 6
Alienation, 2, 5
  and the master story, 168–69
  and professional ethics, 179
  as utopian, 122
  not a moral disease, 121
  pilgrim as alien, 121
Alienated theology, see Theology
Aliens, see Strangers
Anarchism, 160
Anti-Judaism, 5, 17, 20, 21, 67, 108
  in the church fathers, 18–19
  myth of supersession, 21, 24, 28, 29, 43, 71
  negative witness theory, 19, 38, 71–72, 81, 85–86, 122–23
Anti-Semitism, 21, 67, 68
Apocalypse, 5, 7
Apocalyptic
  dangers, 6
  self-destruction, 5
  threat, 13
Auschwitz, 5, 7, 15, 23
  and Hiroshima, 12, 14
  refining fires of, 27

Babel, tower of, 4
Banality of evil, 104
Bhagavad Gita, 3
Buddhism, 7, 13–14

Caesura, 22, 129
  See also Demonic
Callinicum, 18
Canon within the canon, 27
Children as new hermeneutic criterion, 40
Church and state, 62–66
Chutzpah, 6, 15–16, 73, 123, 126, 187–88
  Abraham as a model of, 52
  and liberation, 167
  as basis for post-Shoah ethic, 54
  as necessary for a just society, 184
  as utopian audacity, 75
  Christian loss of, 62–66
  defined, 51–52
  Ellul's ethic of audacity/chutzpah, 156–57, 161
  Hirsch's counterfeit chutzpah, 80

in defense of human dignity, 58
  Job as a model of, 52
  Wiesel as bearer of, 56
Commanding voice from Auschwitz, 56, 71
Conversion, 76, 111–12, 175–78
Covenant
  as a two-way street, 51

Death camps, 131
Demonic, 13, 26, 102, 110, 132, 133
  Christianity as, 43
  demythologized, 143–51
  human capacity for, 6, 130
  possession by alien forces, 102
  See also Doubling; Self-Deception
Desacralize, see Sacred
Deutsch Christians, 72, 79–81
Doubling
  and demonic doubling defined, 136, 138–40
  and Luther's two-kingdom ethic, 141–43
  and NeoPlatonism, 143–46
  and Paul, 148
  and society's cast of characters, 181–82
  and the "wrestling with God" narrative tradition, 142–43
  as cowardice, 140
  as key to human evil, 140
  Augustine's two selves, 115
  Augustine in relation to doubling and conversion, 148–49
  developing an Auschwitz self, 136
  realism as the language of the demonic, 147
  See also Demonic; Self-Deception
Doubt, 4, 6, 11, 15, 53–54, 80, 115, 116, 119, 123, 124, 126–27, 166–67, 168–69
Dignity, 61, 74–75
  See also Ethics

Edict of Toleration, 18
Emotions, 116–17
Ethics, 2, 50, 64–66, 83–84, 122

and doubling, 136, 138, 169
  and dreams, 176–77
  and efficiency, 154, 160
  and human dignity, 170
  and idolatry, 86
  and social roles, 168–85
  and the city, inner and outer, 174
  and the socio-ecology of conscience, 168–78
  and technical bureaucracy, 99, 102–4, 130–31, 133–40, 146–48, 154, 168–85
  anthropological and cosmological ethics, 9–11, 82, 153–85
  as critique of culture, 9, 12
  beyond unquestioning obedience, 71, 80, 154
  Buddhist, 7, 82
  character, 94
  Christian, 7
  chutzpah, 58, 74–75, 77
  comparative, 6, 8
  cosmological, 9, 81, 89, 94, 106, 146–47, 153–55, 163–64, 169, 171–73, 182
  dignity as the measure of ethics, 58–59
  emotivism and relativism, 92–93, 181
  ethics without choice, 84
  failure of Christian ethics, 49–50, 70–71
  faith and ethics, two different models, 49–50
  Hirsch's counterfeit ethic of wrestling with God, 81
  Holocaust as a test case for Christian ethics, 105
  holy community as ethical option, 81–82, 108
  Jewish, 7, 15
  justice and the ecology of conscience, 174
  liberation ethics as utopian, 165–66
  Lutheran and sectarian models, 153–61
  Luther's two-kingdom ethic, 16, 77–78, 153–61
  narrative, 6, 89–97
  no moral ground outside the system, 104
  of collectivism and individualism, 78
  of hospitality, 82–83

of minorities and majorities, 163–68
of obedience, 49–50, 63
of sacred and the holy, 2, 72, 82–83, 86, 150
of two realms or kingdoms, 9–11, 77, 82, 154, 158–62, 169
of welcoming the stranger in the NT, 85
professional ethics, 161, 178–85
relativism, 92–93, 109
rite and right, 89
sacred society ethic, 81, 153–54
secular, 7
self–deception and personal responsibility, 97
Socratic, 9
social, 9, 12, 15
standard post-Enlightenment account of, 90
theological, 6
universal ethics leads to violence, 106–7
values, a scale of, 183–85
See also Holy; Sacred; Values
Evil, 131, 132
See also Demonic Doubling

Faith, 49, 58, 72, 82, 116, 118–19, 123–24, 125
See also Doubt
Final Solution, 22

Genocide, 21, 131, 188, 194
Gleichschaltung, 172
Gnostic, 74, 76
See also Manichaean

Hiroshima, 5, 7, 12, 14
Holocaust, 22
Holy, 10–11, 43, 46, 68, 81–82, 155, 175
Holy Other, 2, 175
Hope, 43, 156–58
Hospitality, see Strangers
Human, 7, 16

Infinite, the, 4, 10

Janus–faced myth, 7
Job, 37–40

Justification by faith, 31–37, 162
Justinian's law code, 19

Killing in order to heal, 7, 13, 70, 76–77, 133–40, 142–43, 149–51, 187, 191
See also Demonic; Doubling
Kristallnacht, 130

Logos, see Doubt
Loyalty, see Obedience

MAD, 5
Manichaean, 20, 74, 76, 112, 116–17, 131, 142, 143–51, 169, 174
See also Gnostic
Messiah, 44–45, 46, 126

Narrative, see Story
Negative witness theory, see Anti-Judaism
Neo-Platonism, 132, 143–51
See also Doubling; Evil
Nonviolence, 3
NSDAP, 100
Nuremberg trials, 104

Obedience, 15, 61–66, 80, 104, 145, 150–51, 154, 191–93
Outcast, 7

Passing over, 3, 13
Peace in the Middle East, 193
Professional identity, 138, 178–85
Public policy, 7, 8

Questions and questioning, see Doubt

Relativism, 6, 8
Remnant, 31
Revelation, 62, 71
Shoah as new revelation, 129
Romans, 24, 29–37

SA, 101
Sacred, 4, 8, 9–11, 14, 21, 41–47, 56, 58, 81–82, 90
and profane populations, 13
and the holy as antonyms, 155
Auschwitz and Hiroshima as sacred events, 13

bureacuratic powers, 146
sacred Christian tradition as profane and demonic, 25
sacred society and holy community as ethical options, 9–11, 81–82
story of secularization as story of three ages, 90
Secular, 4, 6, 8, 68
See sacred
Self-Deception, 96–105
See also Doubling
Self-knowledge, 1–2
Sermon on the Mount, 62
Shoah, 22, 26–27, 37
Story, 9–11, 84, 86, 89, 90, 94, 95, 96, 97, 99, 104–5, 108–14, 116, 118, 119, 120–27, 148–51, 168–69, 170–71, 173–74, 191–92, 193–94
Strangers, 1–4, 27, 67, 85, 192–93
Christians as, 164
hospitality to, 16
in our dreams and in society, 178
openness to, 6
Supersession, see anti-Judaism

Technical imperative, 12
Theodosian law code, 19
Theology, 1–5, 6, 8–9, 12, 15, 106–7, 125, 126, 127, 166–67
Transcendence, 5
Tremendum, 22, 130

Universalism, 107
Utopia, 7, 58, 82
Utopian, 4, 5, 6, 7, 10, 11, 13, 14, 21, 94, 119, 121, 122, 165–66

Values, 9, 10, 14, 78–79
See also Ethics
Vatican II
Nostra Aetate, 24

Welcoming the Stranger, 82, 97, 185, 192
Wholly Other, 2, 5, 10
Will to power, see Values
Wrestling with the Stranger/God, 1–2, 54–55, 75, 76–77, 80–81, 123, 125, 142–43, 149–51, 187–94

NORMANDALE COMMUNITY COLLEGE
LIBRARY
9700 FRANCE AVENUE SOUTH
BLOOMINGTON, MN 55431-4399